SHADES OF LAURA

Shades of Laura

Vladimir Nabokov's Last Novel
The Original of Laura

Edited by

YURI LEVING

McGill-Queen's University Press
Montreal & Kingston · London · Ithaca

ISBN 978-0-7735-4263-1 (cloth)
ISBN 978-0-7735-4264-8 (paper)
ISBN 978-0-7735-8967-4 (ePDF)
ISBN 978-0-7735-8968-1 (ePUB)

Legal deposit fourth quarter 2013
Bibliothèque nationale du Québec

Printed in Canada on acid-free paper that is 100% ancient forest free (100% post-consumer recycled), processed chlorine free

McGill-Queen's University Press acknowledges the support of the Canada Council for the Arts for our publishing program. We also acknowledge the financial support of the Government of Canada through the Canada Book Fund for our publishing activities.

Library and Archives Canada Cataloguing in Publication

Shades of Laura: Vladimir Nabokov's last novel the Original of Laura / edited by Yuri Leving.

Includes bibliographical references and index.
Issued in print and electronic formats.
ISBN 978-0-7735-4263-1 (bound). – ISBN 978-0-7735-4264-8 (pbk.). – ISBN 978-0-7735-8967-4 (ePDF). – ISBN 978-0-7735-8968-1 (ePUB)

1. Nabokov, Vladimir Vladimirovich, 1899–1977. Original of Laura. 2. Nabokov, Vladimir Vladimirovich, 1899–1977 – Criticism and interpretation. I. Leving, Yuri, 1975–, writer of introduction, editor of compilation

PS3527.A15O7568 2013   813'.54   C2013-904324-1
                                     C2013-904325-X

Typeset by Jay Tee Graphics Ltd. in 11/14 Adobe Garamond

To Ella, Lola, and Leva,
for making shades visible

Contents

Acknowledgments

I wish to thank my editors, Jonathan Crago and Ryan Van Huijstee, at McGill-Queen's University Press for their professionalism and patience with this project, as well as the external reviewers of the manuscript, whose insightful comments led to many improvements in this collective exploration of one of the most controversial works ever published posthumously.

I also would like to extend a thank-you to Frederick H. White for our long and fruitful discussions about the marketing of literature and posthumous legacies; these exchanges indirectly influenced the concept of this collection. I also thank Theresa Heath and Anne Marie Todkill, who helped with the copy-editing of the work while it was in progress, and Hilary Drummond for preparing the index.

On 22 February 2012, Dmitri Nabokov, son of Vladimir and lone heir of the Nabokov estate, died in Switzerland. Dmitri was solely responsible for publishing his father's unfinished novel and showed a keen interest in this project. Although Dmitri died before its publication, his advice was greatly appreciated, and this book benefited from his input.

Reprinting the reviews of Nabokov's last novel in fragments would have proved impossible without the kind cooperation of the authors and their respective publishers, who gave permission to include articles in the section on the critical reception of *The Original of Laura*. I appreciate their understanding that, because even digital editions can accumulate dust, the immediate history should be a matter of scholarship.

Research for this volume was conducted with the help of a grant from the Social Sciences and Humanities Research Council of Canada

(SSHRC). I wish to express my deepest gratitude to the *Nabokov Online Journal*, as well as to the SSHRC Aid to Scholarly Journals program and Dalhousie University for the financial support that made this publication possible.

Yuri Leving
Halifax, Nova Scotia
January 2013

SHADES OF LAURA

Introduction: Nabokov's "Swan Song"

YURI LEVING

Vladimir Nabokov's unfinished novel in fragments, *The Original of Laura* (hereafter referred to as *Laura*), was published after a prolonged public debate, sparking controversy even before it was brought out by Knopf and Penguin in the original English and then, almost simultaneously, in numerous translations.[1] It was dubbed "the most eagerly awaited literary novel of this fledgling century ... the posthumous and fragmentary work of the greatest writer of the second half of the last century."[2] Nabokov planned the novel in 1973, began writing in 1975, and was working on it in 1977 when he became ill and died, leaving instructions that the manuscript be destroyed. The book was printed in 2009, and the manuscript, comprising 138 index cards, was put up for auction at Christie's for $400,000 to $600,000 three weeks after its worldwide release.

The plot concerns Flora, the daughter of an artistic couple, who becomes the subject of a scandalous novel, *My Laura*. Flora's husband, Philip Wild, is engaged in a "process of self-obliteration" in which he attempts to erase himself from existence through the powers of the imagination, and the novel generally explores the subjects of death and the afterlife. As John Banville points out, "the book is deeply interesting, not so much for what it thinks itself to be as for what we know it is: a master's final work."[3] The editing and packaging of *The Original of Laura*, together with the subtitle "Dying Is Fun" and the list of synonyms at the end (from *efface* to *obliterate*), suggest a concerted effort by the publishers to exploit Nabokov's own disintegration.

When, after more than three decades of ripening, Nabokov's last novel was finally made public, literary connoisseurs did not spare quills.

Respectable Western periodicals presented refined opinions – often expressed with zest, and exposing not only a rich palette of tastes but also, amid talk of greedy publishers and rebellious heirs, revealing the vices of the modern book market that stem from the exigencies of promotion and the pressure of readers' expectations. Consider the following sample of complaints:

> [The book] feels like a brittle little fable composed on automatic pilot. (Michiko Kakutani, *The New York Times*)

> [The book] has the necrophiliac tendencies of the precocious short stories, obsessed with living death. (John Updike, *The New Yorker*)

> [The book is] so brief that the reader feels short-changed. Even so, the book is beautifully executed, and it has a sort of moral. Great loves often force people to confront unpleasant truths about themselves, but since the great love in this case is not available for comment, the rebirth is entirely the old man's work. (*The Economist*)

> [T]his is a tale of obsession. (Marie Arana, *The Washington Post*)

> The circular narrative is oblique and hard to follow, but it undeniably builds up an eccentric momentum, all the while dropping in pearls of what might be wisdom, or might just be senile dementia. (Theo Tait, *Sunday Telegraph*)

To put things into perspective, I suggest conflating this long-awaited literary event – the publication of *The Original of Laura* – with the appearance of two works authored by other heavyweights of twentieth-century prose. Both were written later than Nabokov's novel and were published in 2004, when talk about saving *Laura* from the flames had gained momentum.

The first is *The Mysterious Flame of Queen Loana,* by Umberto Eco[4] – Italian semiotician, literary critic, and novelist (as well as author of a short parody of *Lolita*, entitled "Nonita"). Eco's novel is about an antiquarian book dealer who, having lost his episodic memory after a stroke, embarks on a quest to piece together his lost past from a fragmented mosaic of personal and cultural references. Richly intertextual, the novel serves as a phantasmagoric counterpart of Nabokov's nascent concept of a narrator who, in contrast to Eco's hero, effaces himself, starting with his own "mental blackboard." Serendipitously, too, the title of Eco's novel works in subtle unison with the posthumous fate of *The Original of Laura*, which Nabokov asked his wife to burn if it remained unfinished at the time of his death.

Gabriel García Márquez's *Memories of My Melancholy Whores* is the other novel that resonates with Nabokov's last work, eerily mirroring the latter's controversial subject.[5] In Márquez's novel, the unnamed narrator's tale arises from a gift he gives himself for his ninetieth birthday: a night with a young virgin.[6] Having never married, the narrator runs a weekly newspaper column, and prides himself on the fact that he has slept with over five hundred women, all of whom he paid for the pleasure. Nevertheless, he is a physically repulsive, weak, and unremarkable man. Nabokov's Philip Wild, "a renowned lecturer and a gentleman of independent means," also has "everything save an attractive exterior" (107). Márquez's book (also published by Knopf, although in a less lavish edition) is as slim and sketchy as *Laura* and, like the readers of the latter, his hero never learns the real name of the girl who transforms him. Additionally, Márquez claimed that this would be his last published work, and that thereafter he would stop writing – another self-effacement of sorts.

Eco was seventy-two when *The Mysterious Flame of Queen Loana* was published, and Márquez was seventy-seven when *Memories of My Melancholy Whores* was unveiled. Five years is a neat lag that approximates the time between Nabokov's conception of his last novel and his death before the work's completion. Neither Eco nor Márquez could have had any inkling of what Nabokov's last mysterious novel was about.

"Now a secret must be imparted," as the narrator of *Pnin* would cunningly say. The reviewers' comments quoted above are not actually concerned with Nabokov's *Laura*. Rather, they were extracted from reviews of *Memories of My Melancholy Whores*: I merely left out the name of the author and hid the work's title.[7] If we compare these comments with the overall tone and even the specific lexical choices of the reviewers of Nabokov's *Laura* (see the "Critical Reception" section in this volume), we will find striking similarities.

The moral of this simple exercise is not to display the triviality of the reproofs that have dominated the critical reception of Nabokov's novel but, rather, to underscore the complexity of contemporary literary practices. Creativity becomes part of a fluctuating artistic process that forms an endless web of interconnections and echoes, regardless of authorial intentions; in the era of digital narratives, post-postmodernist mixed media, and spoof authorships, Nabokov's unrealized novel seems to embody a perfect conceptual act, while its publication represents a self-contained public performance.

His estate, loyal critics, and scholars *nolens volens* all contribute to raising the value of Nabokov's reputation by bringing him into a known and renowned existence.[8] By means of this invisible collusion, Nabokov has been consecrated and his works have been inducted into the literary canon. He was and continues to be venerated in exhibitions, prestigious collections, and museums, and his stature is validated in record-breaking auction prices. If one were to apply Pierre Bourdieu's notions of "literary field" to the *Laura* case, it becomes apparent that without reports on various national radio and television networks, and without the impressive volume of blog commentaries in respected online publications worldwide,[9] the whole *Laura* dilemma would be "nothing but a crazy or insignificant gesture without the universe of celebrants and believers who are ready to produce it as endowed with meaning and value by reference to the entire tradition which produced their categories of perception and appreciation."[10]

Perhaps the greatest unwritten metafictional novel of the mature Nabokov, *The Original of Laura* is also intriguing to readers by virtue of its fragmentary nature. The present collection offers a wide range of perspectives using a variety of methodological approaches ranging from a selection of reviews to investigative pieces that address the novel's plot, structure, imagery, and motifs (to the extent possible when treating a fragment of a work of art in progress); questions of canonicity and the place of the novel in relation to Nabokov's other works; Nabokov as a literary phenomenon; how his art will be viewed in light of this posthumous publication; and, finally, the very poetics of incompleteness.

The question frequently asked is whether this novel should have been published. Michael Dirda, a critic for *The Washington Post*, believes that "all the work of a great writer like Vladimir Nabokov ought to be available to scholars and interested readers ... Dmitri Nabokov was clearly right to ignore his dying father's request that he destroy these fragments of an unfinished novel."[11] But the same author quickly adds that this does not mean that *The Original of Laura* actually deserves the attention of "anyone but the most rabid Nabokov fanatic."[12] How valid is such an assessment? Indeed, the international sales of *Laura* (the number one bestseller in Russia for several weeks, with hundreds of thousands of copies sold; massive sales of both the Knopf and Penguin editions in the United States, Canada, and the United Kingdom; serial publication of the novel in *Playboy* magazine; simultaneous releases of translated versions in France and Italy, followed by translations in the Netherlands, Brazil, Israel, and Japan) all testify to the commercial success of what was dubbed a "fragmented" and "unfinished" work among the general readership, and not merely in the circles of "rabid Nabokov fanatics."

Nabokov Studies is a dynamic field that has lately enjoyed immense growth: new monographs are published every month, major international conferences are held almost annually (Kyoto, Japan, in April 2010; Auckland, New Zealand, in January 2012; St. Petersburg, Russia, in April 2012; Paris, France, in June 2013). The novel's presence in public discourse suggests that there is a wide potential readership for the first scholarly volume on this controversial literary work. Because *The Original of Laura* is the only one of Nabokov's novels that has not been treated in a full-length English-language scholarly edition so far, this collection should fill an important gap and will shed new light on the literary prestige that Nabokov currently enjoys, a prestige connected in no small part to the controversial release of *The Original of Laura*.

This collection opens with Brian Boyd and Yuri Leving's "Chronology of the Novel in Fragments," which sketches much more than just a publication history of *The Original of Laura*; based on unpublished archival evidence, it gives a rare behind-the-scenes look at Nabokov working against time in a desperate struggle to complete the "swan song" of his career.

The book is divided into two major parts – "Approaches to Analysis" and "Critical Reception" – supplemented by round table discussions, an unfamiliar genre in scholarly book publications. These discussions are not round tables in the strict meaning of the term but, rather, are carefully orchestrated written exchanges between prominent scholars invited to contribute to the volume.[13] As it is not always possible to commission lengthy academic chapters on given topics from representatives of different disciplines, these cross-disciplinary conversations enable the expression of diverse views on the subject in a somewhat informal but nonetheless revealing and insightful way. Additionally, these round tables were developed with the distinct aim of providing a valuable exchange on topics of common interest between scholars who have supported the decision to publish Nabokov's last novel, and those who have been critical of its publication. "Publishing *Laura*" brings together Professors Galya Diment, Leland de la Durantaye, Michael Juliar, Eric Naiman, and Olga Voronina – all leading Nabokov experts – who evaluate the marketing strategies employed by *Laura*'s publishers, including the designs of various editions by Knopf, Penguin, Rowohlt, and others; they also examine the roles and responsibilities of literary heirs regarding publishing decisions that involve posthumous legacies. The round table participants discuss the aesthetic merits and flaws of the published novel, and raise controversial issues (e.g., the monetary value of Nabokov's manuscripts and their relevance to his popular status) that they might otherwise have been reluctant to probe, given that such issues often require a lapse of time before an academic investigation can be undertaken. (This is a familiar problem in the study of contemporary literature.)

The "Publishing *Laura*" round table is complemented by another, "Translating *Laura*," which has been placed toward the end of the collection in the part entitled "A Toolbox." This discussion features the translators of Nabokov's novel into Russian, French, Italian, Dutch, and Japanese. Gennady Barabtarlo, Maurice Couturier, Anna Raffetto, Rien Verhoef, and Tadashi Wakashima share their personal experiences related to translating Nabokov and, more specifically, their methods while working on translations of *Laura* (e.g., a linear vs non-systematic approach, working with a typed vs hand written document, the use of dictionaries); they also discuss unique challenges that arose in the process of translating this idiosyncratic text, particularly in comparison with their work on other, finished writings by Nabokov. This conversation delivers the unique vantage point of a translators' laboratory, and elucidates many technical methods used to adequately capture Nabokov's enigmatic and flamboyant style. Some aspects of this round table perhaps cater to a more specialized audience; nonetheless, the efforts of the five leading translators should interest readers of *Laura* because, as Umberto Eco has stated on another occasion, "a translation is an actualized and manifested interpretation,"[14] and it is precisely in grappling with the incompleteness of Nabokov's last novel that this critical discourse yields innovative approaches to bringing the cryptic *Laura* into targeted languages. Scholarly and non-scholarly audiences alike will appreciate such insightful dialogue, and the dynamic question-and-answer format complements the scholarly exploration presented within the standard chapters of this collection.

The main part of this collection contains analytical studies of Nabokov's last novel by literary scholars whose overall approach and academic jargon stand in stark contrast to the section devoted to the critical reception of *The Original of Laura*. In a playful homage to Nabokov's alternative title, this main section is titled "Reading Is Fun: Approaches to Analysis." Its seven contributors are renowned international Nabokovians who claim, in contrast to the often-slighting tone of newspaper and periodical reviewers, that sketchiness and incompleteness notwithstanding *The Original of Laura* is a significant literary work that deserves careful handling and serious academic attention.

In his "Vanishing Fragments," Michael Wood probes the structure of Nabokov's unfinished novel, suggesting that the author clearly planned to insert a novel written by the narrator of the opening pages – that is, a person who knows Flora and turns her into a thinly disguised character called Laura or FLaura. The fundamental epistemological problem here, according to Wood, is that someone, possibly the same writer, is describing Flora as she was before and outside the book. Indeed, Flora herself reads, or almost reads, the book. She purchases it when she is, once again, between trains, at a place called Sex, "a delightful Swiss resort famed for its crimson plums" (223), but loses it to a friend who wants to show her the passage with her "wonderful death." A train takes the friend and the book away, along with many other questions shrewdly posed by Wood.

Gennady Barabtarlo is not merely a translator of *Laura* into Russian: He closely monitored the editorial process and made several crucial conjectures regarding the possible architectonics of the novel's composition that influenced the way the Russian edition was published. "Terminating the Phrase" is Barabtarlo's attempt to describe the fragmented and unfinished book from several angles, with particular attention to its extant state and discernible design. It is based on the author's experience of studying the manuscript during the preliminary deliberation stage early in 2008 and subsequent translating it into Russian. Barabtarlo ultimately reconstructs the pre-history of the project from a personal viewpoint, assesses the state of the index cards, and compiles a brief logical history of *Laura*'s composition. Additionally, Barabtarlo's essay outlines themes suggested by the striation of cards, addresses the specific problem of fragmentation, and suggests *Laura*'s possible *literary* originals in works by Petrarch, Pushkin, and Primavera. Most significantly, he also proposes a potential structural solution to the enigmatic novel: that is, its possible ending.

The numerous "shades" of *Laura* are examined by Ellen Pifer in "Worlds Apart: Lolita, Laura, and the Shadows of Difference." Pifer asserts that there are echoes of *Lolita* in *The Original of Laura*, and Flora's kinship with Nabokov's nymphet seems obvious, just as the name of her mother's middle-aged lover, Hubert H. Hubert, confirms his identity as a child molester. However, warns Pifer, confronted by a text as fragmented as *Laura*'s, the readiness of critics to detect obvious, perhaps *too* obvious, resemblances between elements of its unstable composition and *Lolita*'s polished structure is, if misguided, at least understandable. These same critics might profit, Pifer argues, from recalling the numerous occasions on which Nabokov cautioned readers on the subject of semblance. She points to a theme writ large in Nabokov's universe: Just as the endless recombination of the twenty-six letters of the English alphabet spawn a living language, so the artist magically spins and weaves these teeming combinations into a world of words to rival nature's own. Resemblance, according to Pifer, establishes likeness by drawing attention away from difference. Granting priority to the general over the particular, it eclipses the specific and unique details that constitute, for Nabokov, the essence of both art and reality. In a less drastic but telling way, facile assumptions regarding Laura's resemblance to Lolita result, Pifer argues, in a misreading of Nabokov's final piece of fiction.

Lara Delage-Toriel, in "Nabokov's Last Smile," re-examines the critical questions raised earlier by Michael Wood and Ellen Pifer from a slightly different point of view. She traces the theme of the part to the whole, or "the head to the body," and resorts, aptly, to Lewis Carroll's metaphor of the Cheshire cat. The integrity of the body is a direct concern in *The Original of Laura*, not only because part of the body of the work is missing, but also because its characters are enmeshed within a complex game of presence and absence, exposure and erasure. "In what kind of game does this engage the reader?" asks Delage-Toriel. Using various examples from Nabokov's fiction, the author testifies that the use of imagery in *Laura* acts as a form of diversion, removing from our sight the less appealing particulars of the flesh. This technique enables Nabokov to divest the body of its material and accidental nature in order to integrate it into a more philosophical realm, within the greater sphere of existence. Conversely, in the same work, Nabokov examines the male body from a clinical, at times even crude, stance, quite bereft of the seductions of metaphor.

The latter philosophical dimension receives further treatment in Michael Rodgers's "*The Original of Laura* and Nietzsche: A Zarathustran Tool?" Rodgers traces in the notes to *The Original of Laura*, under the heading "the art of self-slaughter" (265), an apparent quotation regarding the misspelled Nietzsche's *Thus Spoke Zarathustra*. He claims that *The Original of Laura*, like Nietzsche's text, can be seen as a "mad neurologist's testament" (3) broaching the topic of mortality. By this view, not only does Nabokov's reference to Zarathustra's outlook on life encapsulate Philip Wild's desire to obliterate himself, but it also encompasses Nabokov's own thoughts regarding his literary and physical demise, his "cancer of oblivion" (45). Given that Zarathustra and Wild both offer tutelage to their prospective students, and that *Thus Spoke Zarathustra* contains chapters such as "Of the Despisers of the Body" and "Of Chastity," the correlations between the two texts become curious. Rodgers explores these similarities and argues that the formation of Nabokov's final work may be more indebted to Nietzsche than the novelist's brief note might at first suggest.

In "Reading the Posthumous Postmodern: *Laura*'s Productive Fragments," Paul Ardoin suggests that a fragmented reading experience not only parallels the thematic elements in *Laura* itself, but also reflects the disruptions to readerly and critical reception that, he argues, Nabokov intended. Diegetic fragmentation, instability, and openings draw focus toward *Laura*'s intra- and inter-textuality, and ultimately direct us to the book's engagement with worlds outside its own textual boundaries. This allows *Laura* to be not just a part of Nabokov's body of work, but also a participant in the critical conversation *about* that body of work.

Barbara Wyllie, in "Looking for Flora: Deviance and Disclosure in Nabokov's *The Original of Laura*," maintains that Nabokov's last work is a book of versions, of fictions within a fiction, a narrative of so many voices that what is true, or original, becomes almost impossible to determine. The novel's elusive quality is compounded by the portrayal of its heroine, Flora Wild. Coldly remote, inscrutable and alienating, she slips out of focus after the first few chapters as the narrative gives way to her husband's excruciatingly extravagant, deviant narcissism and his accounts of his bizarre experiments in auto-dissolution. But why does Flora suffer this effacement? Merely to satisfy her various lovers' grievances? Meanwhile, Wyllie purports, the text at once seduces and repels the reader. Its narrators sustain a fragile balance between sympathy and spite, tragedy and bathos, comedy and irony, serving to conceal the ultimate banality of their worlds but also to draw the reader's attention away from the significant details of the text. Considered in light of Nabokov's other, deeply fraudulent narratives, the reader's response to this can be only one of cautious scepticism. Wyllie concludes that the narrative's obfuscating facade is at once undermined by resistance, exposing the text's significant details – the strelitzias in Chapter One, for example, or the Blue Fountain Forest in Chapter Three – which indicate the presence of a distinct perspective, that of Nabokov's "gliding eye," whose principal interest is to reveal the true Flora.

The second part of this collection is a showcase of selected public responses to *The Original of Laura*. The sheer volume of criticism surrounding the subject of the novel's publication and then its actual release constitutes a peculiar case of reader-response activity, both in print media and in the blogosphere. Some of the immediate tendencies shaping the massive wave of reviews in the wake of the novel's long-awaited appearance have already been surveyed.[15] Review articles representing opposing trends in the novel's reception, and a selection of the most notable critical pieces, are reprinted here in their original form. This assortment offers a peculiarly synchronic slice of responses across the board, featuring both supporters and critics of Dmitri Nabokov's difficult decision to disobey his father's last wish. These reviews were written by journalists and scholars, as well as by celebrated novelists of our time such as Martin Amis, John Banville, and Alexander Theroux. Furthermore, this section sheds light on the vibrant relationship that exists between the principal decision-makers (the Nabokov estate), the intermediaries (literary agencies, scholars), the lobbying groups (mass media, bloggers, the writer's fans, and so on), and the general readership (consumers). Although some of these reviews are available electronically, virtual publications can be short-lived. This section is therefore intended to capture and preserve the remarkable critical attention generated by this text both before and after its publication, and which has been crucial in shaping public opinion regarding a manuscript that narrowly escaped the incinerator. The sample review articles will prove handy to both scholars and aficionados of Nabokov, while omitted items have been incorporated in Marijeta Bozovic's overview of the critical reception of Nabokov's *Laura*. Bozovic offers identifying remarks about the reviewers and contextualizes the debate in wider cultural, social, and literary-historical perspectives. To preserve the diversity of opinion, Bozovic includes critical responses featured in venues that range, geographically and socially, from the *Boston Review, Los Angeles Times, Washington Post*, and *Christian Science Monitor*, to *PopMatters, Paste Magazine*, and *Frieze Magazine*.

Concluding this volume is an afterword by Brian Boyd, "The Last Word – Or Not? On Some Cards Named *Laura*." Nabokov's best biographer and the first scholar outside of the Nabokov family who gained access to the secret unpublished manuscript, Boyd convincingly demonstrates the open nature of Nabokov's novel and discloses the history surrounding its notorious publication. His thrilling story unfolds as he comes to terms with the seven "disappointments" or "concerns" that characterized his first reading of Nabokov's *The Original of Laura*.

I met Dmitri Nabokov for the last time in June 2010, in his sunny apartment in the hills of Montreux, while I was filming a documentary about his father. Among other issues we touched upon off-camera was the present collection, then in progress. In a somewhat defensive move, Dmitri considered contributing a piece and possibly squaring off with numerous critics of his controversial decision to publish *Laura*. However, his quickly deteriorating health would prevent him from doing so.

On the afternoon of our meeting Dmitri was in a good mood: He murmured a Russian song; his French-speaking female assistant served us chilled white wine; in the distance beyond the windows we could hear the cheerful celebrations of football fans (it was the summer of the

World Cup). "I do not usually read critics," Dmitri scornfully stated at the beginning of our conversation. Then, sitting in a wheelchair in front of me, he slowly – taking longer than I had expected – went through the draft summary of the published *Laura*-related titles and commented on every single newspaper or journal review article included in that list (not denying himself the pleasure of offering, from time to time, a piquant remark about this or that critic). It quickly became apparent that, despite his own earlier declaration, he was intimately familiar with everything that had been printed so far in the world media concerning his father's last novel. Every now and then Dmitri would reach out for a tissue in a blue paper box on a miniature side table. At certain point I followed the direction of his hand and was struck to notice the brand name on the box: "LAURA." A coincidence, apparently, but I was secretly amused. I wondered, how Dmitri would respond if I brought this quirk to his attention, but quickly suppressed the impulse. Now that he is not longer around, I keep thinking that perhaps I should have gambled and asked him; after all, like his father, the late Dmitri Nabokov possessed an excellent sense of humour.

Experts and sceptics agree that swans do not actually sing as they die. Who knows, maybe Vladimir Nabokov's final effort proves them wrong. On the other hand, perhaps a swan song is audible only to those who wish – or are able – to listen. Or, as in the present case, to read.

A Picture in Fragments

Saving *The Original of Laura* from the flames: Nabokov's manuscript existed as a series of index cards in no obvious order. The Knopf edition consists of reproductions of the handwritten cards, with a printed transcription of their text below. (Photograph © 2011 Yuri Leving)

Chronology of the Novel in Fragments: Composition, Publication, Reception

BRIAN BOYD AND YURI LEVING

1973

Vladimir Nabokov (VN) has the first idea for his next novel after *Look at the Harlequins!*

VN TO GEORGE WEIDENFELD, 24 SEPTEMBER:[1] [turning down 75th birthday celebration] "I feel that I need all my strength to complete the novel I am writing now which may take me up to one more year, and I already have another book planned for immediately after."

1974

VÉRA NABOKOV TO ALFRED APPEL, JR, 18 MARCH: "Let us plan for some time in the second half of June or in July (probably somewhere in Italy). August would not be a good month as VN will probably be writing then his *next* book."

VN TO FRED HILLS (McGRAW-HILL), 10 MAY: "P.S. I was finishing this letter when your cable of May 9 came like a sunburst, dear Mr. Hills. This prompts me to add a postscriptum. I have a new novel mapped out rather clearly for next year, and therefore I beg you to publish *LATH* [*Look at the Harlequins!*] at the very earliest date possible. In fact, I have cancelled c. June–July vacation in Italy so as to prevent the awful vagaries of its mail from interfering with the proofs etc. of *LATH* this summer."

VN DIARY, 15 MAY: "Inspiration. Radiant insomnia. The flavor and snows of beloved alpine slopes. A novel *without* an I, without a he, but with the narrator, *the gliding eye*, being implied throughout."
VN TO FRED HILLS, 4 NOVEMBER: "I want to get rid of all translations (including the harrowing French ADA! [*Ada*]) before settling down to a new novel that keeps adding nightly a couple of hours to my habitual insomnias."
DECEMBER: Records the tentative title of the future work in his diary: *The Original of Laura: Dying Is Fun.*

1975

VÉRA NABOKOV TO GORDON LISH (*ESQUIRE*), 11 FEBRUARY: "[VN can't write a little piece for them because] for a year now he has been obliged to attend to various tasks (such as revising the French translation of ADA [*Ada*] etc.) which prevented him from doing his own writing and that he can't wait to finish with them and go back to the only thing that is important to him: his new book."
VN TO BEVERLEY LOO (McGRAW-HILL), 24 JULY: "PROCEED ... JUNE TENTATIVE DELIVERY DATE FOR NEW NOVEL"
BEVERLEY LOO TO VN, 22 AUGUST: "Franklin Library developing new de luxe book club called first edition society through which they will mail to members high priced custom leather bound so called first editions of new books by distinguished authors such mailings to coincide with publishers publication date they are only in test mailing stage now [$1000 for name to be used on mailing, $25,000 eventual advance against royalty of $2 per copy] and also let us know approximate delivery date of manuscript."
VN TO FRED HILLS, 14 NOVEMBER: "I am recuperating steadily but slowly and shall hardly be able to get back to my new novel before Christmas."
BEVERLY LOO TO VN, 8 DECEMBER: "in re Franklin library ... happy to report have now worked out with Franklin library new credit phraseology as follows: a private limited edition has been separately published assume we may now have your approval to proceed with contract which you will recall will be an option of dlrs 1,000 against dlrs 25,000 book club advance book referred to is your new manuscript passing fancy."

VN TO BEVERLY LOO, 8 DECEMBER: "I ACCEPT YOUR SUGGESTION ... RE FRANKLIN LIBRARY OFFER FOR MY NOVEL IN PROGRESS A PASSING FASHION."

VN TO FRED HILLS, 14 DECEMBER: [sending *Details of a Sunset* proofs and a separate correction list] "I am now returning zestfully to the abyss of my new novel."

1976

VN DIARY, 1 JANUARY: "Writing since 10 Dec '75 at least 3 cards of new novel."

VN DIARY, 21 JANUARY: Véra Nabokov informs the publisher Carl Proffer that "at this moment [Vladimir] is completely absorbed in his new novel, which is going full swing."

VN TO FRED HILLS, 23 JANUARY: "I am deep in my new novel."

VN DIARY, 26 JANUARY: "Novel progressing nicely but insomnia worse and worse."

VÉRA NABOKOV TO BEVERLY LOO, 28 JANUARY: "My husband is deep in his new novel, and also otherwise everything is O.K."

VN TO SAMUEL ROSOFF, 31 JANUARY: "I am better, except for hopeless insomnia. I have gradually gotten back to my writing, and am working on the first third of a new novel."

VN DIARY, 2 FEBRUARY:

"New novel more or less completed and copied 54 cards.
In 4 batches from different parts of the novel.
Plus notes and drafts
50 cards since Dec 10, 75. Not too much."

VN TO FRED HILLS, 16 FEBRUARY: "I am having a marvelous time with my new novel whose tentative title has been changed from A PASSING FASHION to THE ORIGINAL OF LAURA."

DAN LACY (MCGRAW-HILL) TO VN, 18 MARCH: "I am grateful to Harvard University for having given me an excuse to call you this morning [presumably an honorary degree]. I am ... pleased that the work on the new novel marches to your satisfaction."

VN DIARY, 3 APRIL: "*TOOL* novel proceeding at the rate of 5 or 6 cards per day but a lot of rewriting"

VN DIARY, 7 APRIL: "*TOOL* transcribed in final form 50 cards + 5000 words"
VN DIARY, 13 APRIL: "bought 500 index cards lined on 1 side"
VÉRA NABOKOV TO FRED HILLS, 20 APRIL: "My husband believes that he has passed the hundred printed-page mark which is about half of *TOOL*. He does not know, he says, what is more brilliant, the novel itself or its acronym – this is as much as he can disclose at the moment."
VN TO ALFRED APPEL, JR, 26 APRIL: "I am not sure I like the idea [of Appel's suggestion to publish a volume of selected short fiction]. A collection is only then valuable when it is complete – and I hope to write a few more stories (after getting rid of my present novel, *The Original of Laura*, which will take most of the summer to finish)."
VÉRA NABOKOV TO GLEB STRUVE, 26 APRIL: [Hoover Véra Nabokov-Struve correspondence] "Seychas, tol'ko chto opravivschis' posle operatsii, on energichno rabotaet nad novym romanom – 'The Original of Laura.'" ["At present, having just recovered after an operation, he's working energetically on a new novel – 'The Original of Laura.'"]
VN TO FRED HILLS, 5 JUNE: "Yes, I intend to affix prefaces to the NABOKOV'S DOZEN and I will also have to add here and there some bright patches to the rest of the introductions, but not before I am through with *TOOL*."
VÉRA NABOKOV TO JOAN DALY (PAUL, WEISS, RIFKIND, WHARTON & GARRISON), 5 JUNE: [both ill earlier in year; VN in hospital with concussion for ten days] "The base salary for 1976 was neither paid nor claimed as my husband has only reached about the middle of the new novel THE ORIGINAL OF LAURA."
BEVERLY LOO TO VÉRA NABOKOV, 17 JUNE: "I have of course assured everyone here that the new novel is well on its way to completion, and that I was privileged with a glance!"
OMAHA WORLD-HERALD, 18 JULY: "The [Book] Digest also says Vladimir Nabokov is halfway through a new novel the title of which he is not yet ready to reveal.

"All the author will say for publication ... is the acronym for the title spells *TOOL*, with each letter standing for one word in it."
VÉRA NABOKOV TO DAN LACY, 28 JULY: "Since his operation in October he has had a long spell of poor health ... He has made three sojourns at the hospital and it is only now that he is really beginning to

regain his health. In these circumstances he will unfortunately need more time to finish his book – at least till Easter, I would say."

VÉRA NABOKOV TO FRED HILLS, 18 AUGUST: "On Vladimir's request I am answering your letter of August 4 on his behalf. He is still rather ill, although very much improved. He is still not supposed to work on the novel. Thus *TOOL* has still to wait."

VN TO VICTOR LUSIANCHI, *NEW YORK TIMES*, 30 OCTOBER: "Here are the three books I read during the three summer months of 1976 while hospitalized in Lausanne:

1. Dante's *Inferno* ...
2. *The Butterflies of North America* by Howes ...
3. *The Original of Laura*, the not quite finished manuscript of a novel which I had begun writing and reworking before my illness and which was completed in my mind: I must have gone through it some fifty times and in my diurnal delirium kept reading it aloud to a small dream audience in a walled garden. My audience consisted of peacocks, pigeons, my long dead parents, two cypresses, several young nurses crouching around, and a family doctor so old as to be almost invisible. Perhaps because of my stumblings and fits of coughing the story of my poor Laura had less success with my listeners than it will have, I hope, with intelligent reviewers when properly published."

VN TO FRED HILLS, 8 NOVEMBER: "My health is coming back gradually. I have been working on *Laura* and have practically finished it in my head; it is the physical effort of writing it down that is still posing a problem. Typing or dictating is out of the question. The writing, however, will take some time yet, as I cannot do very much of it at a stretch, even though all traces of concussion have disappeared months ago. But I am still weak, still recovering from three months of high fever and weeks of delirium cause by a stubborn infection of the urinary tract which it took the doctors unbelievably long to diagnose and to treat."

HUGH MULLIGAN (ASSOCIATED PRESS) TO VN, 16 NOVEMBER: Typescript, interview, 30 November, 1976:

1. *What is the Nabokov diet these days, both literary and caloric?*

My caloric diet usually consists of bread and butter, transparent honey, wine, roast duck with red whortleberry jam, and similar plain fare.

My literary regime is more fancy, but two hours of meditation, between 2 AM and 4 AM (when the effect of a first sleeping pill evaporates and that of a second one has not begun) and a spell of writing in the afternoon, are about all my new novel (*The Original of Laura*) needs.

1977

VÉRA NABOKOV TO BERNARD DE FALLOIS (JULLIARD), 3 JANUARY: "He is very busy with the new book he is writing so he asks me to tell you that he is quite satisfied with the blurb you sent him."
VÉRA NABOKOV TO JONATHAN GILLET, 25 FEBRUARY: "I hasten to advise you that, although my husband's book is advancing nicely, he would not like to commit himself to any definite date. He suffers very much from insomnias and after sleepless nights has to forgo his daily writing."
30 JUNE: Nabokov is taken into intensive care at a Swiss hospital. He instructs Véra that if he dies before finishing the book, the draft is to be destroyed.
2 JULY: The writer dies; his directive remains unfulfilled.

1981

JAQUELINE CALLIER [VN'S AND VÉRA NABOKOV'S SECRETARY] TO BRIAN BOYD, 11 DECEMBER: "When I saw him in hospital, he said that 'The Original of Laura' would be the best of his works."

1984

DECEMBER: Véra Nabokov promises to show the manuscript of the unfinished novel to Brian Boyd, who is gathering materials for a new biography of her late husband.

1987

FEBRUARY: Véra finally fulfils her promise, and Brian Boyd is the first person other than Nabokov's widow and his son Dmitri to read *The Original of Laura*. Upon reading the manuscript, the biographer initially recommends against its publication.

LATE 1980S

Dmitri Nabokov has the manuscript typed out.

1991

14 FEBRUARY: Elena Sikorski, Nabokov's sister, inquires of Gennady Barabtarlo (the book's future translator into Russian): "You ... have read *The Original of Laura* in Boyd's paraphrase. Do you suppose that it would be indiscreet of you to give me the content of that book in a nutshell?" (See Barabtarlo's article in this collection.)
7 APRIL: Véra Nabokov dies, leaving the burden of making the final decision to Dmitri, the Nabokovs' only heir.

1990S

Dmitri Nabokov deposits index cards bearing the text of the novel in a safety deposit box in a Swiss vault.

1998

Jeff Edmunds, the editor of *Zembla* (a website devoted to Nabokov), composes an impressive pseudo-excerpt, signed by an invented scholar "Michel Desommelier." The phantom author claims that he received the fragments of *The Original of Laura* from a young nurse who attended a fatally ill Nabokov, who, in his delirium, was reciting passages from his unfinished work (see entry for 30 October 1976, above).
10–12 SEPTEMBER: During the Nabokov Centenary Festival at Cornell University, Ithaca, Dmitri Nabokov reads fragments of the unpublished novel to the conference audience.

1999

JANUARY: The editors of *The Nabokovian* announce a "Nabokov Prose-Alike Centennial Contest." The Nabokov Estate provides two, nearly page-long, passages taken from *The Original of Laura*, unidentified, to be intermingled with the "genuine" finalists.

19 APRIL: According to an interview, Dmitri Nabokov seriously considers preserving the manuscript in an institutional library to be accessed only by a limited circle of scholars.[2]
SPRING: *The Nabokovian* (no. 42) publishes five selected passages of prose, three of which are imitations of Nabokov, in addition to the real excerpts from *The Original of Laura*.
DECEMBER: No one is able to correctly identify Nabokov's authentic writings in the *Nabokovian* prose-alike contest.

2000–2001

Dmitri Nabokov has the manuscript of *The Original of Laura* transferred to digital format and sends the text to a few chosen scholars, soliciting their opinion about the novel.

2005

27 NOVEMBER: New York columnist Ron Rosenbaum, known for his interest in literature (especially Nabokov and Shakespeare) and his appetite for publicity, starts a prolonged public campaign in favour of saving the text of Nabokov's last novel from the flames (*The New York Observer, The Spectator / Slate*). Intense debate ensues.

2008

14 FEBRUARY: *The Times* of London asks two famous contemporary literati about the manuscript's fate. The novelist John Banville advises: "If I were Dmitri Nabokov, which thank goodness I am not, I would have the fragment typed up and given to two or three reputable and sympathetic critics – e.g., James Wood, Harold Bloom – and perhaps also a writer or two – John Updike, Martin Amis – for their opinion on whether it should be published." Playwright Sir Tom Stoppard pronounces his verdict: "It's perfectly straightforward: Nabokov wanted it burnt, so burn it."
MARCH: A final round of consultations with Nabokov experts takes place behind the scenes.

23 APRIL: In an interview for the *Nabokov Online Journal*, Dmitri Nabokov announces his dramatic decision to publish the novel.
SUMMER–FALL: International controversy surrounding the issue of publishing of Nabokov's unfinished work is covered by NPR (National Public Radio), the BBC (British Broadcasting Corporation), the CBC (Canadian Broadcasting Corporation) and the ABC (Australian Broadcasting Corporation) radio and television stations, among others.
SUMMER: The Vladimir Nabokov Literary Estate, represented by the three-person literary agency Smith-Skolnik, moves to the large and actively expanding Wylie Agency, based in London and New York.
18 NOVEMBER: Exactly a year before the book is unveiled, the celebrated cards are shown briefly in Dmitri Nabokov's hands during a BBC televised report (*Newsnight*, "Nabokov's final work saved").

2009

JANUARY–JUNE: An undisclosed pool of international translators approved by the Nabokov estate simultaneously work on the translations of the novel into several languages. The initial plan is for simultaneous worldwide publication.
10 NOVEMBER: A 5,000-word excerpt appears in *Playboy* magazine, the first serial publication of *The Original of Laura*.
17 NOVEMBER: *The Original of Laura* is published in English by Knopf in the United States and Penguin in the United Kingdom.
27 NOVEMBER: The Russian translation is released by Azbooka.
DECEMBER: Three weeks after its worldwide release, the manuscript of *The Original of Laura* is auctioned at Christie's in New York (estimated sale price $400,000–$600,000), but fails to sell.

In Russia, *The Original of Laura* is reported number one in sales as over 50,000 copies are sold within a few weeks; the deluxe edition is briefly number two on the bestseller list at the same time.

Immediately after the book's publication, more than three dozen critical responses are published by the leading press, including the *Financial Times*, the *Los Angeles Times*, *The New York Review of Books*, *The New York Times*, *The Observer*, *San Francisco Chronicle*, *Süddeutsche Zeitung*, *The Sunday Times*, *The Telegraph*, *The Washington Times*, and

Die Zeit. (A selection of these reviews are reproduced in the present volume.)

2010

23 NOVEMBER: An autographed manuscript of *The Original of Laura* (lot 26) is finally sold for £78,050 ($124,334) at Christie's, London (sale 7882). The price realized is below the low presale estimate of $160,000.
DECEMBER: John Banville regrets his earlier call to save the book and seems to be particularly offended by its preface: "Reading these introductory pages is like being trapped in an airless room with a priggish adolescent dressed up in his father's outsize clothes – tails, white tie, spats, and all – who expatiates on the awfulness of the masters at his school while puffing on one of Daddy's finest cigars and turning slowly green."[3]

2011

14 FEBRUARY: Staying with Dmitri Nabokov in Montreux, Brian Boyd recognizes as part of *The Original of Laura* 21 hitherto unknown index cards found by Dmitri's archivist, Antonio Epicoco. They reflect various stages of composition, but 600 words of almost 1200 form a single draft scene.

Publishing *Laura*

GALYA DIMENT, LELAND DE LA DURANTAYE,
MICHAEL JULIAR, ERIC NAIMAN, AND OLGA VORONINA

YURI LEVING: *Publication of the unfinished novel was surely a sensational event, but there is still plenty of unpublished correspondence, Russian poetry in need of translation, and uncollected critical essays among the archival legacy of Vladimir Nabokov. Could you illuminate some possible challenges of bringing out the newly discovered Nabokov from institutional and private archives?*

OLGA VORONINA: The biggest challenge, in my opinion, consists of fitting the unpublished Nabokov in with the poems, essays, and letters that have already appeared in print. Some of the editorial work done in the 1970–1980s suffered from the editors' inability to access all of the archival materials necessary for preparing the footnotes and introductions. Brian Boyd's monumental biography, which provides a solid chronological and factual foundation for any kind of manuscript-focused Nabokov scholarship, came out after many of VN's works had been published posthumously. A new volume of painstakingly prepared and more complete Nabokoviana will not necessarily cancel the earlier editions, which have already earned a reputation as canonical texts. The new translations will be quoted along with the old ones, possibly spreading panic among scholars who are used to most Nabokov translations being "definitive." The *Letters to Véra*, which I am currently preparing for publication with Brian Boyd and Dmitri Nabokov, are more or less unknown, save the few that came out in 1989 in *Vladimir Nabokov: Selected Letters, 1940–1977*. But there are, as far as I know, quite a few unpublished lectures on literature, which will have to be assimilated with the already known essays edited by

Fredson Bowers. Other books may also be in the works, with their editors confronting a healthy number of purely Nabokovian challenges.

GALYA DIMENT: When it comes to unpublished materials other than *The Original of Laura*, none of them (with the possible exception of some letters) have similar potential to be sensational or, even more importantly, to be sensationalized. I personally hope that most of the correspondence and critical essays get published. As to his Russian poetry, I would probably leave it untranslated, mostly in deference to Nabokov's own post–*Three Poets* views about translating poetry, and also because I largely share them.

ERIC NAIMAN: When *The Original of Laura* appeared, it was beautiful and should have been a cause for celebration. How many novelists dead over thirty years get this lovely a casket? The roll-out of the book was like the exhumation and reburial of Rousseau. He has long been in the Pantheon, but this was fresh proof that Nabokov still matters: people still care about his legacy, and they care so much that they can grow irate or become misty-eyed about this latest book.

Part of the logic – if not the packaging – of the publication of *Laura* is that everything Nabokov wrote is precious – at least to scholars. I would hope that a similar logic applies to the publication of Nabokov's correspondence, particularly with his wife and his mother. (What we have seen so far, in [the Russian magazine] *Snob*, is to my mind just as interesting as *Laura;* here we have Nabokov playing with narrative technique in his intimate correspondence.[1] Love letters as a laboratory for future works). I would suggest that the only rationale for suppressing parts of the correspondence is injury to the living. There is probably very little risk that the publication of Nabokov's more intimate documents will do for him what the Soviet edition did for Chernyshevsky. What I would also like to see are documents that help provide a clearer picture of how Nabokov worked with his co-translators. A scholarly edition of the initial work by Michael Scammell and Dmitri Nabokov – along with Nabokov's responses to them – might play a significant role in shaping our reading of the English texts and help us determine whether the original Russian versions might not be more – or, at least, differently – authentic.

For those editing Nabokov's work, it is important to resist the temptation to retain knowledge unavailable to other scholars. Where editing is concerned, the less we have of authority and mystery, the more we will see of miracles.

YURI LEVING: *What are the rules of thumb and potential pitfalls associated with preparing the scholarly apparatus for Nabokov's editions (introductions, commentary, and other readers' aids)?*

OLGA VORONINA: Nabokov's ability to attract the "mass reader" (a phantom of the imagination, but not of revenue, on the part of the publisher, who believes that "masses" do not need glosses), along with connoisseurs eager to suck his prose to the bare bones and savour every bit of it, can corner even an experienced editor. How much commentary is too much, and how few readers' aids are too little? Personally, I like the stark Vintage editions, but my students cannot get enough of *The Annotated Lolita*,[2] which provides them with a safety net for exploring the novel's dizzying heights. Not every Nabokov paperback should be "Appelized," but the appeal of *Pale Fire, Transparent Things*, and *Look at the Harlequins!* for the lay reader and maven alike would be greater if the novels contained a foreword suggesting the reading strategy as well as a commentary that directed the "wild goose chase." The main pitfall to avoid, of course, is to numb the thrill by revealing too much. *Ada Online* is one of the possible solutions to this dilemma. This website contains everything one needs to decipher the riddles in the novel; readers can portion the aids and do a vigorous cross-search to weave their own web of subtextual and intertextual associations. As for editions of Nabokov's non-fiction, they need everything: the introduction, the commentary, and the afterword. It is high time that *Strong Opinions* was reissued in a new, "scholasticized" format, including the index already put together by Dieter Zimmer. Perhaps it could become another Nabokov online project.

ERIC NAIMAN: The wonderful thing about some of the annotated editions – particularly those by Appel and Barabtarlo – is that they capture many of the anxieties and thrills of reading Nabokov. These are examples of the kinds of good readers that Nabokov creates. If you teach *The Annotated Lolita*, Appel emerges not only as a figure of authority, but as a character in his own right, one situated at a level between the author and his readers. Olga describes his critical apparatus as a "safety net," but it can also be seen as a product of over-eagerness to control the meaning of the text. The Berg Collection contains part of Appel's correspondence with Nabokov, and we can see the origin of those anti-annotations in interpretations suggested to and rejected by the annotator's teacher. One can read them as Appel's attempt to put these meanings into circulation anyway, a gesture akin to the critical citations of émigré scholars in Soviet days. His commentary and Barabtarlo's are so wonderful because they capture the complex dynamics of readerly temptation, resistance, and submission. Like all good works of scholarship, they should be read not as ensuring the reader's safety but as encouraging a mixture of scepticism and excited admiration. "Ok, now let me drive."

YURI LEVING: *The cover or jacket of a book conveys a message about its contents, influencing both the retailer who stocks the book and the potential purchaser in the shop.*[3] *Can Nabokov's covers be "read" to reveal the assumptions that publishers make about the markets they are targeting? How has Nabokov, as an established author, been repositioned over time?*

LELAND DE LA DURANTAYE: Unquestionably. *Lolita* offers the most striking instances, as both Duncan White and Dieter Zimmer have shown (Zimmer's archive of cover images is particularly revealing in this regard), with the roles played by soft lighting, full lips, long legs, bobby socks, saddle shoes and the rest. More generally, the air of impish mystery conveyed by the entire series of Vintage International covers not only reflects the assumptions of publishers but seems to have shaped – or, at least, reinforced – a certain image of Nabokov as an impishly mysterious author. The graphic designs of foreign editions of Nabokov's works – from Brazil to Turkey and beyond – offer fascinating glimpses of such assumptions, as well as showcasing remarkable talent.

OLGA VORONINA: Up until the mid-1990s, only a few Nabokov covers suffered from overstatement. The recent trend, however, has been toward visual embellishment, if not exaggeration. The latest hoopla about Vintage paperbacks is especially alarming.[4] Not only are John Gall's "collector boxes" an unacknowledged rip-off (the installation artist Barbara Bloom came up with this box format ten years ago, in a series of exhibits dedicated to Nabokov), they have also succumbed to one of the interpretative sins most loathed by VN: generalization. I can't imagine a Nabokovian novice or a pro who wouldn't be scared off by the cover of *Laughter in the Dark* with its crude cut-and-paste vampire; the new Vintage *Look at the Harlequins!* is just as garish and fallacious.

MICHAEL JULIAR: I agree in part with Olga: the new Vintage *Laughter in the Dark* cover makes me grimace. (By the way, there is no new Vintage *Look at the the Harlequins!* yet). But what's really annoying and worse, misleading, is the new set of Penguin covers. I do like their various patterned backgrounds – very Nabokovian. But the light touches of the pen-and-ink and watercolour illustrations are more suggestive of something from Barbara Pym and don't give any hint of the directness and energy in Nabokov's works.

GALYA DIMENT: Older dust jackets at least ran the gamut from the ridiculous to the sublime. In the ridiculous category were Fawcett's mass market paperback editions of *Glory* (1973) and *King, Queen, Knave* (1969), both featuring a couple, one quite naked, the other quite clothed, locked in a passionate kiss. The covers looked indistinguishable from cheap Harlequin Romances. Among the sublime I count my favourites: Milton Glaser's rendition of *Pnin* which, as we know now from Mr Glaser's testimony, was heavily influenced by Nabokov's aid and instructions, and also the cover of the first Avon paperback edition of the same novel. Now the covers are, for the most part, neither truly outrageous nor wittily intelligent but mostly predictable and mediocre. At some point book illustrators must have held a conference and resolved that disembodied parts of the female face, especially lips, and female limbs, in particular knees, somehow do the trick. Thus *Lolita* and *Anna Karenina* have become linked through their knees, although Karenina's in the 2004 Penguin edition are definitely plumper.

ERIC NAIMAN: Recently, Sandy Klein posted on Nabokv-L a link to a photo of Natalie Portman holding her Lolita "clutch" – a pocket book designed from the original Paris cover by the aptly named Olympia Le-Tan.[5] That first cover is still one of the best, introducing nothing extraneous except the allure of what is inside and now the cultural memory of the book's first encounter with the world. It is hard to imagine Le-Tan having used a later design.[6] One could put the Portman photo on a future cover, reasserting the power of text over fashion – or at least commingling their different modes of appeal. Then the conjurer's purse would once more be almost intact. (That was an anti-annotation – I don't think I could bring myself to buy or assign such a thing, but the picture could go up on the bulletin board next to my office door, surrounded by index cards detached from *Laura*).

YURI LEVING: *What do you think of the design of* The Original of Laura *by Knopf, Penguin, Rowohlt, and other publishing companies?*

MICHAEL JULIAR: I am ambivalent about the Knopf design. On the one hand, it feels like overkill. It is too much of a thing: it is stark, with poster-hard blacks, whites, and reds among a suffusion of grey pages; it is gimmicky, with a perforation theme that includes printed dashed lines where no perforating is possible;[7] it is show-offish, with the odd red page that faces the table of contents, the playing-card–like design at the end, and the index-card binding. On the other hand, I love this brimming-over of Chip Kidd's imagination. If my brain were so fertile, I would have designed *The Original of Laura* in much the same overwrought manner.

LELAND DE LA DURANTAYE: The Knopf cover is very elegant and apt, fading to black as the reader's eyes move from right to left, grading into the darkness of death.

GALYA DIMENT: I do think the Knopf / Penguin edition was artfully done, and I understand that university presses, given the harsh economic times right now, could hardly have afforded similar treatments. But in this particular case, no matter how beautiful and creative the book looked, I agree with Michael that it was overkill given what was contained between the covers.

OLGA VORONINA: Against the latest Vintage background, the solemn jacket and the underlying manuscriptic binding of *Laura* by Knopf offers a solace to the eye. But I agree with Michael: there is too much of a good thing. Rowohlt's exquisitely ascetic edition is more appealing: it glorifies the text without sacrificing the texture.

YURI LEVING: *Jason Epstein, Nabokov's publisher turned friend, writes: "With books no longer imprisoned for life within fixed bindings the opportunities are endless for the creation of new, useful, and profitable products by Internet publishers. For Walt Whitman and his ever-changing editions of* Leaves of Grass *the Web would have been ideal. So would it have been for Theodore Dreiser and Vladimir Nabokov, plagued with squeamish and ignorant publishers, as it would also have been for* samizdat *writers in the former Soviet Union and will be for their counterparts under today's tyrannies."*[8] *What do you think of Internet prospects for Nabokov's works (although it has recently been reported that no Nabokov digital editions are in the offing)?*

MICHAEL JULIAR: Obviously not just *Ada* (see Boyd's *Ada Online*) but all of Nabokov's works cry out for hypertext annotations. Of course, online versions of Nabokov's works (and, illegal though they are, there are many already) will lead to mash-ups, variations, take-offs, and possible samplings in the form of *Lolita, My Zombie Love* and *Pnin Pninned* and goodness knows what else. I'm sure that Nabokov would have been highly amused by this doodling in the margins of his works, as long as it didn't corrupt his texts. And I believe it wouldn't have and won't. I'll bet that *Pride and Prejudice and Zombies* and *Sense and Sensibility and Sea Monsters* have driven thousands of readers to peek into and to discover the riches of the originals. So why not a *Look at the Horrible Harlequins!*? Or *Lolita, My Demon Love*? Or *Slaughter in the Dark*? Or *The Bloody Eye*? Or ... someone please stop me!

OLGA VORONINA: Sooner or later, the Internet will embrace Nabokov – or vice versa. The problem I see with VN's internet prospects concerns not the dissolution of "fixed bindings," which the master himself, serendipitously, has already dissolved (with *The Gift* and *Ada* being perhaps the most representative examples of Nabokov's aerial boundlessness) as much as the establishment of firm boundaries for those who would not mind inscribing themselves in the texts. I don't think Nabokov would have been "amused" by a plethora of virtual co-authors, especially in view of the fact that the online Nabokov *samizdat* these days is predominantly pornographic. One needs to make a heroic intellectual effort to counterbalance it. *Ada Online*, I have already mentioned, is an engaging example of how things could be done on the Internet.

YURI LEVING: *Discuss the issues of copyright and illustrative material in their application to the potential publishing of Nabokov's writings.*

OLGA VORONINA: Nabokov not only doodled like Pushkin, his cards themselves can be seen as an art form. And yet, publishing another novel as a facsimile of VN's manuscripts would be a mistake. There are some fascinating images on the *Lolita* cards, but I doubt that they would heighten the reader's pleasure. Maps, however, might be a kind of "illustrative material" that would amplify our reading experience. Dmitri Nabokov writes in his introduction to *The Original of Laura* about the tragic loss of his father's maps of the United States marked with references to Lolita's journey with Humbert Humbert. But what if other such "visuals" have been preserved? I would love to see, for example, maps of Demonia and Antiterra as drafted by Nabokov. After all, his *Lectures* have lavish cartographic illustrations – a hint that that's how Nabokov wanted us to read his works, too.

GALYA DIMENT: I would like to see the butterflies from Nabokov's dedications flit freely between various editions.

REINVENTING NABOKOV: POSTHUMOUS LEGACIES

YURI LEVING: *Could you address the marketing strategy for Nabokov's writings in general and the recent publicity campaign for* The Original of Laura *in particular? (For example, Dmitri Nabokov's interviews or Ron Rosenbaum's series of publications, the* Playboy *engagement, publicity pages on publishers' websites, short pieces devoted to the forthcoming novel in fragments running in glossy magazines such as American* GQ *or the Russian entertainment weekly* Plus TV, *etc.).*

LELAND DE LA DURANTAYE: In a word, savvy.

OLGA VORONINA: Patrick Forsyth and Robin Birn claim that marketing is "no more than common sense." According to these mavericks, "not simply trying to sell what we happened to produce" should be a credo of any publisher.[9] Even if this is the rule of the game, Nabokov would have surely winced at Forsyth's and Birn's claim. Its underlying idea (writing is accidental, promotion rules) transfers agency from writer to publisher, for whom "common sense" often, indeed, becomes the main aesthetic criterion.

And yet there is an analogy that might help us understand why Vladimir Nabokov, and later Dmitri, would not shun marketing as a means of delivering as many books as possible into the hands of as many as readers as possible. The paragraph dedicated to soccer in *Speak, Memory*, describes Nabokov's alter ego as a detached participant in the game, the rules of which he did not invent. "I would ... think of myself as of a fabulous exotic being in an English footballer's disguise, composing verse in a tongue nobody understood about a remote country nobody knew. Small wonder I was not very popular with my teammates."[10]

The Nabokovian marketing strategy seems to me exactly this: it is a form of detached participation that ensures the positive outcome of the game while minimizing the emotional involvement of the player. Or, rather, the goalie. He might not be in total control of the match, but he certainly pounces on the ball at the critical moment, hopefully catching it just in time.

MICHAEL JULIAR: *The Original of Laura* was a niche book in the American market. Knopf/Wylie/Dmitri Nabokov oversold it and positioned it incorrectly. It belonged on the literature/college reading shelves and not on bookstores' hot-book-of-the-week front tables. I give them credit for getting *Playboy* to put down very good money for the first serial rights.

The publicity campaign, though, was remarkable. Radio talk shows, blogs, magazine and newspaper reviewers – all jumped in and created a tremendous buzz. I was pleasantly amazed. The book didn't have, unfortunately, carrying power; it couldn't develop the word of mouth that a finished version of a completed, cohesive story would have generated. Consider: The outtakes of a just-discovered and unfinished Fellini film would have met the same fate.

ERIC NAIMAN: *The Original of Laura* was difficult to read in *Playboy*. The word *squinty* – in the font used by the magazine to print the work – would fit easily within Sasha Grey's nipples in the photo spread that accompanied the abridged fragments. (And those nipples – Flora's – were soon everywhere, in just about all the reviews that disparaged the writing and found it impossible to forgive, as though nobody had ever noticed "the vacuous expression of breasts.") *Playboy* surrounded the text with so many sidebars that the reader would have been hard pressed to read it in any sort of attentive fashion. In the old days, when Nabokov was still alive, the distractions were the cartoons on facing pages, or the photos – an odd number of girls, or even? – one had to overlook in the process of turning the pages to reach the continuation of the story. Here, however, the story was hemmed in, indeed hounded by curatorial tenderness that probably left some readers feeling claustrophobic rather than aroused.

In *Playboy* the text itself had many embellishments of the sort that Nabokov was paid by Heffner to add – "the super-Oriental doctor with long gentle fingers," "her nightly dreams of erotic torture in so-called 'labs,' major and minor laboratories with red curtains," the "lace-edged rag on the moss," one of "the only signs of an earlier period of literature."[11] Nabokov played these games before, but then the reader had been encouraged to *read* them. A new novel by the author of *Lolita* shouldn't have to rely on a photo spread in homage to that earlier book, although Nabokov surely would have enjoyed the pairing of a nude cross-over model with a completely anodyne text by Roger Ebert about Kubrick's movie. Ebert might have been paid more for his name had he realized that anyone who actually did read the story could not help but equate him – his words lying on the page next to Grey – with Flora's Philip Wild.

GALYA DIMENT: As Nabokov's life was coming to an end, he probably thought that while – like Philip Wild – he could not control his rapidly deteriorating body, he could at least control the fate of his unfinished and thus vulnerable manuscript. So while, as a Nabokov specialist, I am grateful to Véra and Dmitri Nabokov for not burning the cards because they will inform my scholarship, as someone who deeply cares about Nabokov's reputation I am also disheartened that instead of making them available in a much more academic fashion Dmitri Nabokov chose to merchandise them. It did create a sensation, yet not one I believe his father would have welcomed. I would add to Eric's vivid description of the *Playboy* layout that they, alas, could not even spell the writer's name correctly in the title of the article ("*The Original of Laura* by Vladimir Nabakov").

YURI LEVING: *Posthumous fame and the economics of culture in the 20th century have acquired a new important dimension: literary estates, heirs, agents, and rights holders play an increasingly dominating role in controlling and disseminating creative works in our society, governed as it is by legal frameworks. Dmitri Nabokov, there is no doubt, has played a major role in the preservation and active promotion of his father's literary legacy over the past four decades – from translating and publishing to editing and commenting on Vladimir Nabokov's writings. To the question of whether he is unique in this role and how one could characterize this kind of activity, which has been dubbed by journalists as anything from selfless devotion to a greedy urge, Dmitri Nabokov aggressively answers: "My reaction, were it legal, would be a swift kick in the teeth."*[12] *Discuss the possible positive and negative effects of the heirs' role in the decision-making process and in the publishing business, especially as they played out in the case of* The Original of Laura.

LELAND DE LA DURANTAYE: Criticism of Dmitri Nabokov's choice to publish the work and of the preface he wrote for it has been sharp and not unfounded. The reasons for the former are obvious, if debatable, and have been rehearsed too often to need repeating here. The harsh reactions of readers of the preface to *The Original of Laura* are also not difficult to understand – from the decorous disappointment heard in reviews like that of Martin Amis, to more fierce expressions, such as John Banville's, who called Dmitri Nabokov's preface "lamentable" and "frequently repellent," to Alexander Theroux's still harsher judgment that it was "nonsensical, snobbish and cruel."[13] That said – and this is something I think it is important to bear in mind – whatever one feels about the case of Laura, it should be recalled that up to the point of its publication Dmitri Nabokov has been a wonderful executor. He had indeed been protective of his father's legacy – as in the Pia Pera incident, to name just one – but that seems to me a natural vigilance. The power he has is easy to misuse, and I think whatever shortcomings he has shown of late are counterbalanced by his earlier decisions and the work – in so many domains, beginning with translation – he has done. When compared with a notoriously thorny character like Stephen Joyce I think that Dmitri Nabokov's general benevolence shines through quite clearly – especially in relation to the question of access to archival data and the granting of legal permissions. For my part, I don't admire his decision to publish, but I do admire the man.

OLGA VORONINA: Dmitri Nabokov was not the only heir who promoted his father's legacy, but he might have been the only one who did so outside of politics and within the limits of the law. Two other cases immediately come to mind. There is the Ayn Rand Institute (ARI), a tenacious protector of Rand's copyright as well as a participant in protests against legislation that the ARI deems "anti-objectivist" (one of the institute's directors, Peter LePort, has co-founded Americans for Free Choice in Medicine, which opposes President Obama's health care reform). And there is Stephen James Joyce, James Joyce's grandson. He has been notorious for his campaigns against performers and scholars who wish to recite, quote, or interpret Joyce in ways he finds unacceptable. Stephen Joyce's lawsuits and mere threats, directed at Ireland's most distinguished institutions, such as the Irish Government and the National Library, have earned him the title of "The Injustice Collector."[14] Rumours circulate that he has destroyed some of the family correspondence, including the documents that he had recalled from the National Library archives. Both Stephen James Joyce and the ARI cite "selfless devotion" as their chief motivation.

MICHAEL JULIAR: Dmitri Nabokov rightfully did all he could to place *The Original of Laura* in front of the reading public. From what I have seen, he did a sharp and aggressive job. His father couldn't have asked for more in the promotion of his legacy.

GALYA DIMENT: I have to take a bit of an issue with Olga. To begin with, there are obviously plenty of other heirs who promote their parents' writings outside of politics. And second, Dmitri did not precisely hide his strong political opinions when he chose to keep a well-publicized blog several years ago. In general, it is inevitable that heirs are in charge of many literary estates. Some, like Dmitri Nabokov (who does not even have other siblings to reckon with) exercise sole power; others allow special committees to share in the decision-making. It is clear that Nabokov himself wanted no one but his wife and son making the calls after his death. It was his right – as it was theirs – not to share the authority with anyone about what to do with the writer's unpublished materials (while seeking occasional advice from some Nabokov scholars, among them Stephen Parker and Brian Boyd). Véra and Dmitri Nabokov mostly appeared to me to have made wise decisions, as when they allowed the publication of Nabokov's *Lectures on Literature, Lectures on Russian Literature,* and *Lectures on Don Quixote*. Nabokov probably would have objected to those publications, since he wanted only polished perfection to appear to his public under his name; however, unlike his novels, these were not his main trade.

OLGA VORONINA: Let's also note here that Dmitri Nabokov's role in the perpetuation of the Nabokov heritage is enormous but, as the publication of *Laura* has demonstrated, he has facilitated rather than limited access to unpublished Nabokoviana. In this particular case no one else would have been able to make the decision about preserving the manuscript and making it available to the public. The notions of "positive" or "negative" effect do not seem to be applicable to this kind of decision-making. Dmitri has allowed Nabokov's readers and critics to judge his father, which is the bravest thing any heir could do.

Now, whether we judge Nabokov's work or Dmitri's involvement in its publication is an entirely different question. What transpired in the post-publication media campaign reflected the critics' desire to participate in deciding the fate of the manuscript. "Is it, as the blurb claims, Nabokov's 'final great book'? No. Does it contain brilliant, funny, astonishing sentences only Nabokov could have written? Yes. Should it have been preserved and published? Definitely."[15] This is David Lodge writing in the *Literary Review*. "It would be ridiculous, of course, to blame the deceased for the estate sale," quips Aleksandar Hemon in *Slate*, blaming Dmitri instead for exposing his father "to a gloating, greedy world of academics, publishers, and the other card-shuffling mediocrities titillated by the sight of a helpless genius."[16] Greedy, mediocre, and card-shuffling, I am with Lodge.

ERIC NAIMAN: Dmitri Nabokov has created an interesting dilemma for the reviewer and scholar, in part because the publication of *The Original of Laura* emphasizes the ways in which those roles may diverge. Is the work an aesthetic miscarriage, or does it make sense to read it as Nabokov's final metafictive word? Most of us who are trained to read closely look first for structural coherence, even if we eventually delight in that coherence's fragility. We all probably doubt that Nabokov would have published this novel in index cards, but here they are, the fragments of a novel, and Nabokov's carefully constructed writing has given me so much pleasure in the past that in opening this book I felt a duty to try to read it as if it were *Pnin*, or at least part of what *Pnin* would have been had the nutcracker fallen just a fraction of an inch to the left. In this respect, the scholar is more fortunate than the reviewer, paradoxically in the position of being able to adopt a more playful attitude toward this text. Many reviewers seem to have had their moral buttons pushed by this edition, as if they had a duty to protect the reader – or Nabokov – from fraudulent merchandise.

YURI LEVING: *Do the matters of facilitating access to archival data, legal permissions, and endorsements have any implications for scholarly research in general and Nabokov studies in particular?*

OLGA VORONINA: Facilitating access to archives would always, in the case of any writer, benefit scholarly research. But the problem often lies not with the heirs or estates, but with the archives themselves. While the New York Public Library has invested significant effort into cataloguing and preserving the Nabokov archive, thus making it a pleasure to work with, the Library of Congress has merely – and rather carelessly – kept its riches. A catalogue of all Nabokov archival holdings would be a blessing to have.

SELLING NABOKOV: ECONOMICS OF CULTURE AND THE MARKET OF LITERARY RARITIES

YURI LEVING: The Original of Laura *was reported number one in sales in Russia when over 50,000 copies sold in November and December 2009. In the United States and the United Kingdom (where, on the day of its release, the book had to compete with Sarah Palin's debut memoir,* Going Rogue*), sales appeared to be much more modest, despite a loud publicity campaign. How would you explain this phenomenon?*

MICHAEL JULIAR: On my bookshelves are more than twenty-one running feet of Nabokov volumes: those published in Russian in the Soviet Union as it was dissolving, and those now published in Russia. Among these hundreds of books from dozens of publishers (when copyright law was flouted) are reprints, reprints of reprints, unauthorized editions, cheap, pulpy affairs, elegant leather-bound volumes, and series of books sporting uniform covers and attempting to encompass the full range of the author's works. And so many of those books were printed in quantities that put our bestseller lists to shame: Runs of a hundred thousand and more at a time were not unusual. Russians love their native author and buy and read him. So *The Original of Laura*, a new Nabokov, even if fragmented, incomplete, and in translation, is a literary event in Russia. But, in America, who cares? Who reads?

GALYA DIMENT: In Russia the reception was, indeed, markedly different – but so was at least one edition. Together with a Russian replica of American and English editions, they also published a much smaller and very inexpensive *Laura i ee original* (Azbooka-klassika, 2010). It contains just 188 4 × 6.5 (as opposed to 6 × 9.5) pages, and that includes more than 50 pages of translator Gennady Barabtarlo's essay in the back. It is defined there as "Fragments of a Novel," and not "A Novel in Fragments," while the "Dying Is Fun" subtitle is altogether missing. The cards (in English) are partly reproduced on four pages (two in the very beginning of the book, and two at the very end), while the narrative is run as a straightforward text. The size of the book and its price (anywhere from 160 to 230 rubles, which is roughly $6–$8) therefore do not artificially inflate its importance, the way English and American editions did. As to Palin, being able to see Russia from her porch in Alaska did not, as far as I know, translate into her being a bestselling author there.

OLGA VORONINA: The idea of Nabokov competing with Sarah Palin is deliciously grotesque. Their readers line up in different queues, with the Nabokov line continuing on the other side of the Atlantic. That said, the half-million figure of Russian sales characterizes not so much the Russian people's disregard for political ego trips as their heightened sense of cultural continuity and national identity as shaped by culture.

Very few Russian readers situate Nabokov in the 1920s to 1970s, the years when he was banned from publication and therefore could not be read openly. For the majority, he belongs to the post-Soviet era of opened literary floodgates, with its spiritual exhilaration and the promise of socio-political renewal. Although that ardour has been dampened, *The Original of Laura* might be attractive as a reminder of the 1990s. There is also a never-ending sentiment of Nabokov's "return" to Russia, something I would hear – and speak of – during my years at the Nabokov Museum in St. Petersburg. Finally (although I should have probably started here), *Laura* attracts Russian audiences because it is a work of literature, a book beyond and above the glorified ghettos of crime, horror, and romance fiction, into which Russian publishers herd their readers these days. For a nation that continues to be taught great books throughout middle and high schools as well as in college, the lack of literary talent on the market is more than obvious.

YURI LEVING: *Nabokov never won the Nobel Prize for literature, and yet he remains one of the best-selling and most studied and admired authors. How would you place Nabokov in the cycle of literary prizes and production values (in Pierre Bourdieu's sense of the politics of culture and the symbolic capital of linguistic utterances)?*

GALYA DIMENT: I personally do not believe Nabokov's legacy is in need of any extraordinary measures (but now it is definitely in need of no more inflicted harm). That Nabokov never won a Nobel Prize puts him in better company (Tolstoy, Joyce, Proust) than had he won one. Nobel Prizes rarely make a writer more admired or studied unless he or she is already held in high esteem. There are few writers who intrigue and gratify discerning readers more that Nabokov – and these are the only readers he ever cared about, and the only readers he truly deserves. They will stay with him for many generations to come.

MICHAEL JULIAR: The Nobel Prize is irrelevant. It is not a prize for popularity, success, literary depth, or academic interest. Its impermanent relevancy is that it pins a badge on the puffed-out covers of the winning author's books and so a few more copies are sold.

OLGA VORONINA: When Nabokov sent a copy of his "Pilgram" ("The Aurelian") in French to the king of Belgium, he described the gesture to Vera as a pleasant walk on "the grass lawn of tradition." Although patronage of the arts has a long and respectable pedigree, literary prizes are mostly a 20th-century phenomenon. The award distinguishes the giver rather than the awardee. Proust, Kafka, Joyce, Mandelstam, and Akhmatova never received the Nobel. Their "symbolic capital," however, continues to soar.

YURI LEVING: *The distinguished manuscript dealer Mary Benjamin wrote: "Autograph collecting, whether in the historical or the literary realm, is more than a hobby. It is a philosophy of quiet pleasure."*[17] *Nabokov seemed always to be quite aware of the future value of his own material. Provide a historical and socio-economic perspective on Nabokov's manuscripts and rare editions for sale.*

OLGA VORONINA: Akhmatova gave out her manuscripts to friends and acquaintances like clippings from an old newspaper. The poet could not keep them all in the battered suitcase that she had to carry around for fear that her archive would be perused and/or confiscated. In the 1940s, she also knew that only the most devoted of her admirers would risk preserving her drafts – even a short autograph could implicate the keeper. Unlike Akhmatova, Nabokov lived (for the most part) in liberal societies where the value of a manuscript matched the popularity of the author. And, unlike her, he knew that liberalism, with its plurality of opinions, could also put an author in danger of having his work posthumously distorted, misinterpreted, or mistranslated. A scholar of Pushkin and Tolstoy and a connoisseur of Shakespeare's legacy, he commented on the failure of authorial control in *Bend Sinister* and *Pale Fire*. A collector himself, he made sure that copies of his books, decorated with his butterfly drawings, would provide "quiet pleasure" for those who possessed them.

In my opinion, VN's autographed first editions, generously given to family and friends, and his closely watched and smartly institutionalized manuscripts represent two ends of the power spectrum. While the butterfly autographs raised the aesthetic and sentimental values of the book that was leaving the author's hands, the tight supervision increased the worth of manuscripts that would, metaphorically speaking, never part with their creator.

YURI LEVING: *The effect of scholarly use and publication on the monetary value of manuscripts is often a factor to consider. Some dealers encourage collectors to disregard requests for use and not permit access, and certainly not publication, because they feel that publication automatically reduces the resale value. On the other hand, the scholar and the editor may suggest that its value would be enhanced by publication in an important and prestigious edition.*[18] *Could you address the market vs. institutional/research value of Nabokoviana (manuscripts, correspondence, rare and inscribed editions)?*

OLGA VORONINA: Both are high and will not deteriorate with time.

GALYA DIMENT: Dmitri Nabokov's answer in the Introduction to *The Original of Laura* is basically that he did what he did simply because he could. Elsewhere in his interviews, the explanation focuses on the otherworldly presence of Vladimir Nabokov giving the son a blessing and seemingly encouraging him to make a nice profit while he was at it. I have no doubt that the loving father in Nabokov would sacrifice everything, including his reputation, for the well-being of his son. I just wish his loving son had not exposed his father to such a barrage of negative publicity, amplified as it was by the hullabaloo accompanying the publication.

ERIC NAIMAN: I nearly always agree with Galya, but not here. Even dead, Nabokov is still a big boy who can take care of himself. The publication of *The Original of Laura* will lead to more reading – and rereading of Nabokov's other works ... and of work about them. In other words, Dmitri's profits will trickle down; all who write about his father will be the richer for it. (Except, perhaps, the inconceivable soul for whom *Laura* would be Nabokov's first book, but the initial edition would have to be very deeply discounted before such a thing could happen.)

GALYA DIMENT: That's a scary thought, especially since one can buy it on Amazon by now for $10.

YURI LEVING: *What, in your judgment, might be the reasons for the flop of Lot 95 (Nabokov's* Laura *manuscript) during the Christie's auction in New York in early December 2009 (held just three weeks after the international release of the long-anticipated book)?*

MICHAEL JULIAR: The manuscript of 138 index cards didn't sell at Christie's on 4 December because it hadn't had time to develop the cultural resonance that arouses a man or woman to spend a large amount of money on a desired object. Simply, the public didn't know the book well enough, didn't care about it enough, and had an image of it being an incomplete artifact. Some years from now (twenty? fifty?), though, I think that people will have come around to "seeing" *The Original of Laura* as the last flowering of Nabokov's genius, as fragmented as it may be, and find it very desirable. And the $280,000 level that the bidding got to isn't to be sniffed at. That was a very fair price, especially in these shallow-pocket times.[19]

LELAND DE LA DURANTAYE: I can only imagine that the failed crying of Lot 95 was the result of the largely negative reviews of the book's publication coupled with the disappointed reactions of so many readers who bought the book during the three weeks between its publication and the auction.

OLGA VORONINA: I don't think that the negative publicity has anything to do with it. The timing of the auction was poor, though. The much-advertised publication of the new (and last) Nabokov novel could have excited an individual buyer but, as Michael says, in this economy individuals continue to part with their money carefully. For an institution, however, the publishing fever and media commotion were not significant enough reasons to justify an expensive purchase. The manuscript of *Laura* might have been sold for $400,000 or even $600,000 a year or years before the publication, with special precautions made with regard to Dmitri Nabokov's sole control of publishing rights.

GALYA DIMENT: I second Leland here. I believe it was the over-the-top marketing campaign in the United States and England that led to the flop of Christie's Lot 95. As a reviewer in *The Independent* stated, to many the auction simply could not "escape the musty air of an estate sale."[20] I would like to see the cards go to the Berg Collection at the New York Public Library or, my distant second choice, the Library of Congress. Even though they have already been reproduced, for many of us there is a special feeling in viewing or holding Nabokov's originals.

YURI LEVING: *The fate of the 138 index cards is still undecided.*[21] *Some believe that, to provide scholars with primary materials for examination of the editing, the holograph cards should be preserved in one of the two major Nabokov manuscript repositories. What is your opinion about this, especially considering that all cards have already been faithfully reproduced in high resolution, reprinted, and sold as simulacra?*

MICHAEL JULIAR: A manuscript is still a unique item no matter how often it is reproduced, photographed, copied, or facsimiled. There is information of real value buried in the original: the paper, the graphite in the pencil, the red and blue lines, the smudge of the eraser. It must all be preserved and made available in an institution.[22]

OLGA VORONINA: I am a big fan of the Berg Collection, which should receive all the kudos for maintaining the Nabokov archive in impeccable order. If Dmitri Nabokov could deposit the cards at the Berg, the institutional value of the collection would certainly go up, while the cards would acquire a safe home. But I don't want to disregard the Nabokov Museum as a possible repository, either. The symbolism of Nabokov's last manuscript returning to the house where the writer was born is rather transparent. And the popularity of *Laura* in Russia just might motivate one of the many Russian oligarchs to buy it for the museum.

YURI LEVING: *What can be said of the writer's manuscripts and memorabilia as mechanisms of generating public interest beyond scholarship?*

OLGA VORONINA: The manuscripts and memorabilia amplify the value of Nabokov's art for those who already appreciate it, but they have little to do with "generating public interest." People who come to the Nabokov Museum (or, at least, used to come there ten years ago) want to see the house and the first editions because they have already read *Speak, Memory*, *Lolita* or "Spring in Fialta." I know a number of readers for whom the encounter with the memorial space and its objects has heightened their appreciation of Nabokov; I know no one in whom the visit has instigated it. This is why I believe that Nabokov's manuscripts or lepidopterized books cannot be "mechanisms" of anything. In my experience, they are visible only to those who have already sprouted a Nabokovian "third eye."

EVALUATING *THE ORIGINAL OF LAURA*: A REPUTATION IN FRAGMENTS?

YURI LEVING: *The public debate concerning whether Nabokov's incomplete novel should be published significantly lacked scholarly voices. While bloggers, journalists and notable fiction writers fiercely exchanged their opinions, participants in the major electronic forum* NABOKV-L, *mainly academics and reputable Nabokov scholars, seemed to be extremely cautious. How would you explain this silence about or even suppression of something that the non-academic world has taken as a vital issue?*

OLGA VORONINA: The non-academic (or, rather, non-Nabokovian) world was curious about the publication of *The Original of Laura* as an act of filial disobedience and a failed case of literary *auto-da-fé*. The academic world waited for the text to be published and now needs time to read it and ponder its riddles. If journalists enjoy the luxury of voicing their opinions before being asked a question, scholars luxuriate in their ability to ask a question no one has thought. It is hard to do this with *Laura*, though. The novel's authorial intent is obscured by Nabokov's last will and by the fact that we can only guess what and how much is missing from the book. Even if the question were asked, its answer would necessarily have to end in ellipsis.

LELAND DE LA DURANTAYE: I don't agree that scholars were silent. Many wrote reviews (one need only think of Brian Boyd and Michael Wood). The caution of the electronic forum is a separate matter, and it should be borne in mind that the majority of major critics rarely enter into those discussions. Brian Boyd is a very notable exception, but does not disprove the rule. If we discount NABOKV-L, what we have are the reviews that have already appeared in major publications by major critics, and the scholarly work that takes time to get into print and which we, thus, have not yet seen.

On another note, those who were what you call cautious should be separated into two camps. The first consists of those who were cautious because they had not read the manuscript – a group that included virtually everyone until the book was published. There were the very few who had had access to the manuscript in the past (such as Brian Boyd, of course), and those who were able to read the proofs in the months leading up to publication, but only those reviewers who were willing to go to Knopf's offices (review copies were not circulated) and read them on site. That this first camp would have been reserved while others debated the manuscript sight unseen in newspapers, blogs, and the like is the most natural thing in the world. The second camp consists of those who were silent or reserved *after* the publication of the work. In many cases I think this can be attributed to the sense that everything relevant had already been said and that it was time to turn to other matters.

GALYA DIMENT: Why have so few, with the exception of Eric Naiman in the *San Francisco Chronicle* and Brian Boyd in the *Financial Times*, rushed to write reviews for the mainstream press? Partly, I believe, it's because while we can argue among ourselves, when confronted with the outside world we tend to treat Nabokov as a member of our own family: If you cannot say something nice, then don't say anything at all. And then there is, of course, the "Dmitri factor." Being called a "moron" in print is nothing compared to his potential refusal to allow one access to the materials or necessary copyright permissions for one's book or article, so angering him can definitely impede one's professional goals.

YURI LEVING: *Let's turn now to the critical reception of* The Original of Laura *upon its publication. What tendencies can be discerned in the massive corpus of reviews that appeared in virtually all major newspapers and magazines?*

ERIC NAIMAN: How to approach *The Original of Laura?* Kindness to which author? One of the principal fault lines running through the initial spate of reviews seems to have been the difficulty of determining whether to treat the book as a unified aesthetic object, and whether it was appropriate to offer an interpretive reading of Nabokov's last gasp. The book is beautiful, the book is a fraud, the book is a toolbox with butterflies or birdies just waiting to fly free – the reader's task is to carefully detach the cards; an act of liberation that can only lead to the necessity of buying another copy. The kindest thing, some readers seem to suggest, would be to give the text a decent burial at the back of a scholarly edition.

LELAND DE LA DURANTAYE: Disappointment. With a few notable exceptions. As for the source of the disappointment, some reviewers attributed this to the waning of the author's powers with age, while others attributed it to the simple fact that Nabokov had not been granted time to bring the work to anything approaching a state of completion. This is an interesting question to reflect upon, but it is ultimately based on the reader's intuition. My personal sense is that Nabokov's final novel, *Look at the Harlequins!* was less compelling than what went before it not because of the authors' waning powers but because of a certain self-indulgence. Consequently, I see no reason to assume that, given world enough and time, *The Original of Laura* could not have developed into as fine a work as, say, *Ada.*

GALYA DIMENT: Many reviews raised largely the same issues: that it is not a novel in fragments but just fragments; that it was oversold and under-delivered; that it features an unhealthy preoccupation with sex with minors (leading such devoted fans as Martin Amis to wonder whether Nabokov was, after all, suffering from "nympholepsy"); that it reveals not just an old and dying human being but a rapidly dying talent; that it is full of immature puns and "fragile spelling," etc., etc. Special acerbity has been reserved for Dmitri Nabokov's introduction, which some critics found "atrocious," "petty," and bent more on revisiting past slights than on framing the work and the decision to publish it in a serious way that would truly respect Nabokov's numerous admirers.

To me, the most curious tendency was some sympathetic reviewers' struggle to come to terms with their conflicting critical emotions. Brian Boyd, for example, recently detailed his initial reaction to *The Original of Laura* ("Destroy it") and how he has come to change his opinion about it ("It's not another *Lolita* or *Pale Fire*, but could have been, and already is, another fascinating Nabokov novel").[23] I usually trust Brian's intuition when it comes to Nabokov, but I do think he tries too hard here to attribute the imperfections of what we have in front of us to Nabokov's wily technique to "mislead our expectations."

OLGA VORONINA: I have already commented on some of the critical responses to *The Original of Laura* and would like to repeat here that, to me, the reviewers' opinions seem surprisingly uniform. Most of the essays pay tribute to sensational journalism rather than literary analysis. The central, and rather comic, trend consists of critics' attempts to summarize the novel's plot to the reader who is warned beforehand that not only is there no story but that there won't be one, no matter how hard we try. Some of the reviewers, perhaps inspired by Peter Brooks' idea that reading (and, by a Freudian analogy, writing) is a gratification of death urge, insist that Nabokov had no desire to finish his novel. ("*The Original of Laura* was never intended to be shuffled into any sequence whatsoever," claims Michael Dirda in *The Washington Post*.)[24] Others, on the contrary, doubt that "A novel in fragments" is an appropriate subtitle. For David Gates of *The New York Times' Sunday Book Review*, *Laura* is not "some deliberate experiment in form" but, rather, a literary puzzle, "arranged in sensible, if debatable, order."[25]

YURI LEVING: *Were you surprised by what emerged in this critical discourse?*

GALYA DIMENT: It should not come as a surprise from everything I stated above that I was not at all surprised by the many dismissive reviews of *The Original of Laura* here in the United States and devastating ones in the United Kingdom. I was actually more intrigued by the exceptions, as when Michiko Kakutani of *The New York Times*, despite her reputation as a tough critic, was rather magnanimous in her evaluation. Likewise, John Lancaster treated it with kid gloves in *The New York Review of Books*.

LELAND DE LA DURANTAYE: No, not really. I was mildly surprised by a few blandly positive reviews, just as I was (less) surprised by the vehemence of a few negative ones – reviews whose vehemence, it should be noted, was directed not at the author but at his son.

OLGA VORONINA: There are a lot of surprises to discuss here. Mine was to discover how many journalists did not even make an attempt to read *The Original of Laura* as a work of literature. Enthralled by Knopf's solution to the problem of the novel's fragmentary nature, they preferred to discuss it as a book and not as text. Sam Anderson in *The New York Magazine* calls *Laura* an "object," "an exquisite thing."[26] Alexander Theroux in the *Wall Street Journal* goes even further. For him, *Laura* has a "play-kit quality," as if there were not enough play kits around Barnes & Nobel aleady. Curiously, for the same reviewer the style of a book about dying should not be anything but tragic. "There are witty Nabokovian moments as well," Theroux exclaims, obviously in shock.[27] The rather artificial, in my opinion, subtitle "Dying is Fun" is probably intended for just this kind of reader.

ERIC NAIMAN: One of the effects surrounding the roll-out of this book has been distraction. Would Dmitri destroy the cards? That fear looks odd now: an initial worry that thirty years from now the text would survive only as a memory in Brian Boyd's brain – or in his notes, a curious Nabokovian equivalent to the Igor Tale[28] – quickly gave way to reviewers' comments that too much was being made of these fragments. The packaging struck some as extravagant. The introduction was too long. But there are some absolutely wonderful things in this book, and the figure of Philip Wild is marvellous – in many respects an imaginative and even logical development of Nabokov's metafictive concerns. This is a character who loves himself to death, as if Nabokov were taking to its extreme the dynamic of creative narcissism which he fascinatingly embraced and parodied throughout his entire career. "One might dissolve completely that way," thinks Fyodor as he is licked all over by the sun,[29] and here, in a wonderful twist on a creator's Savage Love for his characters, Wild usurps the authorial power to do away with his characters, becoming the metafictive version of [Dostoyevsky's] Kirillov. The edition captures this sense of a dissolving, collapsing text. Dmitri Nabokov and [the book designer] Chip Kidd seem to have understood this aspect of the novel's potential and teased it out. The resulting impression is not so much of an unfinished text as it is of a remainder – of the novel whose hero has managed to flee the text as well as of the now deceased author himself. This sensation will only be enhanced in the future, when we encounter in secondhand bookshops (or online) copies of the book from which some of the cards have been removed and gone missing.

YURI LEVING: *When we asked the two chief curators of the largest institutional depositories of Nabokov materials (the Library of Congress and the Berg Collection of the New York Public Library) if they expect that a publication of* The Original of Laura *would give an additional impetus to future discoveries and publications related to Nabokov's archival materials, both seemed sceptical.*[30] *What is your take on that issue, especially after the revelation of the text of* The Original of Laura?

LELAND DE LA DURANTAYE: I see every reason to trust their judgment (and no reason not to).

OLGA VORONINA: I do, too. Future Nabokovian discoveries are not the same thing as the future publications of previously unavailable Nabokov manuscripts. It is hard for me to imagine how the appearance of *The Original of Laura* could significantly contribute to our reinterpretation of, say, *Pale Fire* or *Look at the Harlequins!*, but I can easily see why publishers, always ready to capitalize on a media frenzy, would now want to investigate other possibilities of issuing the yet unpublished Nabokov.

YURI LEVING: *Nabokov, the canon, and the "common reader." How do you think this triangular relationship has been affected in the wake of the recent campaign that accompanied the publication of* The Original of Laura *and Nabokov's general rebranding?*

OLGA VORONINA: I wonder who "branded" Nabokov in the first place. "Common reader" is for "common ideas," Nabokov would say, while any truly original literature requires a reader with "uncommon visage." *Laura* will probably never be canonized, but it will take its rightful place in the niche reserved for unfinished books with a tragic fate, such as Kafka's writings, published by Max Brod, "Hero and Leander" by Christopher Marlowe, *Weir of Hermiston* by Robert Louis Stevenson, and *Answered Prayers* by Truman Capote.

LELAND DE LA DURANTAYE: Oh, not at all. Not durably, at least. I've made clear elsewhere that I was not in favour of publication, but I tried to be equally clear about there being no durable harm that publication could do to Nabokov's reputation – and thus none to his place in any canon or to his relationship to readers.

MICHAEL JULIAR: It is all nothing but a tiny splash in a distant northern lake.

GALYA DIMENT: Well said. It will be soon forgotten by all but Nabokov specialists.

ERIC NAIMAN: I'm not so sure the impact of *The Original of Laura* will be negligible. There is a tendency in Nabokov studies for scholars to take a single work and read all of Nabokov's oeuvre back through it. Boyd's take on Nabokov is heavily indebted to "The Vane Sisters," Nafisi's to *Invitation to a Beheading* and, for all we know, they might be right. It would be equally possible – and justifiably preposterous in a Nabokovian sense – to inflect an interpretation of Nabokov's earlier fiction through this final work. Many new aspects of the older works might be illuminated in a fascinating and unexpected light.

Reading Is Fun: Approaches to Analysis

Vanishing Fragments[1]

MICHAEL WOOD

One of the attractions of Nabokov's view of literature is that although (or because) he scoffed at any idea of readerly independence he scarcely ever wanted to separate the writer's interests from the reader's. He was prepared to indulge in a kind of crazed fusion of the two in his commentary on *Eugene Onegin,* and to parody that same craziness in *Pale Fire*. When he defined his ideal of "aesthetic bliss" in literature, in his afterword to *Lolita,* he was speaking as a reader and a writer – to be precise, as "neither a reader nor a writer of didactic fiction" but of something else[2] – and when late in life he told a journalist from *The New York Times* what he was currently reading he listed three books: a translation of Dante's *Inferno,* a book on North American butterflies, and his own novel *The Original of Laura.*

Wait a minute. If he was reading it, why can't we? It wasn't finished, of course, and Nabokov's expressed wish was that it be destroyed. But it wasn't destroyed, and it is now published in a handsome, not to say lavish, edition. So why can't we read it, or read more of it? Why are we stranded with a small handful of fragments, some of them luminous, some of them mysterious, and some of them quite opaque? Well, of course Nabokov was reading the novel as he wrote it. The work was, as he said, "completed in [his] mind," and like many writers he was slightly exaggerating his progress in getting it down on the page, or in his case the index card. He was working, he reported, on a "not quite finished manuscript of a novel."[3] Those words "completed" and "not quite" have become far more significant, more moving, and more ambiguous, than they were when first written.

Nabokov was ill, and the stylish and playful continuation of his response to the query from the journalist revealed an unmistakable worry. He chose to stage his fever, to dramatize for his readers what he called his "diurnal delirium." He was not only reading but "reading ... aloud to a small dream audience in a walled garden. My audience consisted of peacocks, pigeons, my long dead parents, two cypresses, several young nurses crouching around, and a family doctor so old as to be almost invisible."[4]

We may think, as Nabokov was pretty certainly thinking, of the scene in *Pnin* where our hero, about to give a lecture, briefly sees, instead of his actual audience, "one of his Baltic aunts," "a dead sweetheart," his dead parents, "both a little blurred but on the whole wonderfully recovered from their recent dissolution," and a crowd of old friends, eloquently described as "murdered, forgotten, unrevenged, incorrupt, immortal."[5] Nabokov's late audience was neither so large nor so steeped in violent history, but it was thoroughly imagined in every detail, and he felt, curiously, that it was rather hard on him. "Perhaps because of my stumblings and fits of coughing the story of my poor Laura had less success with my listeners than it will have, I hope, with intelligent reviewers when properly published."[6]

Even allowing for the neat advertisement for the book to come, this sentence shows a writer who has his doubts. He can't help the coughing, but why is he stumbling as he reads? Doesn't he have a completed book in his mind? And what about the listeners he sets before us with such care? Cypresses can be tough critics, I'm sure. Peacocks and pigeons are not going to listen properly. I can't imagine what the "crouching" nurses are doing, and the doctor, as we shall see in a moment, appears to have slipped out of the novel itself. That leaves only his parents, and perhaps they will have been shocked by the high level of sexual content, or by the dreary lack of sexual enjoyment. What Nabokov's little tale suggests is that he knew – had always known, whatever performances of imperial confidence he regularly chose to put on – how fragile the bridge is that leads from thoughts to written words, and how long the journey can be from a mentally finished book to something an editor can take away and print.

Too fragile, and too long, in this case. Nabokov had the idea for *The Original of Laura* as early as April 1974. The letter to the journalist from the *New York Times* is dated October 1976. He died in July 1977. In

February 1976, he noted in his diary, "New novel more or less completed and copied 54 cards. In 4 batches from different parts of the novel. Plus notes and drafts."[7] "More or less" is like the "not quite" I quoted earlier, and I think we have to take "completed" and "copied" as meaning what the rest of us might call "thoroughly planned" and "written." Nabokov was not deceiving himself or his publisher, but his notes suggest he desperately wanted to overtake the time that was running away from him so fast, and to provide those tough listeners in the garden with something that would make them happier. In April 1976, he informed his diary that he had "transcribed in final form 50 cards = 5000 words."[8] By this accounting, a novel of, say, 60,000 words would require 600 cards. The set published by Knopf and Penguin,[9] which includes quite a bit of material manifestly not "in final form," has 138 cards. Not a novel in fragments, as the subtitle ingeniously has it, and not even fragments of a novel, because we can't see what the novel is: just fragments, treasurable, tantalizing, and desperately looking for the narrative home they will never have.

The 50 or 54 cards Nabokov mentions, or some number thereabouts, are relatively easy to identify in the published text. There is a clean copy of chapters one and two (38 cards), and there are beginnings of chapters three, four and five (6, 4, and 5 cards respectively). There is the beginning of another chapter five with the "five" crossed out, so presumably this one was to be renumbered. The rest of the cards show material together under letters or names or themes (Ex, D, Wild, legs). There are two intelligible stories here, or at least the beginnings of two such stories, and there are hints of several more. The first intelligible story, that of the opening five chapters, concerns a twenty-four-year-old woman called Flora, her charm, her physical attraction, her scatterbrained promiscuity and her early life. The other story is about a neurologist called Philip Wild, a man of a certain age and an even more certain obesity. He writes in the first person of what he calls "the art of self-slaughter" (265) – not suicide, but a form of mental magic in which he makes his unloved body disappear bit by bit, only to resurrect it at the end of the session, ready for another vanishing the next day, or when he feels like it.

Flora and Philip are married, and are clearly a deep disappointment to each other. He has some of the fame and fortune she wished to wed, but not enough; and he is used to her infidelities without ceasing to be pained by them. "She saw their travels in terms of adverts and a long talcum-white beach with the tropical breeze tossing the palms and her hair; he saw it [sic] in terms of forbidden foods, frittered away time, and ghastly expenses" (115).

They're made for each other, in a way: locked in their own cheap myths and clichés. Philip does have a villa on the Riviera, but it has no swimming pool and only one bathroom. If Flora started to make changes, "he would emit a kind of mild creak or squeak, and his brown eyes brimmed with sudden tears" (113). The creak or squeak is very fine, and now we feel sorry for him, repellent as he is. When he talks to her "between trains, between planes, between lovers," she says things like "You really ought to lose some weight" or "I hope you transferred that money as I indicated." And then, as Wild writes, "all doors closed again" (263). Nabokov has a great gift for making us care about the unloved characters in his novels – but only briefly. We'd rather hang out with the abandoners than the abandoned, and we can enjoy Flora's company because we're not married to her and because, as Woody Allen would say, she's only fictional.

Into this mix Nabokov clearly planned to insert a novel written by the narrator of the opening pages; that is, a person who knows (and sleeps with) Flora and turns her into a thinly disguised character called Laura. Or actually called FLaura at one point, when Nabokov is beginning to mix his fictions. *Laura*, or *My Laura* as it is called at times, perhaps written by one Ivan Vaughan, a name not without a resemblance to that of Van Veen in *Ada*, is a bestseller, and hangs on in the charts for three months or so. Does it portray Flora in Laura? The picture is "statically" faithful, we are told, but its final story is that of "a neurotic and hesitant man of letters who destroys his mistress in the act of portraying her" (121). But then someone, possibly the same writer, is describing Flora as she was before and outside the book. Indeed Flora herself reads the book, or almost reads the book. She buys it when she is, once again, between trains, this time (or maybe as always) at a place called Sex, "a delightful Swiss resort famed for its crimson plums" (223), but loses it to a friend who has read it and wants to show her the passage with her "wonderful death." The work, the friend says, "is, of course, fictionalized and all that but you'll come face to face with yourself at every other corner" (225). At every corner, one might think, but that's fiction for you. A train takes the friend and the book away.

We have no way of knowing how the three texts – *My Laura*, Wild's memoir, and the narrative that surrounds them – would finally have meshed, or what they would have added up to. We are on firm ground with the opening chapters, though, which strike me as quite remarkable, a sort of experiment in the purveyance of what Ada calls, in the novel named after her, "rapid narrative information," along the lines of "you recall Brown, don't you, Smith?"[10] The work begins "Her husband, she answered, was a writer, too – at least, after a fashion. Fat men beat their wives, it is said, and he certainly looked fierce, when he caught her riffling through his papers. He pretended to slam down a marble paperweight and crush this weak little hand (displaying the little hand in febrile motion)[.] Actually she was searching for a silly business letter – and not in the least trying to decipher his mysterious manuscript. Oh no, it was not a work of fiction which one dashes off, you know, to make money; it was a mad neurologist's testament, a kind of Poisonous Opus as in that film" (1–3).[11]

We know the conversation has already started, since our heroine is answering someone who has presumably said he is a writer. The aphorism about fat men seems to come from the narrator but turns out be Flora's contribution in free, indirect speech. It is irrelevant anyway, since the event she is reporting involves a pretend threat and no sort of regular beating. It's true that the claim that fat men occasionally pretend to crush their wives' hands is less compelling, even if you can wave the hand in question. We gather that Flora knows her husband is a writer because she accidentally found his work, and the whole ditzy show is either the way she goes about flirting or just the effect of her being a little drunk, as we soon learn she is. Either way, she manages casually to insult her interlocutor, the presumed writer ("you know, to make money"), and slip in an allusion to a movie I feel we are supposed to recognize but can't – or at least I can't. We now discover, in another piece of indirect speech, that "she wished to be taken home or preferably to some cool quiet place with a clean bed and room service," and then, for the first time, the narrator gets a word in. "She wore a strapless gown and slippers of black velvet. Her bare insteps were as white as her young shoulders" (3–5). But then we're off into Flora's perspective again: "The party seemed to have degenerated into a lot of sober eyes staring at her with nasty compassion from every corner, every cushion and ashtray, and even from the hills of the spring night framed in the open french window" (5).

"Nasty compassion" makes us (or at least me) sympathetic to Flora, however irritating she might be otherwise. She is taken to the clean bed she is looking for, and sleeps with the narrator, who describes her naked body as if he were Humbert Humbert taking a creative writing class: "Her frail, docile frame when turned over by hand revealed new marvels" (19). It seems as if we might already have moved into *My Laura*, or into a zone where the original and the copy have melted into language; but no, we are in some meta-place where Flora is a not a character in a book, or a model for such a character, but a person for whom a certain kind of book is the only metaphor: "Only by identifying her with an unwritten, half-written, rewritten difficult book could one hope to render at last what contemporary descriptions of intercourse so seldom convey ... Readers are directed to that book – on a very high shelf, in a very bad light – but already existing, as magic exists, and death" (21–5).

Even here, Flora and the book are only part of the story – the future tale of a sexual moment that can't fully exist until it has become history and memory.

This is a lot to do on a few index cards, and there is more. If much of the description of Flora's body resembles the linguistic drooling of Humbert, this is partly because Nabokov feels that drooling has its pathos, and partly because Flora is Lolita with an altered genealogy – Russian ballerina mother, photographer father; in one of Nabokov's finer casual extinctions, this man commits suicide after discovering "that the boy he loved had strangled another, unattainable boy whom he loved even more" (47–9) – and a different sexual history. Here a version of Humbert, conveniently called Hubert, makes a pass at Flora at age twelve and gets kicked in the crotch. The narrator was never going to linger here, since, he says, "There is little to add about the incidental, but not unattractive Mr Hubert H Hubert. He lodged for another happy year in that cosy house and died of a stroke in a hotel lift after a business dinner. Going up, one would like to surmise" (75). One would.

So what happens to Flora, apart from her many affairs and her appearance in a novel? Well, there is a hint of her becoming religious. All we really know in any detail from the rest of the cards is her husband's game of self-cancellation. A card cleverly placed at the end of the book (and copied at the beginning as a sort of announcement) lists the words "efface, expunge, erase, delete, rub out, wipe out, obliterate" (vii, 275). A poem forsooth, as Humbert might say, and a brilliant suggestion that these fragments have all been heading somewhere, even if that somewhere is nowhere. But there's no real indication that Wild's exercise is at the heart of the book, or is more important or interesting than anything else. Of course, a dream of annihilation written by a dying man is a pretty powerful proposition, but Nabokov would be the first to say the biographical detail can't rescue or alter a piece of writing. "The best part of a writer's biography is ... the story of his style," he once remarked;[12] and style is a not a bid for sympathy.

This is not to say that Wild's game is without interest. Here's how it works: "The student who desires to die should learn first of all to project a mental image of himself upon his inner blackboard" (131). Then you knock off pieces of the image as the fancy takes you. Wild believes that "the process of dying by auto-dissolution [affords] the greatest ecstasy known to man" (171), but of course you'd have to have a severe distaste for your own body to get such a kick out of its mental disappearance. "By now I have died up to my navel fifty times in less than three years and my fifty resurrections have shown that no damage is done to the organs involved when breaking in time out of the trance" (267). "To break the trance all you do is to restore in every chalk-bright details [sic] the simple picture of yourself a stylized skeleton on your men[t]al blackboard. One should remember, however, that the divine delight in destroying, say[,] one's breastbone should not be indulged in. Enjoy the destruction but do not linger over your own ruins lest you develop an incurable illness, or die before you are ready to die" (181).

Ah yes, the student who desires to die only desires to "die," to watch himself killing himself off. There is an echo here of *Ada,* where the genealogical chart at the beginning lists no death dates for Van or Ada, even though we are told on the following page that, with some exceptions, "all the persons mentioned by name in this are dead."[13] Van and Ada don't die in the book, they die into the book ("into the prose of the book or the poetry of its blurb"[14]), and Wild presumably has no intention of dying outside of his mind until he is ready, if he ever is. We can guess where this line of the plot is going – toward an accidental overdose of imagined destruction, surely – and there is mention of Wild's "fatal heart attack" (187). But the guess doesn't tell us what will happen to the liberated Flora or how she is to survive her "wonderful" fictional death or her turn to religion.

There really isn't much more. Well, there *is* a description of the only "position of copulation" Wild and Flora can manage: "he reclining on cushions: she sitting in the fauteuil of his flesh with her back to him. The procedure – a few bounces over very small humps – meant nothing to her[.] She looked at the snow-scape on the footboard of the bed – at the [curtains]; and he holding her in front of him like a child being given a sleighride down a short slope by a kind stranger, he saw her back, her hip[s] between his hands" (197–9).

The procedure, the fauteuil, the "sleighride": the comically awkward act is both sterilized and sentimentally distanced. Her indifference almost calls for his rather creepy invocation of the kind stranger, and their two imaginations do vaguely meet in the pictured snow. The marriage of untrue minds. Nabokov played out sexual despair in *Lolita,* and evoked untroubled or barely troubled sexual bliss in *Ada.* Here he seems to have been after something else: the desolation of habit, the banality of what used to be an adventure, even a taboo.

Terminating the Phrase

GENNADY BARABTARLO

... we ought really to rest thankful that at this deleteful hour of dungflies dawning we have even a written on with dried ink scrap of paper at all to show for ourselves, tare it or leaf it ...

Finnegans Wake

The more or less synchronized appearance of *The Original of Laura* in a dozen languages was preceded by an unexampled multilingual disputation, in print and pixel, the latter, of course, especially clangorous and wild. Never before had an unfinished piece of fiction been put, before its publication, to a speculative treatment so protracted and of such grotesquery. The sensational shape these speculations took not so much defies summary as makes it tedious. Since none of the contributors to those preliminary discussions had read one word of the book, their remarks were mostly of a broken-line variety (as in the telephone game), passing around, with much blur and blotch, the origins of *The Original of Laura* and its presumed subject matter. Now, of course, the story of its appearance is reasonably well known, and I shall tag only the basic facts, adding a few from personal recollection.

Nabokov would not publish what he wrote until he had polished and buffed it to his singularly high standard of perfection. By December of 1975 he had apparently finished composing this new book in his head, as was his wont, and then proceeded to write out its various parts on pocketable index cards, most out of the sequential order of the storyline.

This process followed the pattern adopted six novels earlier, but this time it was spastic: he was interrupted every now and then by an illness that required frequent hospitalizations and from which he never recovered fully enough to complete the setting-down of his latest conception. One of the early working titles was *Dying Is Fun.* In *Invitation to a Beheading,* one of Nabokov's *impersonae*, a joker, drops as if by accident a musical resolution to the plot which the death-row hero does not grasp, and which, when properly decoded, states that death is sweet, but that secret must not be revealed.[1]

Four years after Nabokov's death, his widow told me of his last, unfinished novel. "I was under orders to burn it" [Мнѣ было велѣно сжечь его], she said with a faint, detached smile, looking at me steadily with that slightly quizzical glance of hers; it dwelled a trice longer than usual. One could suppose that she was restaging mentally that conversation with her dying husband, and that the matter troubled her. The invariable loving formula gracing almost all of his English dedication pages – "*To Véra*" – expanded in this case into the urgency of a last wish: "burn it." This conversation took place during one of our Russian *Pnin* editing sessions in Nabokov's small study at one end of their suite at the Montreux Palace, with a tall oval window giving out on the lake. "But I have not done it yet." She did not offer, and I did not seek, any follow-up, perhaps out of a silently shared sense that this angular secret should remain undisturbed by curiosity. In his preface to the original edition, Dmitri Nabokov says that his mother was prevented from destroying the manuscript by procrastination – "procrastination due to age, weakness, and immeasurable love."

The storyline surfaced eight years after that initial conversation, when Brian Boyd sent me the manuscript of his Nabokov biography for comment. That pre-publication version relayed the contents of *Laura* in detail that I thought was too ample for something that was meant to vanish without much trace. My opinion alone would scarcely have mattered, but as it turned out, Véra Nabokov later demanded that the description be whittled down to a bare-bones account, and that was what Boyd published. At the time (the late 1980s) nobody but the widow, the son, and Boyd had read the cards, and indeed few knew of their existence. Here is strong proof: in 1991, Nabokov's sister Elena Sikorski, who knew his art deeper than many specialists, wrote to me: "You [...] have read *The*

Original of Laura in Boyd's paraphrase. Do you suppose that it would be indiscreet of you to give me the content of that book in a nutshell? I shall of course keep it in strictest confidence."

In his preface, Dmitri Nabokov points to the recurrent theme of fire, and his nettled choice reminds one of the dilemmatic episode from *The Real Life of Sebastian Knight*, in which the narrator sits before the fireplace with a batch of intimate letters that his dead half-brother willed to be destroyed, unread. Ethically speaking, there must, however, be a solid difference between private letters and a presumed masterpiece, even if unfinished. It must be doubly hard to annihilate the last composition of a supreme genius, a work that, by the logic of artistic evolution unmarred by impotence or senility, was likely to outdo in certain important ways (formal control, for instance) all the previous. Indeed, the chief argument of those who advised Dmitri Nabokov to publish, over the advice of those who thought he should not, was that the stylistic brilliance preserved in some of the fragments outweighed the clear lack of integrity and critical mass. There is, of course, a vast no-man's ground between burning a manuscript and publishing it, a non-burning and non-publishing murky grey area, a death row of sorts, where *Laura* had languished for many years, first in the Palace storeroom and then in a Swiss bank strongbox. And now an unfinished masterwork, condemned to die by the master, was being released on appeal.

A particularly noxious canard infected the Russian-language media pre-publication coverage: that the book had a hidden *autobiographical* current, and that *that* was the secret reason why it had been suppressed for so long. Naked ignorance and veiled vulgarity always suspect that a good novel must be an exhibition of re-tagged self-portraits, but it takes a singularly unhappy combination of these vices to look for proof of such nonsense in Nabokov's books. Anyone with minimal knowledge of his artistic principles knows that, except for his memoir, Nabokov's fiction steers clear of charting an autobiographical storyline, most certainly in the usual sense of the notion.[2] True, one may argue that *all* his compositions are autobiographical in the sense in which rain in Cannes can be responsible for the mist evaporated over the Mediterranean – in other words, it can be said metaphorically. The real, and the only clear, personal thematic line in *The Original of Laura* is the line of death, a dotted line from the end all the way to the beginning of a book whose writing was stopped short by the writer's departure – and this could become known only post mortem.

ENDING AS A DEPARTURE POINT

In his "Philosophy of Composition," Poe explains that he began composing "The Raven" from the end, "where all works of art should begin." Had Nabokov been building his last novel in sequence from the foundation up, the finished third might have been enough for a plausible contouring of the whole edifice. If, on the other hand, he had been a run-of-the-mill award-winning writer, whose chief method consisted in connecting the immense halls of down-to-earth dialogue by way of narrow descriptive passages, then certain recognizable traits and combinations found in those descriptions would have enabled an expert to plot the rest with believable approximation. But Nabokov's prose tends to avoid dialogue and is emphatically neither friable nor porous, and, of special weight here, he composed and kept in his mind not only the design but the entire book in much detail. Thus, when he started setting it down on paper he would not follow a sequential story but rather a plan for general ordonnance, teasing out, affixing, and adjusting this or that episode with lesser or greater care, now from the middle of the plot, now close to the entrance or the exit. These latter two could have been worked out first. He repeatedly likened his habit of writing to the processing of a photographic film: it preserves in darkness the entire series of exposed pictures waiting to be chemically treated, then printed in random order, and finally sorted out – composed – in the strictest, preordained sequence.

It is possible, therefore, to say with confidence that the extant fragments of *The Original of Laura* make up more or less joined, or rather more or less disparate, descriptions and scenes rendered from the sign language of imagination onto one hundred and thirty-eight 9 cm × 12 cm cards, and that as such they permit no trustworthy conjecture about the book's plot. These cards are numbered, presumably, in the order in which they were found, and since the incremental numeration is not by Nabokov's hand, that order in many instances does not establish the position of this or that episode in the novel. Dmitri Nabokov writes that his father "lovingly arranged and shuffled the cards of his new novel." The original edition comes with cards perforated all round,[3] with no through-numeration, allowing, even bidding the reader to extract them and play out his own pensive solitaire. One can imagine second-hand copies surfacing years later with a neat rectangular cavity inside – perfect for stashing away from a burglar's eye the crown jewels of a king deposed by mutinous rabble, or a will, or a stack of notes for an unfinished novel.

SHUFFLING THE DECK

In May 1974, even before Nabokov's last published novel, *Look at the Harlequins!*, came out, he had mapped his next book mentally. Other tasks interfered: translations, new editions of the old books, collections of short stories flogged on by a lucrative but pressing contract with McGraw-Hill. A May 15 entry in his diary reads: "Inspiration. Radiant insomnia. The flavour and snows of beloved alpine slopes. A novel *without* an I, without a he, but with the narrator, *the gliding eye*, being implied throughout."[4] Boyd thought that this was meant for a project following *The Original of Laura*, but this plan fits well the narrative mode of the novel about Laura nested within another, about Flora.

Throughout 1974 and in the first months of 1975 Nabokov expends much time and effort editing the French *Ada*. Yet between December of that year and February of the next he writes three cards of *The Original of Laura* a day – not every day, however, and often rewriting his drafts. Tradition has it that Virgil wrote three verses of *The Aeneid* a day, and seeing that he could not finish it before he died, asked that the manuscript be burned; Augustus, his imperial friend, did not heed his request. In February 1976, Nabokov writes in his diary: "New novel more or less completed and copied 54 cards. In 4 batches from different parts of the novel. Plus notes and drafts. 50 days since Dec. 10, 1975. Not too much."[5] Yet at about the same time he writes to his publisher that he has put together an equivalent of about "a hundred pages of print, or about half of the novel". Either he miscalculated badly, or else included in the count his drafts, which he might have destroyed after all, for the 138 surviving cards make up hardly forty pages of regular print (even thirty-four, by Dieter Zimmer's careful estimation).[6] Early in April he writes "five or six cards per day, but a lot of rewriting" and then notes in his diary that he "transcribed in final form 50 cards = 5000 words."[7] But the existing 138 cards comprise 10,209 words in total; thus, his count of a hundred words per card is clearly off the mark, in part because many cards are but half filled.

Toward the end of Petrarch's life "his illnesses gathered: fevers, fainting spells, foot trouble, the itch. He was so thin he was afraid of vanishing."[8] By contrast, Philip Wild is so fat that of vanishing he has no fear; indeed, vanishing is what he longs for. Nabokov, who might well have read these words by his friend, doubtless marked the f-alliteration. Dying is no fun. Wild's funereal pun is that living is deleterious. In his preface to *The Original of Laura*, Dmitri Nabokov recalls that the year 1975 – almost exactly 600 years after the distant admirer of Laura de Noves and the first poet laureate died – "seemed to set off a period of illness which never quite receded ... a harrowing search for the noisome germ began [the supposed cause of the recurrent fever. – *G.B.*] ... his steps became short and insecure ... [among his sufferings] were incessant inflammations under and around his toenails." His life-long insomnia grew worse, the trial-and-error rotation of sleeping pills provided but short relief, and after his fall on a Swiss slope and an unrelated surgery in July of 1975 he was noticeably infirm. Even the physical routine of writing became toilsome. Boccaccio advised the old and ailing Petrarch to give up the labour of writing; the poet replied that nothing weighed less than a pen and nothing gave more pleasure; but even a pen may be too cumbrous to lift.

In 1977 Nabokov could engage in writing *The Original of Laura* only fitfully and only until mid-March, when he came down with a viral cold and spent many weeks in a Lausanne hospital. Even in his sickbed he tried to keep processing the script that was stored in the safe of his imagination, but on July 2 he passed on.

LOOSE ENDS

It should not, then, be unreasonable to propose that the text that Nabokov set down on 138 index cards is largely a once- or twice-revised draft of various pieces of a novel that was designed to grow three- or fourfold. However, there is a sharp division among scholars on this point. While Dieter Zimmer (who translated *The Original of Laura* into German) has independently arrived at the same conclusion as given here, Brian Boyd, along with the Japanese translator (joined later by Martin Amis), thinks that the text amounts to 60 to 70 per cent of the whole, a thin novelette.

Three points run against this position: (1) Nabokov's own calculations, given above; (2) the absence of any seventy-page novel among his English fiction;[9] and (3) most significantly, the large number of inchoate lines and loose ends requiring considerable space to be sorted, linked, and tied up – tasks that Nabokov invariably did with utmost care.

The first five chapters take up 58 (or 63) cards; they propel a dynamic description of Flora's person in a natural sequence, with almost no digression, in which the elaboration of detail noticeably dwindles from chapter to chapter:

Chapter One: Exposition: Flora's Russian lover (20 cards).
Chapter Two: Flora's lineage and childhood (18).
Chapter Three: Flora's youth and deflowering (11, with large gaps).
Chapter Four: Flora's mother exits; enter Philip Wild (4, just the beginning).
Chapter Five: Flora Lind marries Philip Wild (5).

It is possible that the five adjacent cards, 59–63, were assigned to chapter 5 as well, but since they engage the internal novel *My Laura,* they may in fact belong to an entirely different part of the book. If so, Flora's line runs through 58 cards.

This is followed by an intermittent series containing Wild's diary entries in which he describes, pizzicato, stages of his autohypnotic self-destructive experiments: cards 64–77, 79–87, 91–2, 96–7, 105–7, 122–7, and 133–6: forty cards in total. Wild's private life and reminiscences, recorded in his diary and related by a third- (or is it fourth-?) person narrator, are set on sixteen more cards (98–104, 115–18, and 128–32). Nine cards account for a-novel-within-a-novel theme (59–63, 93–4, and 110–11). What I take to be the novel's intended finale is written on three cards: 112, 113, and 114 (more on this later). Working notes and quotations are found on seven cards (78, 90, 108, 109, 137, 138). In addition, there are five cards on which three key episodes are barely sketched: "Medical Intermezzo" (88–9); the first scene revisited (95, which could be a variant of the beginning); and a very important and enigmatic setting on cards 120 and 121, which is either the starting point of a completely new line or a sharp turn of the main one.

Thus, 114 cards out of 131 (discounting the reference notes, etc.), or almost nine-tenths of the whole batch, are divided about evenly between the still mostly preliminary line of Flora and the dotted one of Philip Wild's diary. The other 17 are sketches of other thematic lines, of which the most important by far – important for the understanding of the book's plot (taken as general design) – is the theme of the nested novel, *My Laura.* It therefore seems improbable that the material in hand comprises anything more than a third of the whole book. In other words, it would take three to four hundred cards *more* to give this material the shape and inner working of a complete Nabokov novel.

Here is an incomplete list of leads that are begun and left dangling, or else only mentioned, cited by card number: Eric (118; could be someone from Flora's seraglio; could be Wild's alias); Nigel Delling[10] (68; could be a new personage, to appear elsewhere, or another Wild alias. Nigel fits anagrammatically into *Delling* – as does Flora's maiden name[11]); A.N.D. (88–9, Medical Intermezzo; *A. N*igel *D*elling? yet another alias of PW?); Ivan Vaughan (59; the author of *My Laura*?); Philip Nikitin (133; the author of *My Laura,* Flora's Russian paramour from the first chapter? Wild's pen name, chosen not only for its Russianness but also for the fact that both name–surname combinations contain only i's for the vowels – a key emblem of Wild's self-annihilating experiment? Or could it be the silent marginal character in *Anna Karenin* imported here for an unknown associative reason?).

All guesses are bound to be more or less wild, for the reader finds himself on a Wonderland hopscotch grid, nonplussed as to which square to hop to next: the numbering is misleading. Yet, since it is doubtful that Philip was meant to have so many pseudonyms, we are moved to conclude that these cards mark several *new* lines in want of development, branching out, grafting, characterization, coordination with others, etc. One of the most mysterious personages is not even named: the first-person narrator on only two cards, 120 and 121. This is arguably the finest passage of the lot, one of those superb stretches of prose with such a strong lyric torque that one understands better why Nabokov's widow and son found it so difficult to wipe out the manuscript for good. Whose voice-over do we hear? Is it that of the author of the book about Laura, Flora's Russian lover? If so, what distant – yet contemporary – war is he talking about? And who is *she*? Could it really be Flora (she is said to be "still married to that hog" – a link to Wild's seeing in his closet glass "an obese bulk with formless features and a sad porcine stare [68]"), the same

Flora for whom taking new lovers is a natural consequence of taking her husband's surname, an obligatory component of any marriage?[12] If so, how can it plausibly be combined with a religious sense so deep-seated and so vulnerable that she is afraid to provoke, by her incautious mention of the "Green Chapel of St Esmeralda," an irreverent quip on the part of her lover and story-teller, whom she apparently knows to be an agnostic? This facet alone would have capitally changed her character, at any rate in the mind of the reader of the first five chapters. Can Laura be so radically unlike her original? And if, on the other hand, this is not Flora, then who is the "she" of cards 120–1? And who is her "hog of a husband"? After all, there are no other stand-alone female roles in the existing draft, and to bring on stage an entirely new heroine with more than a walk-on role would require more chapters, set with interconnecting wiring.

THE PUZZLE

One principal difficulty in bringing out these fragments inevitably has to do with the fact that Nabokov's highest artistic achievement lies not in the rich intricacy of style and sheer power of expression, in which he has few equals, but precisely and especially in the art of composition, where he has none. Not so much the fretwork of words as the plexure of periods, passages, parts, planes of narration, thematic backroads, and skyways. Nabokov understood astonishingly early what many first-rate writers never do: that art, in a high metonymic sense, is an elaborate intercourse of liberty and deliberation, a stream freely running over bumpy ground after a torrential rain, and that it is at the same time, viewed from a different vantage point, a complex of connecting, bypassing, and draining canals. Not everything is subordinated and fixed within the well-furnished space of a Nabokov novel. There is enough room for a free and unthematic unfolding of an image or a description as well as for a tightly woven thematic fabric, and the art of reading Nabokov consists, among other demands, in the ability to tell one from the other: not forcing a connection where none is meant yet finding and tracing all such connections where their latticework is part of the design.[13]

In the absence of a finished structure, however, the latter operation is hardly possible. The weave and interaction of parts and particulars cannot be traced and tried; transitions, reciprocities, and other familiar Nabokovian landmarks are all but absent, and we cannot see again, from a high look-out on the twisty road, the spot that we passed a score of pages earlier. With *The Original of Laura* we cannot say that an unfinished book breaks off at the most interesting place, a cliff-hanger, because cliffs are everywhere and many places are ruptures. Our text lacks *textility* and at the same time topography, a system of linkages required for the understanding of the correlation between the inner narration (*My Laura*) and the embracing one (*Dying Is Fun*), and also between these two, on the one hand, and the all-encompassing, roving-eye narration of *The Original of Laura*, on the other. Needless to say, without such understanding no sound judgement of the book's plotted content is possible; in this state it is much more like the archaic torso of the Miletus Apollo, whose legendary head, Rilke says, we cannot know (nor can we see three-fourths of his limbs), than the Milos Venus, her arms missing rather fetchingly. We therefore can by no means be certain that the placement of the cards as they were found after the author's death follows the assigned sequence in the book that he had already composed mentally.[14] Nor can we, as the original edition tempts us to do, rearrange them ourselves with enough justification, try as we may to find in the ghostly contour of an imagined book the assigned place for a single card or a series. Sasha Luzhin, putting together a jigsaw puzzle, "would try to determine by scarcely perceptible signs the essence of the [whole] picture in advance" (38).[15] We have a puzzle for which not only two-thirds of the pieces are missing but, more important, missing is the box with the model picture: we don't quite know whether we are assembling a man or a mansion. Many scalloped pieces can be interlocked to form isles of bright and clear sense, and some of those can be indisputably joined, or placed side by side, to hint at an outline of a larger archipelago. But there also are many single tesserae that fit nothing.

And yet it is all too easy to forget that what is published as *The Original of Laura* is not a collocation of shards, nor excerpts of an unfinished novel, but rather fragments *from* a novel – one already structurally composed in the architect's mind but only partly written down. What that structure was to be is anybody's guess and nobody's surety. In my Russian edition I followed the numbered order of the original, with two significant exceptions. First, all seven working notes obviously extraneous to the novel's body were removed to an appendix. Second, the fragments were fitted with a putative conclusion.

Whereas the initial series of fifty-eight cards presents an incontestable beginning (they are so marked by the author: Ch. One, Two, etc.), it is scarcely less clear that the last text-bearing cards in the stack, nos. 135 and 136, which describe one of the earlier stages of Wild's experiments, not only could not possibly mark the end of the book but are logically out of sequence with the whole lot. Of course, one cannot expect a manuscript in this state of incompletion to have anything resembling a finale. However, I think that by luck we happen to have a closing – at least a provisional one.

MISSING THE TRAIN

Poe's paradox underscores that in a top-level work of durational art the ending is the *point d'appui* of the whole thing, and sometimes also its departure point. Ivan Luzhin, a flabby writer, discovers Poe's principle at the end of his life but dies before he can begin writing his new book (about his son's genius). Nabokov's endings often nudge the reader to go back to the book's opening in order to view it in a different light and from a higher vantage point – and then yield to the salutary urge to reread the entire novel. Soon after his migration to America, Nabokov published his ending to Pushkin's unfinished *Rusalka* (*River Nymph*), not merely as a sporting homage to his favourite poet but also, I think, because of his desire to see the *whole*, even if in a fantastic frame of his own fabrication. Of course, there is a difference in integral worth between a mermaid without the tail and a tail without the mermaid.

Even on my first, superficial reading of the text I thought that cards 112–14 were quite possibly designed to end the novel. For one thing, one cannot ignore that they are inscribed "*Last §*" (Nabokov's customary mark for chapters, e.g. in the manuscript of *The Real Life of Sebastian Knight*) and "Z, Z2, Z3" respectively on each of the three cards. At the bottom of no.114 a fat line is drawn. True, a few other cards bear this sort of bottom line; moreover, card 93 is also marked "Last chapter." However, there is a significant, if oblique, evidence in favour of the proposition that the text on cards 112–114 was designed as the tail of the book – a working tail, perhaps. Just above that bold line appears what might have been the novel's final sentence: "You'll miss your train." Nabokov fielded this double-entendre (as in "to miss the boat," to miss the train of thought or events) in a number of books and in several variations. In his first English novel, Nina Rechnoy, a *sirène fatale* of exceptional seductive power, who had already enthralled and brought down Sebastian Knight and was now busy spellbinding his half-brother, the supposed narrator, whom she has lured to her estate, tells her husband while getting rid of him for the day so as to clear the stage for the final act of her mesmeric séance: "*Mon ami*, you'll miss that train." Of course, it is the narrator who misses the train in more senses than one at the novel's end; this is forestalled, as are many other events in V.'s unreal life, by a mysterious voice resembling Knight's that mumbled that he regretted having missed *trains, allusions and opportunities.*[16] The semantic string here is precisely what that short sentence in *The Original of Laura* was, I think, charged to imply. We see something similar in *Pnin,* which opens on a story of the hero getting on the wrong train, which becomes a metaphoric emblem of much of what is to unfold. When Pnin does not understand an American idiom (in the second chapter) he replies malapropos, thus "missing one bus but boarding the next."

Could Flora's words to her girlfriend, who is dying to show her the place in *My Laura* where Laura's "wonderful death" is described, be designed to alert us that we have missed something of great moment? Perhaps we would do well to catch the next train to the beginning and start the book over, guided by the knowledge collected on the first run. We shall very likely never know whether this was to be the book's *finis*; it is certain, however, that the islets and keys that form *The Original of Laura* contain no ending that would be more Nabokovian.

HARLEQUINS IN A RECEDING CAVALCADE

Two curious traits stand out at once, even at first reading. One is euphonic: besides the thematic rhyming and telescoping of the names *Laura* and *Flora* (her original) – with the sidekick Cora, Flora's maid – Nabokov all too often resorts to the weak alliteration of the initial consonant in words that come in pairs, threesomes, or sometimes even larger clumps. The cards are mottled with these; phrases such as "beaming bum," "banal bevy," "firm form," "high heather," "rubber and rot," "sketchy skeleton," "pain and poison," and "Carlton Courts in Cannes" are so inordinately frequent (I counted nearly forty instances, i.e., about one per standard page) as to annoy by their persistent buzz, much as shimmering and sparkling harries the eye of a seafarer.

The other feature is more interesting and almost as persistent: *The Original of Laura* is striated as densely as the much larger space of *Look at the Harlequins!*, Nabokov's last finished novel, with references to "other works by the author." Any reasonably well-read lover of Nabokov's fiction will at once recognize various names and situations from all but one of his previous English novels, here elastically deformed or canted. Where in *Lolita* Humbert Humbert's wife is killed by a car, instantly making him Dolly's only earthly guardian, *Laura*'s Hubert Hubert's presumed daughter Daisy is killed by a lorry backing up (the nameless nympherast in *The Enchanter* also dies under the wheels of a huge truck). Aurora Lee immediately brings up her near namesake Annabel Leigh, Humbert's child love, and their common Poe-tic 1849 source, *Annabel Lee*.[17] In *Pnin*'s second chapter the methodical Freudians Eric and Liza Wind gather various wives and husbands "in two parallel psycho-asinine discussion groups where the former with absolute frankness compare notes on the plusses and minuses of the latter: Well, girls, when George last night ..."; *Laura*'s third chapter stages a similar, if more ribald, scene in a different setting: there, on the grass in Fontainebleau, "[t]he girls would compare the dimensions of their companions. Exchanges would be enjoyed with giggles and cries of surprise" (no. 42). The manuscript of the last chapter of Wild's opus is filched by a person unknown (to us, in any event) while the author is dying of a heart attack (no. 94) – the manuscript of Shade's long poem "Pale Fire" is snatched by Kinbote (a masked personage, to us) and inlaid within his own grandiose story, disguised as commentary to the poem but related to it only by fanciful contacts devised by a brilliant madman. Continuing chronologically, *Ada*'s agonist Van (Ivan) Veen has here a phonetic counterpart: Ivan Vaughan appears in an intriguing place unattached to anything elsewhere. Flora's matter-of-fact adultery and her husband's desperate resignation are perhaps closer psychologically to the situation we see in *Transparent Things* than in *Invitation to a Beheading*.

One can find in *The Original of Laura* a number of Russian reminiscences as well, although in their English attire some may look questionable. In one of his first short stories "Revenge" (1924), Nabokov presents a tightly compressed plot of jealousy in its last, irrevocable stage (madness leading to murder). Here, as in *The Original of Laura*, a savant invents a professional and original method of dispatching his wife. In "Revenge" a biology professor places a skeleton in the conjugal bed, and his supersensitive wife dies of fright; in *The Original of Laura,* a neurology professor (or perhaps the author of *My Laura)* seems to proceed from experiments in gradual self-erasure to a methodical telepathic annihilation of his lecherous wife who dies a "wonderful death" (nos. 61, 113–14). The great difference between the two is that in the early story the wife is innocent; she has mystical rather than philistine proclivities, and her husband, not unlike Othello, is a victim rather of self-mystification than of blind jealousy alone.

A clearer-cut, if more difficult to extract, self reference can be found early in Chapter One: Flora's new lover is taking her home in a cab strategically stopped "at the corner of Heine street," where "a young man with a macintosh over his white pyjamas was wringing his hands" (nos. 16 and 17). This young man, apparently Flora's preceding beau dismissed half-an-hour earlier by phone, is a visitor from Nabokov's 1918 rendition of Heine's *Der Doppelgänger* (so called by Schubert, who made a romance out of it) where

Da steht auch ein Mensch und starrt in die Höhe,
Und ringt die Hände, vor Schmerzensgewalt;

[A man stands there and stares into heaven,
And wrings his hands, overcome with pain.]

Heine's man is a praeter ego, standing long ago on a quiet street, on a still night, near the house of his love. "Heine street" on card 16 appears over an erased variant, where "street" was preceded by a shorter word ("calm"?). There seem to be rich possibilities here.[18]

In the titles of Flora's grandfather's paintings, "April in Yalta" and "The Old Bridge," Nabokov's reader will recognize, respectively, "Spring in Fialta" and Nabokov's favourite poem of the same period, "The Swallow" (from *The Gift*): "One night between sunset and river / On the old bridge we stood, you and I." Hubert Hubert dies in a hotel lift that was "[g]oing up, one would like to surmise" (no. 38), and one may recall an especially magnetic place in *The Defence,* where a hydraulic house elevator, having delivered Luzhin's corpulent French governess upstairs, came down empty: "Goodness knows what had happened to her – perhaps she had travelled up to heaven and remained there."[19] *Laura*'s provisional title (*Dying Is Fun*) is a colloquial remake of an encoded key phrase in *Invitation to a Beheading* (mentioned at the beginning of this essay). The gliding eye of the narrator resembles a similar device in *The Eye* and the beginning of "Spring in Fialta." And a shadow of the idea of self-induced dissolution of one's body makes a fleeting appearance in a strange poem written in the same year as *The Real Life of Sebastian Knight* (1938): here, too, the grand mystery of man's existence is solved in a dream:

Рѣшенье чистое, простое.
О чемъ я думалъ столько лѣтъ?
Пожалуй и вставать не стоитъ:
Ни тѣла, ни постели нѣтъ.

[A clean and simple resolution.
What was I thinking of so long?
Why even bother getting up –
My body and my bed are gone.]

All of which reminds one of Nabokov's stratagem in his last published novel: it opens on a list of "other works by the narrator," which differs from that of his author by the exquisite rephrasing of the titles and slightly displaced chronology. One should resist the temptation to look in these cards for the tracks of *all* Nabokov's books listed in *Look at the Harlequins!*, a temptation that grows stronger as one imagines that *The Original of Laura* might be meant as the last review of his *harlequins,* the figments of his rich imagination, as he calls them in his last poem, parading in cavalcade before they recede from his sight:

Ахъ, угонятъ ихъ въ степь, арлекиновъ моихъ,
Въ буераки, къ чужимъ атаманамъ ...

[O, my harlequins! they will be driven away
to the gullies and plains, to strange chieftains ...]

This is exactly the sort of final inspection to which Sebastian Knight, in his farewell novel, briskly marshals most of his books and themes and images.

LAURA AND HER ORIGINAL

The portrait's fine – th' original is dreadful.

Mikhail Lermontov, *The Masquerade*

Since the text at our disposal was in nowise meant to be at our disposal, we face enigmas wherever we turn our attention: doors leading to pitfalls, corridors ending in pit-faces, windows giving out onto naught. A highly classified, suddenly abandoned construction site has been turned into an archaeological dig open to the public, and a visitor must tread here with utmost circumspection. We cannot even be certain about the important question of what exactly the title means.[20] Does the original refer to the small-headed, small-minded Flora Wild, a model for the doubly fictional Laura? Is it the outer structure that wraps round the internal novel, *My Laura*, a dream within a dream? Or could it be something else, an unsupposed third possibility of which no one can know anything with firmity?

The name Laura, in its Franco–English pronunciation, is phonetically contained within her prototype (which makes its translation into most languages a conundrum). "Everything about [Flora] is bound to remain blurry, even her name which seems to have been made expressly to have another one modelled upon it by a fantastically lucky artist" (no. 43). If everything does not deceive, this Laura cannot be attached without a deforming stretch to either Petrarch's beloved, "radiant in her virtues," or to Pushkin's frothy girl from *The Guest of Stone*, who, inconstant as she is, "cannot love two men at once."[21] On the other hand, not having the entire book, one cannot assert even that. As in Petrarch, an idealized poetic subject is slipcased into a (perhaps) starkly differing protagonist, a thematic thread of metamorphosis basting its course through what existent length of the text we have; Petrarch's favourite punning on Laura: *L'aura* (breeze), *L'auro* (gold)[22] somehow correlates with the Flora – Laura – L'Aurora [Lee] series. The fifth sonnet in his *Rime sparse* is an elaborate play on her name in Latinized French, Laurette: *Lau-re-ta*, one syllable hidden in the third, fifth, and seventh lines of the octave, then repeated in a different pattern in the sestet (ineluctably bringing to mind the syllabic intoning of *Lo-li-ta* in the opening paragraph of that other novel). It may be worth noting that an excellent Harvard edition of Petrarch's lyric poems by Robert Durling came out in 1976, when *The Original of Laura* was in the works; that Cornell University, Nabokov's academic stead for ten years, is home to the great Petrarch Collection (fully catalogued in 1974); and that Nabokov's closest friend at Cornell, Professor Morris Bishop, was a renowned Petrarch expert and the author of the famous 1963 book *Petrarch and His World* ("highly readable but unreliable," shrugs Durling).

There may, however, be a more natural precedent for the heroine's name and the book's title. Even though what we have is only a patchy piece of fabric, it bears discernible traces of what can be taken for the weave of a floral motif, from Flora's *linden* maiden name and the "banal bevy of birds-of-paradise flowers" in the entrance hall (nos. 18–19, 20) to the wild brambles in a ditch at the bottom of the batch (no. 136). In the episodes we have left this motif serves only as a pastel background or shimmering backlighting, but who knows how it would have blossomed and whither led, had the other two or three acts been written. This thematic floral design – an anthemion, as Nabokov once intended to title the book of his memoirs – inevitably takes one to the prototype of all Floras, the Roman goddess of flowers, and to her peerless image on Botticelli's *Primavera.* There she stands primped up with wild flowers and bestrewn with wreaths and anthemia, and her facial features and expression overlap with the description of Flora Wild, that scentless wild flower of Nabokov's last novel. Botticelli made her almost microcephalic, more so than the other figures in the painting, because it was supposed to hang above eye level (over a *lettuccio,* an exceedingly elaborate settee on a pedestal, in a chamber in the Medici town palace) – and Nabokov gives his Flora a markedly little head (no. 9) for her "strange little mind" (no. 117). The painted Flora's eyes are not close-set, and although they were painted blue, they grew drab olive-green over the past five centuries.[23] But the ruthless sensuality of her slightly open mouth (cf. no. 43) is strikingly there, and so is the pulling force of her imperturbable but parlous attraction and the strangely *modern* general air about her entire appearance. She is depicted as a married woman wearing, as was the custom in the

1400s, a *ghirlanda* on her head and a floral girdle high round her waist. With her left hand she is holding up a fold of her dress making a pouch for the roses that she is about to strew out with her right hand, and that gesture seems somehow a graceful foil to one rum place in *The Original of Laura*: "Statically – if one can put it that way – the portrait [of Flora] is a faithful one. Such fixed details as her trick of opening her mouth when towelling her inguen or of closing her eyes when smelling an inodorous rose are absolutely true to the original" (no. 61).

Nabokov must have known this painting thoroughly. In April of 1966 he spent a fortnight in Florence hunting for butterflies on the canvases of the old masters for his book on the subject. That he had taken time to study *Primavera* can be seen from the following passage in his last published novel, thus immediately preceding *The Original of Laura*: "I want you to celebrate your resemblance to the fifth girl from left to right, the flower-decked blonde with the straight nose and serious gray eyes, in Botticelli's *Primavera,* an allegory of Spring, my love, my allegory."[24] In *Look at the Harlequins!* Anna Blagovo, an unclever virgin to whom these words from Vadim Vadimych N.'s letter are addressed, is Flora Wild's opposite in everything, excepting this strange outward affinity.

In this fantastic masterpiece, great in both senses of the word (it is a 7' × 10' megalorama), Botticelli adjoins two temporal planes: Flora is standing next to her own younger self as she was when, a nymph called Chloris, she was deflowered by the oddly ghoulish, ashen-greenish Zephyr, who then, according to Ovid, made her his wife and thereby promoted her to the goddess of flowers.[25] This prologue takes place in a laurel thicket, rather than in a citrus grove where the rest of the picture is set, which serves as a visual cue to the deliberate anachronism of the scene. In an adjacent myth, nymphet Daphne, pursued by Apollo, metamorphs into a laurel tree (*daphne* means laurel in Greek); hence the bay wreath on Apollo's brow; hence, by extension, the custom of laureating poets; hence, also by extension, a laurel tree is never struck by lightning.

TERMINATING THE PHRASE

Once again, without a map of the unrealized novel we cannot inspect its grounds; not knowing the system of its inlet and outlet canals we cannot even admire, let alone navigate it.[26] Yet if some road signs can be taken for pointers, they may suggest a possible solution: a hazy convergence of the only two arterial themes we can detect here, that of Flora's fiction-writing lover and that of her husband's vanishing act. By comparing the detailed descriptions of Wild's self-annulling experiments with the mention of some unparalleled, *wonderful* death of Laura, a fictional character modelled on his wayward wife, one can cautiously propose that Nabokov might have had in mind the Pygmalion story turned the wrong way round: an artist telepathically reducing a live Galatea to nil, while making of her an immortal marble statue.[27]

The book's very first sentence is Flora's reply to a courtesy question about her husband's occupation, put to her, presumably, by a Russian writer, who is to become her lover that very night. "Her husband, she answered, was a writer, *too* – at least, after a fashion" (italics mine). Next we learn that what he is secretly writing is not fiction but rather "a mad neurologist's testament, a kind of Poisonous Opus as in that film" (no. 2). She no doubt knows of that "absolute secret" because she, contrary to her pointed denial, *did* go through his notes. But what is this opus, and in what film? Among many more or less plausible candidates[28] there is a 1972 screen version by Rogelio González of "The Oval Portrait," a story within a short story by Poe, which in its first publication in 1842 was entitled "Life in Death." In it, an artist is painting a portrait of his wife, who dies while sitting for him, but the portrait turns out to be horrifically lifelike. The plot had of course been trotted out in, and before, Gogol's "The Portrait" and was not avoided even after Wilde's definitive *The Picture of Dorian Gray*, but the following enigmatic phrase found on card no. 61 gives support to my conjecture about *Laura*'s possible storyline: "The 'I' of the book is a neurotic and hesitant man of letters, who destroys his mistress in the act of portraying her."

The word *obliterate* is the very last one on the last card of Nabokov's last novel (in the sequence as it has been now reproduced). It was an accessory card, of a different, graph-paper stock, on which he jotted down a long column of synonyms for *efface*. He put most of these to use. The theme of obliteration enters, of course, the main line: Professor Philip Wild, a man of letters, is an *oblittérateur,* as it were – a singular notion that lends itself to the weird concept of obliterature: the art of erasing what has been written. And this is precisely what Wild does: wipes, by sheer willpower, the lower parts of his whitish "I" off his mental blackboard.

The key conclusion to a carefully written record of this experiment has been stolen (perhaps by another writer) and thus, in a sense, also effaced.

We cannot know exactly why Nabokov wished that the cards with the unfinished *The Original of Laura* be destroyed: out of a disinclination to appear in public in a dressing-gown, thus out of decency mated to authorial dignity or vanity; or perhaps because, when death is in sight, long-held views on matters such as the fate of *The Aeneid* (had it been burned as willed), or of *Dead Souls* (had the second volume *not* been burned by Gogol before he died), or of one's own drafts – especially one's own drafts – may undergo a sudden and radical change.

In almost every novel since his third, *The Defence* (1929), Nabokov inserts as a secret signature one theme that he varies in shape and application but never really develops: the theme of the imperceptible but effective intercourse of the souls of personae who died within the book's limns with the doings and destinies of the characters still quick. Having held one Nabokov book up to the light and seen the pattern of this theme, the reader is conditioned to look for it in others, acknowledging its recurrent signs.[29] This is a strange, one-way spiritism whose influence is completely inaccessible to the characters fallen under its spell and can be discerned only by a keen observer outside the book, and then only after he has acquired the knack. The death that released a gently guiding or watchfully guarding ghost is usually mentioned in passing, within a long period, often in the pluperfect, but the reader should learn how to collect such things, for the understanding of higher planes of the story. Dying in a Nabokov novel may not be fun, but it is no *fin* either.

On the other hand, Nabokov – unlike Tolstoy, for example – never shows death itself at close range, in a physically realistic description. Philip Wild dies of a heart attack, apparently at home, far away from the reader's eye, while Laura's "wonderful death", within the confines of an intramural novel, remains in the end an enigma even for her original. In 1951, after his spectrally shimmering story "The Vane Sisters" had been misunderstood and rejected, Nabokov confided to Katharine White, editor of *The New Yorker* and a good friend, that his fiction followed "a system wherein a second (main) story is woven into, or placed behind, the superficial semitransparent one."[30]

A more or less universal law of any artistic act is that it is essentially driven by *l'amore che muove* the artist's pen or brush. The fuel is a greatly variable mixture of love and vanity: the last soaring lines of *Paradiso* disentangling themselves from the vicious circles of *Inferno*. "Both Homer and *la mer* are driven by *l'amore*," in Mandelstam's precise formula, from his famous insomnia poem. Earthlier love, being terminal, is the drivetrain of a classical tragedy, and Nabokov so beautifully ponders this antinomy, insoluble on earth, in a long, wistful, keenly lyric passage in his memoir, recollecting one morning in May of 1934 when his son was born. It can be said that all Nabokov's novels are tragedies in at least one narrow sense: love and death, as their subject and predicate, span the tenses from the past perfect to the indefinite future. As early as 1923, when he was about to begin his amazingly rapid transformation from a gifted young poet of dependent sonorities and frangible strength into a strangely mature, masterful artist, he wrote to his love, the future singular second person of his *Conclusive Evidence*: "When you and I were last at the cemetery,[31] I realized with such incisive clarity that you knew everything, you knew what would come after death ... and that is why I am so happy with you."[32]

From the very beginning to the very end of his lifelong exploration of the mystery of life, death, and afterdeath in the laboratory of fiction, Nabokov tried and tweaked the formula "*death is ... X*." Since his brilliant 1924 *Tragedy of Mr Morn*, where a curiously well-informed personage says that "death is curious," he let characters of varying intelligence and trustworthiness rephrase it – into the strangely encrypted "death is sweet" (*Invitation to a Beheading*), or the deceptively banal "death is inevitable" (*The Gift*, epigraph), or the oddly doubled, as in incantation, "death is divestment, death is communion" (*Pnin*), or the desperately grumbling "death is silly, death is degrading" (*Look at the Harlequins!*). His famous maxim that death [in a novel] is a question of style is at once shallow and deep, depending on the angle of view. Looking straight down, how far can one penetrate Nabokov's aerial design, having just these ten thousand words to work, or to play, with? Was the death of Philip Wild to give his ghost a special role further on in the tale, a corrective assignment in the lives of Flora or her literary lover? A minimally educated guess depends in part on the place reserved for card 94, where Philip Wild's death from a fatal heart attack is reported in the subordinate clause, while the main clause momentarily produces an anonym who deftly plucked from Wild's typist the manuscript of the last chapter of his opus. It is entirely possible that in that chapter Wild recorded his attempt to touch his heart with a mental eraser.

Death is divestment, proclaims Vladimir Vladimirovich N., an inventive narrator in *Pnin*. Death is silly, murmurs Vadim Vadimych N., a confused narrator in *Look at the Harlequins!* Philip Wild proposes that dying by divesting oneself of one's flaccid body, whether head or feet first, is fun, even ecstatic. Death in fiction may be a matter of style, but in fiction, too, Nabokov kept otherworldly concerns above the worldly ones. Pushkin, at a low ebb before his marriage, in the last lines of his hastily finished or, rather, finished-off, *Eugene Onegin*, a novel in verse seven-and-a-half years in the making, quite unexpectedly calls life a feast that one would do well to leave early, with one's glass of wine half-full: better to stop reading life's novel before reaching the end. Pushkin was Nabokov's weakness: he admired him almost uncritically, but this notion that an early departure may be a blessing was wholly alien to him. Unlike the other poet, he knew no ennui, "life's noise" (in Pushkin's famous 1828 lyric poem) did not "torment him with anguish," and the "gift of life" was not only not "in vain" and "a matter of chance" but, on the contrary, promised new marvels, joyous and *not* accidental to the point of tears. He fell almost literally with "a heavenly butterfly in his net, on the top of a wild mountain," to quote from a clairvoyant poem about the possible setting of his death, written three years before the incident.[33] The net leapt out of his hand and got caught up in a tree branch, "like Ovid's lyre" (Why Ovid, by the way, and not Orpheus, the original enchanter?), and could not be retrieved. But he died two years later, on a hospital bed, *pace* Gumilev (whose poem was the model for his "heavenly butterfly" remake), and shortly before the end his eyes welled with tears, perhaps at the realization, according to his son, that he would never see again a certain earthly butterfly that was on the wing – not that his book was left unfinished, but at the thought that his life's book was about to end and that he would soon have to part with it, at which point the notion of parting with "my Laura"[34] might have receded into "tomorrow's haze."

Worlds Apart: Lolita, Laura, and the Shadows of Difference

ELLEN PIFER

In *The Original of Laura,* Philip Wild experiments with ways to cheat death by bringing off his own. As preoccupied with dying as Wild is, *Laura* evinces Nabokov's lifelong fascination with the dynamics of transformation and renewal in both life and art. Ignoring or downplaying this aspect of the text, early critics of *Laura* have pronounced it a shabby cousin of Nabokov's previous fiction – its recycled characters and themes testifying to the enfeebled state of the aging author and his concomitant "lapse in judgment."[1] Most often noted by critics is the fact that Philip Wild's twenty-four-year-old wife Flora has the nubile body and breasts of a twelve-year-old and that, as a child of twelve, she was harassed by her widowed mother's middle-aged lover. Such bold echoes of *Lolita* make Flora's kinship with Nabokov's nymphet seem obvious, just as the name of her mother's middle-aged lover, Hubert H. Hubert, seems to confirm his identity as a child molester. Barring one consonant, his moniker is identical to that of *Lolita*'s Humbert Humbert.[2] The most damning verdict has been issued by no less an admirer of Nabokov's "inspiring genius" than the British novelist, Martin Amis. In *Laura*, Amis regretfully concludes, Nabokov recycles the motif of child molestation without a trace of the moral resonance found in *Lolita.* Having "insufficiently honoured the innocence" of "12-year-old-girls" during the "last period" of his career, Nabokov leaves even his "keenest" admirers to wrestle with "a problem from hell": the author's morally dubious obsession with pedophilia.[3]

Confronted by a text as fragmented as *Laura*'s, the critics' readiness to detect obvious, perhaps *too* obvious, resemblances between elements of its unstable composition and *Lolita*'s elegant structure is unfortunate, if understandable. They would do well to consider the author's own words on the subject of semblance. The difference between the "comic" and "cosmic," Nabokov observed, depends on a lone "sibilant."[4] Here he points to a theme writ large in his universe: just as the endless recombination of twenty-six letters of the English alphabet spawn a living language, so the artist magically spins and weaves these teeming combinations into a world of words to rival Nature's own. In each live new world of fiction, the contrasting poles of human experience, perception, and meaning are registered in words that, however different in value and effect, may be separated by no more than a single letter: the lone sibilant dividing *comic* from *cosmic* or, for that matter, the lone consonant distinguishing *word* from *world.* In some cases the difference is even less apparent to the eye or ear: as Humbert slyly observes in one of his many attempts to whitewash his sexual conduct toward the child, "The rapist was Charlie Holmes; I am the therapist – a matter of nice spacing in the way of distinction."[5] In the world of words, a mere space on the page or pause in pronunciation divides *the rapist* from his ethical opposite, the *therapist.* Taking such observations into consideration, readers may find that the lone consonant dividing Humbert's name from Hubert's alerts us to crucial differences between the two characters, ones that shadowy semblance obscures from view.[6]

Resemblance emerges when attention is diverted from contrast and difference. Granting priority to the general over the particular, it eclipses the specific, unique details that constitute, for Nabokov, the essence of both art and reality. Like clichés, those verbal husks of once-vital perception, resemblances are inherently static.[7] No longer informed or renewed by the dynamics of change, transformation, or differentiation, resemblances lack the most vital signs of (literary) life. In *Pale Fire,* John Shade aptly observes to a colleague, "Resemblances are the shadows of differences. Different people see different similarities and similar differences."[8] In *Despair*, the painter Ardalion makes a similar point: "You forget," he tells Hermann, "that what the artist perceives is primarily the *difference* between things. It is the vulgar who note their resemblance."[9] Hopelessly vulgar in this respect, Hermann nurtures a growing obsession with his presumed "double" and, in a drastic misreading of reality, murders a man who turns out to look nothing like him. In a less drastic but telling way, facile assumptions regarding *Laura*'s resemblance to *Lolita* result, I shall argue, in misreading the fragments of Nabokov's last novel.

In *Laura,* the most frequently noted resemblances to *Lolita* occur in scenes that render Flora's childhood encounters with Hubert H. Hubert, the "elderly but still vigorous" Englishman who is her mother's live-in lover. "He was what used to be termed a *charmeur*. His name, no doubt assumed, was Hubert H. Hubert" (53). That Flora, as opposed to her mother, does not regard Hubert as charming is evinced by her vivid recollections of their encounters. These memories constitute some of the "fragments of her past" that, as readers are later informed, "Flora of the close-set dark-blue eyes and cruel mouth recollect[s] in her midtwenties" (85). Here, and throughout the text, grown-up Flora is repeatedly characterized as cold and cruel, indifferent to both art and love. Assuming that her adult personality bears some relevance to the nature of her memories of childhood – particularly of her encounters with Mr Hubert – readers are well advised to heed Flora's character and conduct as a young woman of twenty-four, of which we gain ample account in Chapter One. Clearly labelled and consecutively numbered, the note cards comprising the first two chapters of *Laura*'s text, unlike the much more fragmentary later sections, appear relatively complete. It is reasonable to assume, therefore, that Nabokov intended to maintain their given sequence in the overall structure of the book. By the time, therefore, that Flora's memories of Mr Hubert are conveyed in the middle of Chapter Two, readers have had an opportunity to witness some telling instances of her callous nature (27).

Chapter One opens at a party, where Flora discusses her absent husband, Philip Wild, with a man, a writer and the apparent narrator of this section, who soon becomes her lover. After taking her, at her request, to a friend's flat, Flora's new lover quickly finds himself in a position to observe in the young woman's "exquisite bone structure" a body so "extravagantly slender" that she appears to possess the "narrow nates" and "mobile omoplates of a child" (19). At the same time, however, he (as well as the reader) can appreciate the deceptiveness of Flora's physical resemblance to a fragile, naive child. The "frail, docile frame" (19) she surrenders to her lover embodies a nature that is anything but delicate or docile. Practised in both promiscuity and infidelity, Flora proceeds, as soon as climax is reached, to "wipe her thighs" and consult her watch. Noting that "it is sufficiently late" to shatter the sleep of a recently rejected lover, with whom she has had "a trivial tiff," she stretches her "swift cruel arm toward the bedside telephone" to dial his number. When he answers, Flora proceeds with "tigerish zest" to denounce him, while the man lying next to her in bed sympathetically envisions the "surprise and distress" of "the poor oaf." Perhaps because the rejected lover's pyjamas were "the idiot subject of the tiff," the narrator imagines those pyjamas turning "from heliotrope to a sickly gray" under Flora's harsh attack. After completing her telephone call, Flora replaces the receiver with dispatch and turns back to her bed partner, who narrates: "Was I game now for another round, she wanted to know. No? Not even a quickie?" Undaunted by this sudden drop in her lover's ardour, Flora again acts with dispatch: "Try to find me some liquor in [the] kitchen," she orders him, "and then take me home" (25–31).

That Flora's new lover declines her invitation for "another round" of lovemaking is hardly surprising, given the zest with which she has just tormented a former paramour. Nor does Flora confine herself to tormenting her lovers. Her husband, Philip Wild, notes of his wife in a later section, "Because [she] was a cruel lady or because she thought I might be clowning on purpose to irritate her, she once hid my slippers" (143). The significance of this seemingly trivial action is borne out by the fact that Wild's "bed slippers" are the only type of footwear he can endure – normal shoes proving a constant source of "agony" and "torture" to his "tiny feet" (139, 141). Just as indifferent to the agonies induced in her husband by a chronic stomach ailment, Flora insists on their traveling to "tropical" resorts where the prospect of having to eat "forbidden foods," which inevitably lead to "heartburn" and "indigestion," fills him with dread (115, 147–9). If, according to the narrator, "Dr Philip Wild had everything save an attractive exterior" (107), the opposite may be said of Flora, whose beauty is her only saving grace: "Of art, of love, of the difference between dreaming and waking she knew nothing" (85–7).

To recall what Nabokov said in another context, Flora knows nothing of those "states of being" – "curiosity, tenderness, kindness, ecstasy" – he himself regarded as the apex of human creativity and consciousness.[10] (The pleasure Flora takes in her unflagging acts of sexual promiscuity – the satiation of physical desire and, perhaps even more thrilling, her sense of power over others – hardly constitutes what Nabokov here refers to as "ecstasy"). Selfish, avaricious, and a "cheat" at school, Flora is exquisite to look at; even the "radial artery" at the top of her hand traces "one of the tenderest areas of her beauty" (91). But while she appears a veritable *objet d'art* to the men who desire her, she is as indifferent to art as she is lacking in love. From the opening sentence of the text, Flora demonstrates her philistine nature: "Her husband, she answered, was a writer, too – at least after a fashion." Unfortunately, his manuscript "was not a work of fiction which one dashes off, you know, to make money ... It had cost him, and would still cost him, years of toil." Indifferent to the values of art or to any less-than-practical pursuit such as philosophy or the higher reaches of science, Flora dismisses such "toil" as fruitless – and deems anyone, including her husband, who dedicates himself to it as "mad" (1–3).

In Chapter Two the narrative leads back in time, providing salient information about Flora's family background. This account leads, in turn, to her personal recollections of childhood. Thus Nabokov's readers share Flora's memories of childhood only *after* they witness her conduct (in Chapter One) as a beautiful but heartless young woman with a keen appetite for promiscuous sex. Flora's "prepubescent years" are recounted in the narrative third-person: "She was often alone in the house with Mr Hubert, who constantly 'prowled' (rodait) around her, humming a monotonous tune and sort of mesmerizing her, envelopping [sic] her, so to speak[,] in some sticky invisible substance and coming closer and closer no matter what way she turned. For instance she did not dare to let her arms hang aimlessly lest her knuckles came into contact with some horrible part of that kindly but smelly and 'pushing' old male" (55–7). Here critics point out that Flora's characterization of Hubert, who exudes "some sticky invisible substance" in order to attract her, resembles Humbert's self-characterization as a spider lying in wait for its prey as twelve-year-old Dolores wanders through the Haze household. Flora's recollection of Hubert's "mesmerizing" power echoes, moreover, the name "Mesmer Mesmer" that Humbert considers using before he decides on Humbert Humbert, which "expresses the nastiness best."[11] The apparent resemblance between Hubert and Humbert culminates in the way Hubert's telltale name is announced: "His name, no doubt assumed, was Hubert H. Hubert." At the same time as the foregoing sentence conveys Flora's doubts as to the authenticity of Hubert's name – his business dealings abroad are "not quite legal," after all – the phrase "no doubt assumed" can be read as a *double entendre*, suggesting that Hubert's name is "assumed," or borrowed, from Humbert's own (53). Before leaping to this conclusion, however, we should recall – as if Nabokov's novels did not offer evidence enough of this fact – the delight that this author took in games of deception: the cunning feints and "fake moves" he was at pains to devise, in order to tantalize readers with the "illusion of a solution."[12]

Part of the pleasure of reading *Laura,* if Nabokov had lived to complete its design, would undoubtedly have derived from the game between author and reader that he staged throughout his fiction. Employing all the devices in his literary arsenal, Nabokov challenged readers to examine their conventional expectations. In *Lolita,* as any careful reader knows, "fake moves" and false leads abound: from the web of allusions to Prosper Mérimée's *Carmen* – fanning the reader's fear that jealous Humbert, like Carmen's lover, Don José, will kill Lolita – to the various hints that he will murder her mother. Nabokov's strategy of catching us out – of thwarting our conventional expectations and thus alerting us to the unique design of the fiction unfolding before us – is already discernible in the fragments of his last novel.. Even the title, *The Original of Laura,* playfully provokes the reader's tendency to seek out an original source, or pre-existing model, from which the fiction at hand derives its characters and themes. Well aware of such tendencies, Nabokov was adamant in his answer to the question early put to him: "Did Lolita herself have an original?" "No," the author flatly replied, "Lolita didn't have any original. She was born in my own mind. She never existed ... Lolita is a figment of my imagination."[13] Given the insinuating, if not insulting, nature of the interviewer's question ("Do you share Humbert's proclivities, Mr Nabokov?"), readers would do well to examine their motives for identifying *Lolita* as a source or model – the original – of *Laura.*

To discover the differences that lurk, so to speak, in the "shadows" of semblance, readers of *Laura* must stay alert to the subtle shifts in tone and point of view that take place in its narrative, as in Nabokov's other novels. In the paragraph following the initial description of Mme Lanskaya's "elderly but still vigorous" lover, Flora's recollections resume: "Flora, a lovely child, as she said herself with a slight shake (dreamy? Incredulous?) of her head every time she spoke of those prepubescent years, had a gray home life marked by ill health, and boredom" (53–5). Here Flora's vantage is signaled by the unambiguous phrase, "as she said herself," supplied by the narrator. As her interlocutor (and lover), he can only guess at her internal response ("dreamy? Incredulous?") to these memories. By her own admission, however, she recalls the gray "boredom" of those "prepubescent years" punctuated by "her nightly dreams of erotic torture in so called 'labs', major and minor laboratories with red curtains" (55). Here, as some critics have noted, the narrator slips in a punning reference to Flora's sexually awakened body – specifically, the major and minor labia, with their distinctive "red curtains." Evidently, these are the "labs," the site or location where the "erotic torture" of "her nightly dreams" is conducted. Continuing the third-person account of Flora's youth, the next sentence of this passage reads, "She did not remember her father and rather disliked her mother." This sentence leads directly into the passage cited earlier – "She was often alone in the house with Mr. Hubert, who constantly 'prowled' (rodait) around her," etc. – that closes with Flora's characterization of Hubert as a "smelly and 'pushing' old male" (57).

By paying close attention to the subtle shifts of point of view in these passages, we glean a crucial difference between *Laura* and *Lolita*: it is twelve-year-old Flora, already experiencing nightly erotic dreams, who perceives Hubert as a sexual enchanter, enveloping her in his mesmerizing power. Here Flora behaves less like Dolores Haze than like Humbert himself, who habitually projects upon the nymphet the "demoniac" power of his own sexual obsessions (*Lolita*, 16, 20). Viewed in this light, Flora's self-confessed sexual fantasies – those "nightly" torments that only a "super-Oriental doctor with long gentle fingers" could possibly slake – can be seen to generate the "invisible" power drawing her dangling "knuckles" into "contact with some horrible" but oddly enticing "part" of Hubert's body. That Flora, rather than Hubert, provides the source of this "mesmerizing" power is further suggested by the telling reappearance of the verb *mesmerize* later in the text. At the opening of Chapter Five (note card Five 1), Flora encounters Dr Philip Wild at Sutton College, where she is a student, and determines to marry him.[14] A "brilliant neurologist, a renowned lecturer," and "a gentleman of independent means," Wild is also an "enormously fat creature." Despite his unseemly bulk, the narrator notes, Dr Wild would "enchant one with his wit. Laura disregarded the wit but was *mesmerized* by his fame and fortune" (107, italics mine).[15]

Here, quite obviously, Flora is the source of the mesmerizing power that draws her to Wild's fame and fortune, as it formerly drew her knuckles into contact with Hubert's body. Given her demanding and promiscuous nature, it is hardly surprising that "after three years of marriage she had enough of his fortune and fame." Disappointed by her husband's failure to live in the luxurious style she had expected, "philistine Flora" deems him "a domestic miser" and consoles herself with an endless series of lovers (25, 111).

Flora's eventual contempt for her husband is also foreshadowed by her twelve-year-old dealings with Mr Hubert. In the passage (note card Two 10) immediately following the one (note card Two 9) in which Flora appears "mesmerized" by her mother's lover, additional information about Hubert is revealed. Here we learn that Hubert is not only a widower but the father of a dead child. In this passage, the shifts in narrative point of view prove crucial:

> He told her stories about his sad life, he told her about his daughter who was just like her, same age – twelve –, same eyelashes – darker than the dark blue of the iris, same hair, blondish or rather palomino, and so silky – if he could be allowed to stroke it, or l'effleurer des levres, like this, thats [sic] all, thank you. Poor Daisy had been crushed to death by a backing lorry on a country road – short cut home from school – through a muddy construction site – abominable tragedy – her mother died of a broken heart. Mr Hubert sat on Flora's bed and nodded his bald head acknowledging all the offences of life, and wiped his eyes with a violet handkerchief which turned orange – a little parlor trick – when he stuffed it back into his heart-pocket, and continued to nod as he tried to adjust his thick outsole to a pattern of the carpet. He now looked like a not too successful conjuror paid to tell fairytales to a sleepy child at bedtime, but he sat a little too close (59–63).

In this passage, Mr Hubert eagerly succumbs to the apparent resemblance between twelve-year-old Flora and his cherished daughter, Daisy, who died at the age of twelve. Not only is Flora's name associated, like Daisy's, with a flower; she too has "dark blue" eyes and "blondish" hair. Hubert even pronounces her eyelashes to be the "same" as his dead daughter's. What Hubert fails to note are the crucial differences between Daisy and Mme Lanskaya's daughter, who lacks any sense of filial affection. Flora, after all, "did not remember her father and rather disliked her mother." Nor does her "mesmerized" sense of attraction-repulsion toward Hubert betray any interest in him as a substitute father. Setting aside the assumption that Hubert is modelled on Humbert, might Hubert's expressed tenderness toward Flora – his desire to touch his lips to that silky hair so like his daughter's – be less predatory than sentimental: the emotional gesture of a grieving father? In the sentence relaying Hubert's fond gesture, he is engaged in telling Flora about "his sad life," a description certainly justified by his having lost both his daughter and his wife, who "died of a broken heart" soon after the loss of their child. It is Hubert who politely asks "if he could be allowed to stroke" Flora's hair or, in a French phrase that echoes her flower-like name, to touch it (*l'effleurer*) with his lips. At this point Hubert appears to do just that, an action indicated by the phrase "like this," which is followed by another polite phrase that puts an end to both the action of Hubert's lips and the sentence itself: "thats [sic] all, thank you."

As Hubert strokes Flora's hair and lightly touches it with his lips, many readers will undoubtedly recall those scenes in *Lolita* when Humbert, still a lodger in the Haze household, is driven to distraction by the tantalizing "nearness" of his nymphet. On one warm summer night, for example, he and "the Haze woman" are seated on "the piazza," Lolita having "squeezed herself" in between them. As "dusk deepened into amorous darkness," Humbert endeavours to distract "the old girl" with an account of his "arctic adventures" as, in "the merciful dark," he slowly advances on the nymphet: "I dared stroke her bare leg along the gooseberry fuzz of her shin, and I chuckled at my own jokes, and trembled, and concealed my tremors, and once or twice felt with my rapid lips the warmth of her hair as I treated her to a quick nuzzling." Carefully parlaying these "ethereal caresses" into more desperate ones, Humbert, "sick with longing," cannot hold back any longer. "I laughed and addressed myself to Haze across Lo's legs to let my hand creep up my nymphet's thin back and feel her skin through her boy's shirt" (*Lolita* 45–6). It is important to note that none of this desperation is evinced by Hubert. In contrast to Humbert, he does not prolong his light kiss of the child's hair or employ this fatherly gesture of affection as a means to initiate a more aggressive embrace. Instead, as a grieving father rather than a predator, he immediately resumes telling Flora about "Poor Daisy," recounting the "abominable tragedy" that took her life and her mother's. As his account draws to a close, Hubert, seated on Flora's bed, nods his "bald head" in acknowledgment of "all the offences of life" and wipes the tears from his eyes with "a violet handkerchief."

Even Hubert's violet handkerchief, which "turned orange – a little parlor trick – when he stuffed it back" in his pocket, recalls his role as Daisy's fond father, still grieving for the child he used to amuse. Just as the handkerchief remains tucked away in his "heart-pocket," so Daisy's memory is lodged in his heart. Then, as the focus shifts from Hubert's sad memories to his sorrowful appearance as he tries "to adjust his thick outsole to the pattern of the carpet," the narrative – imbued with Flora's characteristic *sangfroid* – resumes her recollections of childhood. Indifferent to the poignant presence of that trick-handkerchief, for which daughterless Hubert no longer has an audience, Flora regards the grieving father as a mere attendant, a "paid" entertainer who has overstepped his bounds: "He looked now like a not too successful conjuror paid to tell fairytales to a sleepy child at bedtime, but he sat a little too close" (61–3). Some readers will detect, in this reference to a "conjuror" telling "fairytales to a sleepy child," yet another allusion to the "enchanted hunter," Humbert Humbert, while others may perceive Hubert as "a not too successful conjuror" in a radically different sense. In Flora he seeks to conjure the ghost of his dead daughter – just as he later attempts, in their brief chess game, "to prepare those magic positions where the ghost of a pawn can be captured on the square it has crossed" (69). To Flora, the possibility that Hubert's attentions are paternal in nature simply does not occur. Instead, she is ready to repel his anticipated advances in no uncertain terms. Thus, in the sentence that closes this passage, we learn that "a very sweet and depraved schoolmate" had "taught her where to kick an enterprising gentleman" (59–63).

According to most critics, Hubert's likeness to Humbert is definitively revealed by the chess game that takes place later on, when twelve-year-old Flora "happened to be laid up with a chest cold." True, this scene is riddled with sexual innuendoes, as is the miniature chess set itself. A gift to Flora from Mr Hubert, the set has "tickly-looking little holes bored in the squares to admit and grip the red and white pieces; the pin-sized pawns penetrated easily, but the slightly larger noblemen had to be forced in with an enervating joggle" (63–5). Here, once again, narrative point of view proves all-important. From whose vantage, we must ask, does the chess set acquire such insinuating sexual characteristics: the "tickly-looking holes" made to "grip" the "pieces" inserted into them? Who is implicitly comparing the sexual members of "pin-sized pawns" that "penetrated easily" to those of the "slightly larger noblemen," which "had to be forced in with an enervating joggle"? Doesn't this perspective, focusing on the relative ease or difficulty with which the male member penetrates the female's, tend to reflect a young girl's (particularly this highly sexed young girl's) curiosity rather than a heterosexual male's? Flora's fascination with the size of the male member is, moreover, soon confirmed. In the following chapter, Flora, "barely fourteen," loses "her virginity to a coeval, a handsome ballboy at the Carlton Courts in Cannes ... She observed with quiet interest the difficulty Jules had of drawing a junior-size sheath over an organ that looked abnormally stout" (77–9). When the "poor boy," exhausted from "a hard day picking up and tossing balls" on the tennis court, suggests that for once they take in a movie rather than have sex, teenage Flora perfunctorily drops him. She quickly moves on to a series of "new lovers" whose "dimensions" she enjoys comparing – to mutual "giggles and cries of surprise" – with another teenage girl, who shares her fascination with the size of the male member (81–3).

The way that Nabokov structures the narrative further suggests that the sexually freighted description of the miniature chess set is the product of Flora's perception. The narrative moves directly from Flora's contemplation of the chess pieces' suggestive "joggle" to mention of her mother, who has not yet returned from the pharmacy where she has gone to buy aspirin for her daughter: "The pharmacy was perhaps closed and she had to go to the one next to the church or else she had met some friend of hers in the street and would never return" (65–7). Far from registering the apprehensive concern of a lover, as the narrative surely would if Hubert's perspective were being conveyed, the prospect of Mme Lanskaya's meeting a "friend" with whom she might disappear, "never" to return, conveys the indifference with which her daughter, Flora, regards her. The unflattering picture of Hubert that immediately follows further signals Flora's perspective. (Overlooking this point, one of Nabokov's most hostile critics attributes Hubert's "smelliness" to his author's having grown "self-indulgently smuttier" and "nastier" with age).[16] Clearly it is Flora who imbibes the "smell [of] tobacco, sweat, rum and bad teeth [that] emanate[s] from [the] poor old harmless" man, just as the close-up of his "fat porous nose with red nostrils full of hair" is vividly rendered through her eyes. (From her extremely young and unforgiving perspective, middle-aged Hubert appears decidedly "old"). "It was all very pathetic," she concludes with disdain, noting that Hubert's nose "nearly touched her bare throat as he helped to prop the pillows behind her shoulders" (65–7). Here, as in the previous scene, Flora both dreads and anticipates coming "into contact with some horrible part of that ... smelly ... old male" (57).

Finally, before the sentence describing the near-touch of Hubert's nose to Flora's bare throat comes to a close, another crucial shift in narrative perspective occurs – this time signalled by a lone comma. The full sentence reads: "His fat porous nose with red nostrils full of hair nearly touched her bare throat as he helped to prop the pillows behind her shoulders, and the muddy road was again, was for ever [sic] a short cut between her and school, between school and death" (67). Here the comma following the word "shoulders" signals a shift from Flora's external view of "pathetic" Hubert to the grieving father's internal perspective. The "muddy road" on which Daisy meets her death looms "again," as it will "forever," in Hubert's consciousness. Once again he replays the afternoon on which his daughter rode her bicycle from school for the last time, taking a "short cut" that leads not to home but to her death. In this passage Nabokov makes clear, as he does in novels from *King, Queen, Knave* to *Pale Fire,* that individuals inhabiting the same dimensions of time and space may exist in radically disparate worlds, each imbued by their unique perceptions and consciousness. At the very moment Flora is registering the touch and smell of Hubert's body, her presence – and perceived likeness to Daisy – carries him far away: to the memory of his daughter and the muddy road where she died. "In this novel of human erasure," Brian Boyd astutely observes, "Daisy's death has *not* been erased for the father who remembers his lost child so painfully, so hopelessly" (Boyd's italics).[17]

In the scene of the chess game that follows, Hubert's thoughts are still with Daisy, who "had loved the *en passant* trick" when father and daughter had played chess together. Hoping to conjure a ghost of those old delights, Hubert prepares to set up the chess-moves and "magic positions" that delighted his dead daughter. But Flora, listless with fever, calls off the game. "She pushed the board away and Mr. Hubert carefully removed it to the chair that supported the tea things. Then, with a father's sudden concern, he said 'I'm afraid you are chilly, my love,' and plunging a hand under the bedclothes from his vantage point at the footboard, he felt her shins[.] Flora uttered a yelp and then a few screams. Freeing themselves from the tumbled sheets her pedalling legs hit him in the crotch" (69–71). Here is the sexual advance that Flora has apparently been waiting for – as have Nabokov's critics, who find in this scene damning evidence of Hubert's likeness to pedophiliac Humbert. Without a moment's hesitation, Flora puts into action the lesson learned from her "depraved schoolmate" and kicks Hubert in the crotch. Before readers accept Flora's or the critics' conclusions, however, they would do well to examine a few salient details, beginning with the comment that introduces this scene: "Fever," the narrator notes, "turns games of skill into the stuff of nightmares. After a few minutes of play Flora grew tired" (69). This is not the first time, after all, that Flora has succumbed to the "stuff of nightmares." Let us recall the detailed account of those "nightly dreams of erotic torture" she has endured, along with Hubert's "mesmerizing" male presence. Should we automatically concur with her feverish assumption that the touch of his hand on her shins, under the bedclothes, is an attempt to grope her? Isn't it possible that, as the narrator indicates, Hubert is moved by "a father's sudden concern" that she has grown "chilly"? He is, after all, seated "at the footboard" of her bed – quite unable to test her forehead for fever or chills. Unaccustomed to such parental concern, Flora, who "did not remember her father and rather disliked her mother," evinces little knowledge of, and less interest in, such forms of affection.

Ignoring such distinctions, ready to assume that Flora has been "victimized" by predatory Hubert, most critics find her mother's reaction to the scene ironic. Returning home from the pharmacy to hear the child's "screams" and the "crash" of tea things that Flora's thrashing legs have jolted off the chair, Mme Lanskaya scolds her daughter for her bad behaviour. After soothing "absolutely furious, deeply insulted Mr Hubert," she tells Flora that Hubert is "a dear man, and his life lay in ruins all around him. He wanted [her] to marry him, saying she was the image of the young actress who had been his wife, and indeed to judge by the photographs she, Madame Lanskaya, did ressemble [sic] poor Daisy's mother" (73–5).

That Hubert desires to marry Flora's mother because of her resemblance to his dead wife reinforces the point, argued earlier, that his tenderness toward her daughter may be similarly based on Flora's resemblance to Daisy.[18] As Chapter Two draws to a close and Mme Lanskaya's perspective dissolves into the more detached vantage of an omniscient narrator, readers are informed of Hubert's ultimate fate. Undermining Flora's contemptuous view of his bad breath and ugly nose, the omniscient narrator reports that this "not unattractive" man continues to lodge "for another happy year" in Mme Lanskaya's household – before dying "of a stroke in a hotel lift." He then adds in a humorous quip, "Going up, one would like to surmise" (75). If Hubert were the pedophile so many critics deem him, would he have continued to live with Mme Lanskaya "for another happy year" – having been literally kicked away by her daughter, with no hope of resuming any close relationship, however furtive, with the child? And would Nabokov have authorized his authorial persona to presume, however playfully, that Hubert meets his maker "going up" – not just to the next floor but to heaven? Nabokov, we know, frequently alluded to the symbolic realms of heaven and hell when depicting a character's moral state or fate. Humbert himself calls the reader's attention to the "hell flames" lining the "paradise" he "elected" to share with his nymphet (*Lolita*, 166). In his Foreword to *Despair*, Nabokov employs these terms to signal a crucial difference between Humbert, who proves capable of remorse for having ruined a child's life, and *Despair*'s unrepentant murderer, Hermann: "Both are neurotic scoundrels, yet there is a green lane in paradise where Humbert is permitted to wander at dusk once a year; but Hell shall never parole Hermann" (*Despair*, 9).

The subtlety with which *Laura*'s narrative shifts from one character's perspective to another's, or to that of an omniscient narrator, is characteristic of Nabokov's late works – one thinks, in particular, of *Transparent Things* – and helps to account, as we have seen, for some of the more egregious misreadings of *Laura* by critics. Their readiness to discover resemblances between Nabokov's unfinished text and his most famous one has also played a part, one that the author himself may have anticipated. After *Lolita*'s success made him a literary celebrity, Nabokov tended to discount the fame attributed to him. "*Lolita* is famous, not I," he told an interviewer. "I am an obscure, doubly obscure, novelist with an unpronounceable name."[19] Aware of the public's tendency, ever after, to associate his works with *Lolita*'s scandalous subject and to characterize his fiction – and worse yet, his personal life – as fraught with pedophiliac tendencies, Nabokov may well have enjoyed playing with readers' expectations.[20] Take, for example, one of the most graphic, seemingly damning passages in *Laura.* Here Nabokov has Philip Wild provocatively describe the only position in which he, monstrously obese, can have sex with his wife. While she sits "in the fauteuil of his flesh with her back to him," he holds "her in front of him like a child being given a sleighride [sic] down a short slope by a kind stranger ... her hip[s] between his hands" (197–9).

Any reader seeking signs of pedophilia will undoubtedly find them in the foregoing passage. In Wild's comparison of his wife, Flora, to a child seated in front of a "kind stranger," Nabokov openly invites readers to associate this act of copulation with the sly pedophile's ultimate aim. Assuming the guise of a kind stranger, the "lecherous creep," to recall one critic's formulation, proffers sweets and games in order to lure the child into his clutches. But here too we must ask: Who in this scene has been ensnared or victimized? Surely not Flora, for whom the "procedure – a few bounces over very small humps – meant nothing." Marking time by gazing at "the snow-scape on the footboard of the bed" and then at the "curtains," she is performing, with characteristic dispatch, a routine duty. Indeed, her appearance in her husband's "bleak bedroom" may signal the start of a new affair with yet another lover: "I alway[s] know she is cheating on me with a new boyfriend," Wild observes, "whenever she visits my bleak bedroom more often than once a month" (193–7). In this passage, it is not indifferent Flora but the inattentive reader who falls prey to entrapment. By insisting on resemblances that, on closer inspection, prove mere "shadows of differences," the unwitting reader is lured into the trap: one of the many false leads designed by the author to ensnare careless readers.

When, in *Pale Fire*, John Shade cautions Kinbote on the subject of semblance, his statement – that "resemblances are the shadows of differences" – alludes to Plato's allegory of the Cave in Book VII of *The Republic.* In it, Socrates describes to Glaucon a group of prisoners, chained by the neck and legs so that they cannot move, staring at a wall on which their shadows, and those of figures and objects moving behind them, are cast by a fire they cannot see. Assuming that the "shadows" they perceive are real, the prisoners evoke our common plight: the failure, in Plato's view, to understand that visible phenomena, the flickering "images" we perceive, are mere illusions – the true "shadows" of true "realities."[21] To mistake these ephemeral images for reality, Plato argues, is to blind ourselves to the light of truth and reason. To submit to the "world of becoming" is to forfeit discovery of the world of "being," the realm of eternal ideas. A practising poet (and we know what Plato thought of poets), Shade implicitly challenges the philosopher's view. Inverting the relationship between visible phenomena and abstract ideas that Plato set forth, he suggests that static notions or *idées fixes* – resemblances – are the true "shadows," or illusions. Reality is found in the world of specific phenomena, a flux of elements ever forming and evolving into untold shapes and substances. Nabokov's fiction celebrates the ceaseless process by which discrete elements, the building blocks of life and language, combine and recombine to spawn new images and forms, entities and creatures.

Precisely because this metamorphic process teems with life, Philip Wild, in his experiments with death by self-erasure, pits himself against it – as though it were a nightmare from which he is trying to awake. In recounting "a recurrent dream" from his childhood, the neurologist envisions escaping life by erasing its "growing shape":

> I used to see a smudge on the wallpaper or on a whitewashed door, a nasty smudge that started to come alive, turning into a crustacean-like monster. As its appendages began to move, a thrill of foolish horror shook me awake; but the same night or the next I would be again facing idly some wall or screen on which a spot of dirt would attract the naive sleeper's attention by starting to grow and make groping and clasping gestures – and again I managed to wake up before its bloated bulk got unstuck from the wall. But one night ... I let the smudge start its evolution and, drawing on an imagined mitten, I simply rubbed out the beast. Three or four times it appeared again in my dreams but now I welcomed its growing shape and gleefully erased it. Finally it gave up – as some day life will give up – bothering me. (249–53)

Imprisoned in a body that torments him, Wild has ceased to take pleasure in life's relentless vitality, the dynamics of change and growth. Like the monster in his childhood nightmares, it threatens to fix him in its "clasping" clutches.

At the time that Wild's author was struggling to complete *Laura*, he was undergoing his own physical torments – some of which are echoed in the text. Yet here too, readers should be wary of searching for semblance when differences – between Wild and his author – are telling. True, Nabokov's own life was drawing to a close at the time he was writing *Laura*; but Wild's preoccupations notwithstanding, the text teems with life-giving energies that animate even the simplest objects: from the pair of slippers, "foetally folded in their zippered pouch," which belong to Flora's new lover in Chapter One, to the "small formless vanity bag, a blind black puppy," that she takes to the party where she meets him (7, 11). On the heels of this metaphorical puppy, a literal dog makes his presence felt: "Mrs. Carr's nephew, Anthony Carr, and his wife Winny were [happy] ... to lend their flat to a friend, any friend, when they and their dog do not happen to need it. Flora spotted at once the alien creams in the bathroom and the open can of Fido's Feast ... in the cluttered fridge" (7–9). In a narrative shift characteristic of Nabokov's technique in *Laura,* the scene instantaneously segues from the party where Flora and the narrator meet to the borrowed flat where they make love. Meanwhile, the existence of the Carr's dog, invoked in the first sentence, is concretely evinced in the second – which notes the open can of dog food in the refrigerator. Later, when the narrator takes Flora home from the flat, another "image" springs to life. In "the shadows of a side alley," the narrator spies "a young man with a mackintosh over his white pyjamas," unhappily "wringing his hands." The lover whom Flora dismissed with such savage zest over the telephone has now materialized. His white pyjamas may not match the "sickly gray" that the narrator had earlier pictured, but the poor fellow's "wringing hands" vividly convey his heartsick condition. When, three days later, the distressed lover turns up – with "three days growth of blond beard" – at Flora's front door, she rudely dismisses him, threatening never to see him again. But by the time he "reached his lodgings," we are told, the "telephone was already ringing ecstatically" – spontaneously signalling, to the already ecstatic lover, that Flora is on the line (33–9).

By means of such devices – including metaphor, personification, and the pathetic fallacy of the ecstatic telephone – Nabokov invests the world of *Laura* with life, even when the subject at hand is death. Perhaps the most striking example of this paradox occurs in a passage, the last one we shall examine here, recounting the fate of the "meticulous masterpieces" painted by Flora's grandfather, Lev Linde. The "glory of Russia, the pride of the people," Linde's landscapes – a collection of which he brought with him when he emigrated from Moscow to New York – fail to win much attention in America. The narrator thus informs us, "Very soon a number of unconsolable [sic] oils found themselves being shipped back to Moscow, while another batch moped in rented flats before trouping up to the attic or creeping down to the marketstall" (41–3). Here the paintings themselves appear to suffer pangs of rejection, inconsolable on their voyage back to Russia or dejectedly moping in storage. In sad defeat the "oils" file up the stairs to an obscure attic or, in humiliation, silently creep down to the market stall to be sold on the cheap. So intense is the shame endured by Linde's personified paintings, that the oblivion to which America consigns them acts as a virulent force, killing off the artist who created them: "What can be sadder," the narrator rhetorically queries, "than a discouraged artist dying not from his own commonplace maladies, but from the cancer of oblivion invading his once famous pictures?" In marked contrast to the intense life of Linde's paintings are the "automatic pictures" that record his son Adam's suicide in a Monte Carlo hotel. A "fashionable photographer" with an "inclination for trick photography," Adam, before shooting himself, rigs his camera "to record the event from different angles. These automatic pictures of his last moments and of a table's lion-paws did not come out to[o] well." Proving once again that bad art never prevented anyone from making good money, Adam's widow "easily sold [the photographs] for the price of a flat in Paris to the local magazine *Pitch*" (45–51). If the fate of both Lev and his "more successful" son is to die of despair, the works they produce are radically different. Both the subject and medium of Adam's "automatic" pictures are lifeless. The rigged camera produces photographs devoid of the vitality animating Lev's landscapes, whose "thawing snow-banks" and "purple heaths" virtually breathe with life (41). In Nabokov's unfinished text, as in his finest novels, resemblances are merely the shadows of differences.

Nabokov's Last Smile

LARA DELAGE-TORIEL

As he embarked upon his final voyage to other shores, Vladimir Nabokov was haunted by the thought of "a certain butterfly [that] was already on the wing" and that he would never see.[1] Yet some eight years earlier, in conversation with Dieter Zimmer, he had compared his own fate to that of a butterfly: "I also intend to collect butterflies ... in Peru or in Iran before I pupate"[2] – as if physical death were but a decisive moment in a process of metamorphosis, leading to a new life.

One might likewise wonder whether *The Original of Laura*, the mere pupa of a novel that was to disappear with its author, might also be given a second lease on life now that its chrysalis has been hatched and that any reader may inspect its carefully preserved innards. Yet such exposure is not without its problems. For one thing, there is precious little to be read, let alone studied. As John Banville has noted, it is "little more than a blurred outline, a preliminary shiver of a novel."[3] Any elaborate commentary will tend to solidify and thus transform the essentially flimsy state in which Nabokov left his text. But then, one may argue, isn't this, perhaps in its extreme form, the natural course any work of art is bound to follow when it is submitted to the public eye?

Although many readers were thrilled at the prospect of getting a glimpse of Nabokov's final opus that had been saved from the flames after being entombed for over thirty years; for others, this was a case of desecration. As a Nabokovian scholar, I stand somewhere in between: I was only mildly excited about the publication, having already read the manuscript some ten years earlier, but I was glad that readers around the world might have the chance to reach a more accurate view of the final stretches of a brilliant writer's trajectory. On the other hand, I did at first balk at dissecting my cherished writer's fiercely guarded privacy. If one heeds the aphoristic pronouncement made in *Pnin* – "Death is divestment, death is communion"[4] – then such exposure is tantamount to sentencing to death a stillborn manuscript. Better still, it marks the symbolic death of the author himself since, oblivious to Nabokov's master plan, to the beauty of the fully-achieved work, I, like any other critic, run the risk of filling the "tempting emptiness" (129) that lies at its heart, not so much with the writer's art as with my own craft. In sum, the publication of *The Original of Laura* exposes *us* to one of the classical "pitfalls" of criticism; that of reading a writer's book by the critic's *own* book. Such risk is increased here by the fact that there is so little to substantiate speculation or interpretation.

If I am now writing about *The Original of Laura* in spite of the caveats I have just raised, it is because a scene from *Alice in Wonderland* has somewhat allayed my qualms regarding the implications of this enterprise. The scene I have in mind is one of those many absurdly comic instances in which Lewis Carroll stands our rational principles on their heads. As one may remember, the Cheshire cat mesmerizes Alice by managing to make its body disappear while teasingly leaving its grin behind it. When, in chapter 8, the cat refuses to kiss the King's hand, it is sentenced to death by the Queen of Hearts, whose answer in cases of conflict is invariably "Off with his [or her] head." However, the cat's vanishing acts play havoc with the planned execution, as the following excerpt makes clear: "The executioner's argument was, that you couldn't cut off a head unless there was a body to cut if off from: that he had never had to do such a thing before, and he wasn't going to begin at *his* time of life. The King's argument was, that anything that had a head could be beheaded, and that you weren't to talk nonsense."[5]

To my mind, there is a metaphorical dimension to this debate that is particularly germane to the situation I have just presented. At the end of the chapter, the cat disappears from the text without further mention of its fate, and one can only surmise that its life has been spared thanks to its ability to will itself away in its uniquely quirky fashion. Likewise, although in Nabokov's case it was fate that willed him away, I feel that despite our attempts to pin down sense and coherence, the writer and his last work will carry on fluttering way above our heads and our reach, offering us only intimations, indeed shades, of the picture he had in mind.[6]

The strange case of the Cheshire cat opens up a multitude of paths for thought. Indeed, what is questioned in the quoted excerpt is the link of the part to the whole, the head to the body. The integrity of the body is a matter of direct concern in *The Original of Laura*, not only because part of the body of the work is missing, but also because its characters are enmeshed within a complex game of presence and absence, exposure and erasure. In what kind of game does this engage the reader? The work constantly dramatizes what William Gass designates as the reader's primary desire, "the penetration of privacy."[7] For Gass, reading at its best is akin to sexual intercourse, but making sentences really sexy is not as simple as it may seem. Indeed, it takes a good writer to fashion a complicity that reaches beyond the reader's basic scopic desire. As he writes, "it is not easy to structure the consciousness of the reader with the real thing, to use one wonder to speak of another, until in the place of the voyeur who reads we have fashioned the reader who sings."[8] Part of this inquiry will investigate the ways in which various kinds of exposure in *The Original of Laura* might make us move from one wonder to another, and from idle consumers to consummate *interprètes*.[9]

The incipit, which classically serves an expository purpose, makes us enter the heart of the matter, not only because it launches us *in medias res* but also because it foregrounds the very situation that Nabokov has been faced with, post-mortem. In point of fact, it presents a double case of trespassing on the writer's private grounds. Flora, the main female protagonist, is literally caught red-handed "riffling through [the] papers" of her husband who "pretend[s] to slam down a marble paper-weight and crush" her hand while she claims she is "not in the least trying to decipher his mysterious manuscript" (1). Her very evocation of this manuscript, which she describes during a party as an unfinished "testament," constitutes a second instance of trespassing since, of course, all this, as she herself admits, is "an absolute secret" (3). Nabokov had already asserted in other works the sanctity of the writer's privacy: *Pale Fire* partly revolves around the obsessive impingement, both physical and intellectual, on a poet's grounds; in *The Real Life of Sebastian Knight*, such impingement is confounded by the protective measures taken before his death by the eponymous writer, deeming that "nothing ought to remain except the perfect achievement: the printed book; that its actual existence is inconsistent with that of its spectre, the uncouth manuscript flaunting its imperfections like a revengeful ghost carrying its own head under its arm; and that for this reason the litter of the workshop, no matter its sentimental or commercial value, must never subsist."[10]

Nabokov was just as adamant in the foreword to his translation of Pushkin's *Eugene Onegin*, claiming that "[r]ough drafts, false scents, half-explored trails, dead ends of inspiration, are of little intrinsic importance. An artist should ruthlessly destroy his manuscripts after publication, lest they mislead academic mediocrities into thinking that it is possible to unravel the mysteries of genius by studying cancelled readings."[11]

It is then no surprise that Nabokov should usher us into his final piece of fiction with such a warning notice, flaunting, in the least attractive guise that may be – by dint of a legerdemain *mise en abyme* – our own penetration of his privacy. The various portraits that sketch out Flora all corroborate this first impression that she is an unworthy model – like Emma Bovary, at once a bad reader and an adulterous woman, superficial and unfaithful.

Paradigmatic of her flaw is her "urge to expose the maximum of naked flesh" (233), an urge that stands poles apart from that of her husband, Philip Wild, whose hatred of his own flesh impels him to repeatedly attempt "self-obliteration" (213) or "self-deletion" (139) or "auto-dissolution" (171). This exacerbated desire to disappear is directly proportional to his physical mass, one of his chief characteristics, as is proved by a zeugma presenting him as "a man of great corpulence and fame" (103); Wild is then described, less elegantly, as an "enormously fat creature" (107) with an "enormous stomack" (231), that he himself compares to a "trunkful of bowels" (149). This dominant trait is passed on to what is presumably his fictional alter ego, Nigel Dalling, or Delling,[12] who sees himself "as an obese bulk with formless features and a sad porcine stare" (135).

Both protagonists are thus engulfed by their own fat, captives within their own body and victims of a dehumanizing processreminiscent of Kafka's *Metamorphosis*, a story in which the main protagonist, Gregor Samsa, turns into a beetle. Interestingly enough, Nabokov feels that Gregor's "beetlehood, while distorting and degrading his body, seems to bring out in him all his human sweetness."[13] Is there likewise some greater "wonder" or meaning to be gained from these characters' excess weight?

Nabokov, for his part, was bent on adding extra sense to his own weight gain by waggishly associating it with the acquisition of his American identity: "my weight went up from my usual 140 to a monumental and cheerful 200. In consequence, I am one-third American – good American flesh keeping me warm and safe."[14] In his fiction, he often endows his own physical ailments with a metaphorical load of sense when passing them on to his characters. A striking instance of this is his recurrently acute dental problems, which both Humbert and Pnin inherit. We are afforded a glimpse of these problems in his correspondence with Edmund Wilson, when he describes the removal of his teeth: "some of them had little red cherries – abscesses – and the man in white was pleased when they came out whole, together with the crimson ivory. My tongue feels like somebody coming home and finding his furniture gone."[15]

The fruit metaphor is magnified and made even more painfully exquisite in Humbert's mouth, since it becomes a maraschino cherry, a cherry steeped in bitter liquor, in part 1, chapter 14 of *Lolita*: "Must have been an enormous molar, with an abscess as big as a maraschino cherry."[16] Whether true or exaggerated, the image serves as a beautiful excuse to steer away from Charlotte's unappetizing baiting manoeuvres but, strategically placed in the aftermath of the davenport scene in the company of her daughter, it also masterfully conjures up the sweet congestion of desire, the "hidden tumor of an unspeakable passion" which has grown upon him and is now distilled through the mellifluous "m's" of his phrase (*m*ust, enor*m*ous *m*olar, *m*araschino) that echo the "milk, molasses, foaming champagne" he has just poured into the little girl's "white purse."[17] It is also very likely that the painfully red molar points to the Quilty motif, which is watermarked in this episode by Charlotte's reference to the dentist Ivor Quilty, his uncle.[18]

In the case of Pnin, the dental issue becomes a metaphor for the condition of the exile, which is directly derived from Nabokov's own feeling of destitution. In *Pnin* (part 4 of chapter 2), the image of the empty house is thus extended to that of a kingdom – an image that aptly ties in with Victor's dream vision of Pnin as a king – now turned into a "terra incognita of gums."[19] The operation marks a symbolic death, since Pnin is "in mourning for an intimate part of himself." Furthermore, the "great dark wound" in his mouth acts as a metaphorical revival of the pain caused by his being abruptly pulled out of Russia, since his teeth stand as the last "battered" remnants of that "brilliant cosmos that seemed all the fresher for having been abolished by one blow of history."[20] However, like Nabokov when joking about his weight gain, Pnin welcomes his new dental plates as a symbol of his successful incorporation of American values; for him they represent "a firm mouthful of efficient, alabastrine, humane America."[21] Note how the steadiness of this new environment is evoked in this last phrase through the repeated use of "f," a consonant made by resting one's upper set of teeth on the lower lip. By highlighting the stability of this new anchor, the author points at the exile's resilience and his capacity to adapt to his new context, thanks, one might assume, to his tongue, which, as its comparison to a seal suggests and as Nabokov's prose amply proves, is a muscular, supple and living thing, able to twist itself in many ways.[22]

Many such correspondences could be developed, notably the enigmatic "shadow behind the heart"[23] that Pnin also inherits from his creator, but these two examples suffice to demonstrate the depths of meaning that Nabokov invites readers to sound when he lets them penetrate the privacy of his characters (and some of his own). The very nature of the mouth, an aperture where words are formed and exchanges between inner and outer world are so manifold, brings us face to face with a kind of intimacy that, quite obviously, cannot satisfy the curiosity of the ordinary voyeur. These two examples testify that the use of imagery acts as a form of diversion, removing from our sight the less appealing particulars of the flesh. It enables the writer to divest the body of its material and accidental nature in order to integrate it into a more philosophical realm, within the greater sphere of existence. Conversely, in *The Original of Laura*, Nabokov examines the male body from a clinical, at times even crude stance, quite bereft of the ornate seductions of metaphor. Physiological observations range from strong odours to digestive disturbances: the "fourfold smell – tobacco, sweat, rum and bad teeth" (67) of Mr Hubert and the "reek" (169) of Wild's presumably rotting feet, to the "first installment of hot filth pouring out of [Delling] in a public toilet" (149). Far from diverting our attention from the less appealing aspects of the flesh, Nabokov insists on their reality *per se*, imposing upon us an intimacy that offers no way of escape into loftier considerations. Nabokov thus thwarts the pleasure afforded by intrusive penetration by flinging privacy directly into our faces.

One of the most remarkable examples in this vein is the dream fantasy in which Philip Wild imagines he is once again coupled with his childhood love, Aurora Lee.

> I saw you again, Aurora Lee, whom as a youth I had pursued with hopeless desire at high-school balls – and whom I have cornered now fifty years later, on a terrace of my dream. Your painted pout and cold gaze were, come to think of it, very like the official lips and eyes of Flora, my wayward wife, and your flimsy frock of black silk might have come from her recent wardrobe. You turned away, but could not escape, trapped as you were among the close-set columns of moonlight and I lifted the hem of your dress – something I never had done in the past – and stroked, moulded, pinched ever so softly your pale prominent nates, while you stood perfectly still as if considering new possibilities of power and pleasure and interior decoration. At the height of your guarded ecstasy I thrust my cupped hand from behind between your consenting thighs and felt the sweat-stuck folds of a long scrotum and then, further in front, the droop of a short member. Speaking as an authority on dreams, I wish to add that this was no homosexual manifestation but a splendid example of terminal gynandrism. Young Aurora Lee (who was to be axed and chopped up at seventeen by an idiot lover, all glasses and beard) and half-impotent old Wild formed for a moment one creature (203–5).

If we pursue William Gass's metaphor, one might suggest that here is Nabokov cocking a snook at readers who thought they would be in for a sex ride, or at least a remake of the Annabel Lee romance in *Lolita*. Indeed, the passage is teasingly reminiscent of Humbert Humbert's first tryst with Annabel Lee, the little girl presented as Lolita's precursor, and already a borrowing from Poe. Yet, as comparison will soon make clear, the two passages stand poles apart and produce a radically different reading experience:

> She trembled and twitched as I kissed the corner of her parted lips and the hot lobe of her ear. A cluster of stars palely glowed above us, between the silhouettes of long thin leaves; that vibrant sky seemed as naked as she was under her light frock. I saw her face in the sky,

> strangely distinct, as if it emitted a faint radiance of its own. Her legs, her lovely live legs, were not too close together, and when my hand located what it sought, a dreamy and eerie expression, half-pleasure, half-pain, came over those childish features. She sat a little higher than I, and whenever in her solitary ecstasy she was led to kiss me, her head would bend with a sleepy, soft, drooping movement that was almost woeful, and her bare knees caught and compressed my wrist, and slackened again; and her quivering mouth, distorted by the acridity of some mysterious potion, with a sibilant intake of breath came near to my face. She would try to relieve the pain of love by first roughly rubbing her dry lips against mine; then my darling would draw away with a nervous toss of her hair, and then again come darkly near and let me feed on her open mouth, while with a generosity that was ready to offer her everything, my heart, my throat, my entrails, I gave her to hold in her awkward fist the scepter of my passion.[24]

Although both passages have nocturnal settings, the atmospheres they conjure up diverge quite significantly. While the stellar backdrop is placed in sympathy with Annabel Lee, by dint of comparisons ("as naked as she was," "as if it emitted a faint radiance of its own"), the moonlight stands for a hostile environment that is complicit in Wild's attempt to corner Aurora Lee ("trapped as you were among the close-set columns of moonlight"). Both girls are wearing the same kind of dress, a "light" or "flimsy" frock that makes them at once alluring and easily accessible, yet their responses to their lover's presence contrast: in *Lolita*, we note a profusion of action verbs, conveying the girl's strong emotional and sensuous involvement, whereas Aurora stands "perfectly still" and casts upon the scene a detached gaze that is ironically highlighted by the yoking together of considerations of "pleasure" and of "interior decoration." Furthermore, the climax features the apparition of the male genitals in both cases, but whereas these are sublimated by metaphorical hyperbole in *Lolita*, they are rendered graphically grotesque in *Laura*. Finally, one also observes an eloquent variance in the modes of ecstasy experienced by the two girls: its intensity is signified in *Lolita* through a broad array of motions that show how the girl is transported outside herself, in accordance with the etymology of the word, which means to stand outside.

The prominent sibilants in the word also contaminate many other words ("solitary," "kiss," "sleepy," "soft," "compressed," "wrist," "slackened," "distorted," "some mysterious"), and fuse organically with her "sibilant intake of breath." Aurora undergoes no such experience, for her ecstasy is decked out with an epithet, "guarded," that entirely deflates what momentum it might have had and turns the one expression of her inner state into a strange oxymoron: "at the height of her guarded ecstasy."

Whereas the overall effect in *Lolita* is to immerse the reader in the shared passion of the two youngsters and thus help to establish a relationship between the older Humbert and the reader, in *The Original of Laura*, the formal style of the neurologist diagnosing this case, added to the disturbingly violent parenthesis and the haughtily indifferent attitude of the girl, debar the reader from any kind of empathy, and many a reader is liable to dismiss this whole fantasy as a rather pathetic compensation for the character's lack of vigour and failed love life.

In sum, whereas in *Lolita* the depiction of this encounter empowers the narrator as he launches upon his story, the dream fantasy in Nabokov's final opus constitutes a cruel admission of Philip Wild's powerlessness, a fact that is spelled out through the reference to his sexual impotence. It is worth noticing, nevertheless, that he is only half impotent, which leaves a fully potent half. At all events, the power of his imagination – to create, but also to destroy, as we shall now see – amply makes up for his physical handicap, and this idea, which runs throughout Nabokov's works, is made all the more poignant and potent in a novel where physical weaknesses are rendered in such an acute fashion. The novel presents a particularly effective polarization of the body, at once debilitated and delible, and of the mind, at once creative and destructive. The most intriguing instance of this polarization concerns Wild's ingrown toenails, the privileged butt of his attacks, both verbal and physical. In the passage featuring Nigel Delling, several cards dwell on the "torture" derived from these extremities, as well as the consequent "ecstatic relief" (139) afforded by their destruction. It is quite striking that these repeated experiences are described in far more lyrical and hyperbolical fashion than any of the sex episodes in the novel.[25] Yet Wild's assault on his toes cannot be considered as merely a quirky perversion aimed at superficially entertaining a certain category of readers. It certainly reflects the intensity of Nabokov's own affliction while composing part of the novel, those "incessant inflammations under and around his toenails" which, according to his son, proved such torment that "he felt almost as if he would rather be rid of them altogether" (xvi). But, as with his dental problems, this incidental ailment becomes a springboard for more fundamental existential issues, which I now investigate briefly.

Toes fulfil a vital function in offering an increased weight-bearing area for our body mass; the great toe in particular is essential for maintaining balance, as various scientific studies prove.[26] Accordingly, when Wild mentally proceeds to exterminate his ten toes, he falls flat on his face, unable to hold his balance. Although his toes are apparently "intact" (165), Wild seems to have managed to detach them from the rest of his body, making them numb, or, as he neatly and alliteratively puts it, "all rubber and rot" (167). This special mental influence on biomechanics reminds one of Vadim Vadimovich's trials with displacement through space in Nabokov's last published novel, *Look at the Harlequins!* Interestingly enough, the protagonist's failure to perform, first only imaginatively, then also physically, a complete turnabout, is interpreted by his companion as a simple confusion between direction and duration: "He speaks of space but he means time ... Nobody can imagine in physical terms the act of reversing the order of time. Time is not reversible."[27]

As Nabokov felt death closing in on him, he must have also grown increasingly distressed at being unable to reverse the order of time – especially since it was after losing his footing on a steep and slippery slope in July 1975 that the march toward his final abode really began – as his son suggests in his Introduction (xi). One might thus surmise that in having his protagonist devise an efficient method of self-destruction, Nabokov, knowing himself to be on his last legs, put all his creative energies into making his protagonist imaginatively perform what reality forbade: put death out of the running in a race against the clock. Like Donne in his tenth Holy Sonnet, quoted in *Pale Fire*, he wished to defy death by sentencing it to its own death – "And death shall be no more; Death, thou shalt die!" Here, by taking such pains to execute his protagonist through an exercise of the mind, from his lower rather than his upper end (the mind thus remaining intact), Nabokov, like the Cheshire cat, asserts his desire to counter fate and thus cut the ground from under Death's feet.

In spite of his disappearance, Nabokov will remain with us through the imposing corpulence of his œuvre, but especially thanks to the many questions its quizzical smile continues to raise in its trail. This final opus, flimsy though it may be, represents a most fitting appendix to the existing corpus. Indeed, the very sketchiness of the manuscript, presented in its most naked state, affords a unique form of intimacy with the writer, since it dovetails not only the intricacies of story and narrative, but also the physical act of writing, torn among creation, destruction, and suspension. Beyond the many instances of sloppy spelling, hesitant wording, smudged deletions, and incoherent scribblings that we have no choice but to stumble upon, this disquieting *corps à corps* with the writer is all the more memorable for its involuntary elusiveness, as well as the vistas it leaves open for every kind of wonder. I am thinking, in particular, of this most beautiful of blanks which, thanks to the hand of fate, grazes infinity and sets all my senses astir, *à fleur de peau*:[28] "In the course of the night I teased off the shrivelled white flesh and contemplated with utmost delight" (167).

The Original of Laura and Nietzsche: A Zarathustran Tool?

MICHAEL RODGERS

Vladimir Nabokov's final novel, *The Original of Laura*, seems to be as much concerned with morality as it is with mortality.[1] The importance of the single letter, reminiscent of *Pale Fire*'s "mountain/fountain" quandary,[2] plays a curious role. Not only does Adam Linde decide to drop the last letter of his name "on the tacite advice of a misprint in a catalogue" (45)[3] but the portmanteau "FLaura" (111) acts to hybridize the ethereality of Laura with the all-too-near presence of Flora. Nabokov's omission (and Dmitri Nabokov's addition) of a letter in the "Notes" of the novel follows this trend:

> the art of self-slaughter
>
> TLS 16-1-76 "Nietz[s]che argued that the man of pure will ... must recognise that there is an appropriate time to die" (265).

Nabokov is alluding to a chapter titled "Voluntary Death" in Friedrich Nietzsche's *Thus Spoke Zarathustra* (*TSZ*), which describes the virtuous action of dying at the right time.[4] Given that Philip Wild talks about trying not to "die before you are ready to die" (181) and that the latter part of the novel explicitly focuses on his existential experiment of "auto-dissolution" (171), this reference takes on greater significance the further we probe.

That Nabokov alludes to Nietzsche but has spelled his name incorrectly is a telling point. Is it simply another spelling mistake among the many in the text, arguably caused by Nabokov's failing health?[5] Could the spelling mistake, like "Montherland" (95), be a ridiculing technique, a "patronizing indifference" to the supposed source?[6] Is it simply that "Nietzsche" is a difficult name to spell, given that it has five consonants in succession? The fact that Nabokov apparently gives a source for the Nietzschean reference – the *Times Literary Supplement* for the week beginning 16 January 1976, published a full year before Nabokov's death – might be expected to clear things up. However, it seems that there is no such reference to Nietzsche in the *TLS* on or around that date.[7] Can we simply explain this as Nabokov wishing us to believe that Nietzsche is included in a review in a broadsheet or should we grant it significance given its charlatan authenticity, its parading of a hermeneutic reference squarely in our faces? As I will illustrate, Nabokov seems to demonstrate more knowledge of Nietzsche than the misspelled allusion might suggest. On this premise, I map the similarities between *Laura* and *TSZ* not only in their thematic correspondences but also in their treatment of death as an ironic source of creativity in which aesthetic delight is privileged over death.

Laura centres around twenty-four-year old Flora Wild – a callous, promiscuous woman, daughter of Madame Lanskaya (a famous ballerina) and the supposed daughter of Adam Lind (a famous photographer) – who is married to the corpulent Philip Wild, a "Lecturer in Experimental Psychology [at the] University of Ganglia" (147). The novel's narrative continually oscillates between numerous characters' perspectives in a fashion reminiscent of Nabokov's early novelette *The Eye* (*Sogliadatai*) (1930). Its opening sequence is told by an anonymous Russian writer (alluded to later in the novel as Ivan Vaughan) who describes his love affair with Flora. This illicit affair is the subject matter for a book that he is writing called "My Laura," described "as a roman à clef with the clef lost for ever" (221). This book, contained in *Laura*, is eventually read by Philip Wild (fictionalized as Philidor Sauvage), and described as a "maddening masterpiece" (ibid). Wild himself is writing a "mad neurologist's testament" (3) concerned with the destruction of the self; of having the will power to intentionally obliterate his body through "luxurious suicide" (243). Wild's experiments seem to suggest his desire to transgress the protocol of death, to determine when his own extinction will occur rather than to leave it in the hands of chance. Indeed, Wild describes undertaking a "process of self-obliteration conducted by an effort of the will" (213).

The idea of willing the self away voluntarily, as I stated earlier, alludes to a passage titled "Voluntary Death" in Nietzsche's philosophical novel *TSZ*. The reference to *TSZ* may seem strange given that "Nietzsche rarely appears in Nabokov's later work," according to John Burt Foster, who does, however, note Nabokov's references to Nietzsche in his earlier works. Discussing *Mary* (1926) and its inclusion of Nietzsche's idea of "eternal return," Foster argues that "Nietzschean ideas were widely current in Russian symbolist and early modernist circles when Nabokov was growing up; and though Nietzsche's books were banned in the Soviet Union, they were obviously still accessible to the émigré audience for which Nabokov was then writing."[8]

Bernice Glatzer Rosenthal argues that "[i]t was not so much the direct influence of Nietzsche's ideas, though that was certainly found, but the persistence, in transmuted form, of ideas and images that had become embedded in the culture before the Bolshevik Revolution ... Russians learned about Nietzsche in the 1890s. His populizers were artists and writers, who hailed Nietzsche as the prophet of a new culture of art and beauty, and of a new kind of human being – courageous, creative, free."[9] The influence of Nietzsche on Russian Silver Age writers such as Andrei Bely, Aleksandr Blok, Ivan Bunin, Vladimir Mayakovsky and Vyacheslav Ivanov is noticeable, and arguably derives from Nietzsche's ability to "distinguish himself from the conventional moralists of the past and to shock his reader into a new awareness of the process of moral valuation."[10] Nabokov's admission that he was "a product of that period" suggests a kind of Nietzschean influence on Nabokov by osmosis[11] – the idea that Nabokov could not read German (despite residing in Berlin between 1922 and 1937) seems, once again, part of his public persona whereby he refuted most suggestions of influence.[12] Indeed, Brian Boyd notes that father-and-son Nabokov both had an interest in Nietzsche, while Thomas Karshan details that, in 1918, Nabokov "made a list of ten 'books which must be read.' One of three books crossed out, and marked as read, is *Thus Spoke Zarathustra*."[13]

In describing the conception of *The Defense* (1930), Foster argues that "[j]ust as Nietzsche recalls first conceiving of eternal recurrence near 'a powerful pyramidal rock,' so Nabokov associates the genesis of his novel with a similar scene: 'I remember with special limpidity a sloping slab of rock, in the ulex and ilex-clad hills, where the main thematic idea of the book first came to me.'"[14] It is important to remember that the motif of the mountain setting of inspiration derives from the conception of *TSZ* and that, rather than being a stranded allusion, Nietzsche's novel has numerous points of contact with Nabokov's final novel.[15]

Unlike a traditional philosophical treatise, *TSZ* is written in dramatic form and explains how the prophet Zarathustra tries to prepare mankind for the coming of the "superman" who will bring meaning to the earth. The superman is someone who will have the ability to "overcome" himself, who will create the values by which he will abide rather than follow the "table of values" that mankind has devised for his own persecution. Interrelated with Nietzsche's other main themes, the superman will be one who possesses an unshakeable "will to power"[16] and wants his life to recur infinitely and identically. Rather than actually *being* the person whom he says will one day arrive on the earth, however, Zarathustra only prepares mankind for his arrival rather than inhabiting its form. The Nietzschean critic Laurence Lampert argues that "God and the immortal soul, the very foundations of virtue, the postulates of moral experience for philosophers as different as Plato, Descartes, and Kant have been rendered incredible by modern life, and Zarathustra comes to announce a new foundation."[17]

From his initial characterization as "fat" (1) to the "rolly polly dandy" (141) in the latter part of the novel, where "the notes sink deeper and deeper into the congenial consciousness of the immaterial husband and anti-materialist thinker, elephantine Philip Wild,"[18] it is clear that Wild is preoccupied with his body or, more specifically, the size of it. The intolerable heaviness of being is catalytic to his desire to obliterate himself. Wild "dislike[s his] toes" (157) and laments his "wretched flesh" (159): the extent to which he holds his body in disregard displays considerable similarities to the chapters titled "Of the Afterworldsmen" and "Despisers of the Body" in *TSZ*. The chapter "Of the Afterworldsmen" defends the conviction that humans should think of themselves as flesh rather than as spirit – that our corporeal self is all that exists, as opposed to the traditional idea of existing alongside a transcendental spirit. Zarathustra proclaims, "Believe me, my brothers! It was the body that despaired of the body – that touched the ultimate walls with the fingers of its deluded spirit."[19] Lampert notes, "This despairing body alleges that it 'heard the belly of being speak to it'; but it is only the body that speaks when gods and afterworlds seem to speak, and it speaks only of its own despair of itself and its need to be delivered."[20] In *Laura*, Wild frequently laments his own physical state; having suffered "for the last seventeen years from a humiliating stomack ailment" (147), he states: "I loathe my belly, that trunkful of bowels, which I have to carry around, and everything connected with it" (149).

The similarities between Wild's attitudes and Zarathustra's condemnations extend further. The preoccupation with the self in *TSZ* continues in the chapter titled "Despisers of the Body." Zarathustra claims that those who believe in the spirit are effectively negating the body in that the self is nothing other than the physical being. Those who reject this position are effectively "despisers of the body." Wild, therefore, cannot be any kind of stepping-stone to the superman that Zarathustra alludes to, given that the latter proclaims, "I do not go your way, you despisers of the body! You are not bridges to the Superman!"[21] Although we are given no substantial insight as to whether Wild accepts any kind of Cartesian dualism, he suggests that the self can be represented as a projected mental image of an individual line: "if I left the flawed line alone, its flaw would be reflected in the condition of this or that part of my body" (159). Similarly, in *TSZ*, Zarathustra explains how the sick claim to be essentially spirit and that, in turn, they reject their visceral self: "But it is a sickly thing to them: and they would dearly like to get out of their skins." The idea that Wild believes that his entire being can be *contained* "on the underside of one's closed eyelids" (131), however, might suggest that Wild is indeed commensurate with Zarathustra's "ideal man": "But the awakened, the enlightened man says: I am body entirely, and nothing beside; and the soul is only a word for something in the body."[22]

Perhaps the biggest single correlation between the two novels is the subject of "voluntary death." Although it is not as major as the "superman" theme, the "will to power" or "eternal recurrence" in *TSZ*, it is nonetheless one of the novel's important ideas. It is alluded to by Nabokov and is effectively what Wild is trying to achieve. Zarathustra proclaims, "Many die too late and some die too early. Still the doctrine sounds strange: 'Die at the right time.'" His proclamation of voluntary death is one, he argues, that will give inspiration to the living – presumably paving the way for the long-awaited superman. He goes on to say, "I shall show you the consummating death, which shall be a spur and a promise to the living … I commend to you my sort of death, voluntary death that comes to me because I wish it." However, rather than fulfilling his promise, Zarathustra contradicts his teaching so that he can see the work of his disciples: "Truly, Zarathustra had a goal, he threw his ball: now may you friends be the heirs of my goal, I throw the golden ball to you. But best of all I like to see you, too, throwing on the golden ball, my friends! So I shall stay on earth a little longer: forgive me for it!"[23] Zarathustra, therefore, appears not to execute the very decree that he says is admirable; this heightens his role as a self-contradictory character rather than as infallible prophet since, after all, "prophets do not argue, they announce."[24] Wild's repeated experiments – "I have died up to my navel some fifty times" (267) – further demonstrate his unwillingness to complete the task at hand.

The relationship between *TSZ* and *Laura* may also help to explain two rather peculiar points in Nabokov's text. The name of Mmẹ Lanskaya, whose own promiscuity has, it seems, been passed on to her daughter, is described by Ivan Vaughan on card Four 1: "Generally speaking, one should carefully preserve in transliteration the feminine ending of a Russian surname (such as -aya, instead of the masculine -iy or -oy) when the woman in question is an artistic celebrity. So let it be 'Landskaya' – land and sky and the melancholy echo of her dancing name … And certainly for no earthly reason does this passage ressemble in r[h]ythm another novel" (100–1). If *Laura* is indeed indebted to *TSZ*, then the narrator's quip that this passage resembles another novel is ironic. As we read through the novel, we are aware that *Laura* contains extracts that will feature in a novel called *My Laura*. This "novel-in-a-novel" format would be an easy way to resolve the riddling statement given above. However, the extent to which the narrator details the name of Mme Lanskaya is unusual. Not only is her name described as "dancing" (a creative act that pervades *TSZ*), but this act of "lightness of spirit" is also described as "melancholy." This descriptive dichotomy of her name (where "land and sky" mix) is suggestive of Nietzsche once again. Lampert, discussing how Zarathustra beholds an eagle with a snake wrapped around its claws, argues that "[t]heir intertwining symbolizes the overcoming of the old dualisms of light and darkness, heaven and earth, good and evil; their intertwining is beyond good and evil, a harmony of earth and sky."[25]

The idea of there being no "earthly reason" as to why the passage resembles another novel is a contentious point. Although the phrase seems too coy to simply describe a non-existent relationship, our arguable "default" answer to this is the *mis-en-abyme* idea of *Laura* and *My Laura*. However, if one keeps the numerous allusions in mind, it may also be that Nabokov is playing with the relationship between *Laura* and *TSZ*.

There is a similarly strange sentence in the description of the ominously named Hubert H. Hubert. He plays a seemingly minor role in *Laura* given that, after 22 pages, we are told that "There is little to add about the incidental, but not unattractive Mr Hubert H. Hubert" (75). A new lover of Flora's after the death of Adam Lind, Hubert, an English wine-trafficker, seems to display more than just a named reference (notice the omission of the single letter) to *Lolita*'s Humbert, given that he "constantly 'prowled' (rodait) around her" (57). Told that Hubert "was a dear man, and his life lay in ruins all around him" (73), we are soon informed that he "died of a stroke in a hotel lift after a business dinner. Going up, one would like to surmise" (75).[26] The apparent lack of explanation as to why Hubert should die "going upward" may again be answered through *TSZ*, specifically in its portrayal of ascendency and descent. Lampert argues that Zarathustra "descends to demonstrate that transcendent things are products of earth and body, thereby calling for a revaluation of both the things descended to and the traditional ideal of ascent, with its hatred of the earthly and the bodily."[27]

Just as Zarathustra wishes to beguile the people into accepting his vision of a world where God no longer exists, and the inversion of values that the superman will herald, Nietzsche seems to invert the traditional Christian idea of connecting ascendency to a higher, "better," realm and descent to a "worse" state of being. If this inversion is projected onto *Laura*, Hubert's "going up" arguably suggests his belief in a better, spiritual life and identifies him as one of the "herd." Lampert describes Zarathustra's prediction as follows: "like a prophet proclaiming the end time as a time of doom, Zarathustra proclaims that the ascendency of the last man will terminate the possibility of human magnificence."[28] If, therefore, Hubert can be seen as the "last man" who ascends, can we argue that his death somehow spells out doom for the "Zarathustran" Wild? The fact that Wild does not achieve his "auto-dissolution" and is, instead, ironically subjected to a perfectly "normal" death by heart attack (187), may add force to this interpretation.

What do we make of the similarities between the two texts? Can we ascribe Wild the role of the prophet Zarathustra given that both are ostensibly learned men trying to give tutelage, only to fail at the task in hand? If so, can it be said that Wild is heralding a superman that is yet to come? Could this figure, ironically, be Flora, the ruthless, promiscuous character who is the only one to survive in a text mired in death but, who, unlike the superman in *TSZ*, already exists among us? Can Hubert be seen as one of the "herd," synonymous with the pity that Zarathustra perceives as a life-denying force? Not least because of the novel's unfinished form and because of the eclecticism of *TSZ*, it would be dangerous to assert that *Laura* adheres unwaveringly to the structure and themes of *TSZ*. Instead, Nabokov has arguably used Nietzsche's text as a source of inspiration whereby the regularity of death can be questioned.

DEATH AS CREATION

The question of *why* Wild decides to embark on his process of "auto-dissolution" is an important one. A possible reason is the feeling of sorrow he feels at accepting that his promiscuous wife is captured in a text detailing her love affairs (despite being fictionalized as Laura). We are told that "Wild read 'Laura'" (125) and thinks of it as a "maddening masterpiece" (221). Noting that "[t]here is, there was, only one girl in my life, an object of terror and tenderness, an object too, of universal compassion on the part of millions who read about her in her lover's books" (151), it appears that Wild is expendable for Flora. In the section "Wild remembers," Wild notes:

> Every now and then she would turn up for a few moments between trains, between planes, between lovers. My morning sleep would be interrupted by heartrending sounds – a window opening, a little bustle downstairs, a trunk coming, a trunk going, distant telephone conversations that seemed to be conducted in conspiratorial whispers. If shivering in my nightshirt I dared to waylay her all she said would be 'you really ought to lose some weight' or 'I hope you transfered [sic] that money as I indicated' – and all doors closed again. (263)

Wild goes on to mention "a separate anecdote in the anthology of humiliation to which, since my marriage, I have been a constant contributor" (219). It could be argued that Wild opts to embark on his "luxurious suicide" because of the feelings that his wife's infidelity and neglect have caused. Where Zarathustra argues that "everyone who wants glory must take leave of honour in good time and practise the difficult art of – going at the right time,"[29] to those wishing to die, Wild offers this instruction: "Enjoy the destruction but do not linger over your own ruins lest you develop an incurable illness, or die before you are ready to die" (181). Lampert addresses this section of *TSZ* explicitly, arguing that "[e] nlightened by Hobbes and Locke to the fear of death as the fundamental fear, Zarathustra's audience is in the process of surrendering all aspiration except for comfortable self-preservation. 'Wretched contentment' is Zarathustra's name for this Lockean ideal."[30] The idea of wretched contentment can account for why Wild opts to begin his experiments when he does and what his experiments or more specifically the risks of his experiments, mean. Although he has an esteemed position and a wife, Nietzsche's idea of "wretched contentment" seems to be applicable here. As Zarathustra advises, the superfluous must decide when the time to die is right.

There seems, however, to be another reason why Wild embarks on his experiment. In *TSZ*, as he enters the town, Zarathustra speaks to a tightrope walker who is about to begin his act. Although the tightrope walker eventually falls and is mortally wounded, Zarathustra argues that his actions are to be praised. Lampert argues that Zarathustra believes "his life is worthy in itself. By making danger his vocation, he has lifted himself high above the crowd and made himself the model for an ideal contrary to the crowd's ideal of risk-free contentment."[31] This privileging of intrepid spirit again relates to the actions of Wild, who notes, "It is the ability to stop the experiment and return intact from the perilous journey that makes all the difference, once its mysterious technique has been mastered by the student of self-annihilation" (245–7). The fact that he has engaged in a task that poses risk reminds us of the distinction that Nietzsche awarded the ancient Greeks for their desire for glory and power. Not content with simple pleasure in living, this risk-taking epitomizes the "will to power" that Nietzsche vehemently promoted. Zarathustra cries, "Your Self wants to perish, and that is why you have become despisers of the body! For no longer are you able to create beyond yourselves." Lampert clarifies, saying "Zarathustra's answer is that the body turns suicidal when it knows itself to be thwarted in its creative essence."[32] Wild also echoes Zarathustra in noting "an act of destruction which develops paradoxically an element of creativeness in the totally new application of totally free will" (213). Thus, the irony that death can offer the ultimate creative gift is rooted in a self-contradictory dilemma that can only effect itself once the person has expired.

APPROPRIATION OF DEATH

Laura's main theme seems to be the appropriation of death – not only is the novel's subtitle "Dying is Fun" but it is a subject of particular importance to Philip Wild who "hit[s] upon the *art* of thinking away my body, my being, mind itself" (243, my italics). Simon argues that Wild "finds comfort in pretending that death is somehow self-imposed."[33] This supposed manipulation of the act of dying is undermined however by his *involuntary* heart attack. James Liu argues that

> the theme of the projected novel seems to be coming to terms [with] death by coming to own it, and what art has to do with that. Flora's grandfather is said to die 'not from his own commonplace malady, but from the cancer of oblivion invading his once famous pictures.' Flora's father kills himself but the profits from capturing that daredevil feat on camera catapults his wife to Europe. A would-be stepfather's own daughter dies offstage (bicycle, truck). Flora's own mother dies after her graduation, also to be caught in a photograph. There is Wild's own deliberate experiments in dissolution, stemming perhaps from his disillusion about his wife, and his real death by a sudden heart attack. Laura is killed off by her author, but Flora survives.[34]

Almost all of the dramatis personae do, indeed, succumb to death, yet it appears that the *capturing* of these deaths is what really matters. Wyllie notes, for example, "As her [Flora's] father's death scene is photographed, so is her mother's."[35] Although the deaths of Mme Lanskaya and Adam Lind are captured on film, the deaths of the other characters are also captured in the *words* that make up *Laura* and *My Laura*. Whether awarded numerous pages or described with laconic bluntness,[36] each death is not only a composite part of a fictional, creative work but, importantly, also controlled. Daisy's relationship with death is especially interesting when Hubert begins to play chess with Flora. The narration alludes to a well-known move in the game: "She [Daisy], too, had 'known the moves', and had loved the en passant trick as one loves a new toy, but it cropped up so seldom, though he tried to prepare those magic positions where the ghost of a pawn can be captured on the square it has crossed" (69).

"En passant" is the ability to capture a pawn, not by the usual move of taking it diagonally, but by being able to take the piece by "moving through" the next diagonal square where it has reached an approaching pawn. Given that this is the only move in chess in which the attacking piece does not move to the square of the captured piece, "en passant" is thus suggestive of being able to capture what is not really there and can therefore be linked to the impalpability of fiction. Durantaye argues that Wild "not only means to take away death's sting, but to make its approach a sensual and intellectual delight."[37] Wild states that he wants to turn vitality on its head by "[l]earning to use the vigor of the body for the purpose of its own deletion" (213). Just like Zarathustra's inversion of morality, Wild's experiment attempts to appropriate death for his own purposes – more specifically, his creative purposes.

WRITING AS DEATH?

The use of the written act to symbolize death is a frequent trope in Nabokov's work. Arguably the most well-known example concerns the character of Cincinnatus from Nabokov's dystopian novel *Invitation to a Beheading* (1938), where we realize that the number of chapters correlates with the number of days he has left to live. As we read on, and *because* we move on, each word acts as further momentum toward his death. On a meta-level then, it is effectively the creative act that tells us of the death, such that the execution of writing acts as figurative execution. Although this may be true, the importance of Cincinnatus's "non-death" must not be forgotten. Embodied in the example where death is crossed out, it can be seen that the written word may also allow for death to be transgressed.[38]

Inversely, the idea of writing as life is a common feature in literature, encapsulated, for example, in Ben Jonson's "On My First Sonne" (1603), and in the works of Milton and Donne, in which writing is often perceived as the living offspring of authors. Whereas *Invitation* also addresses the connection between creativity and life,[39] *Laura* explicitly plays with this relationship. It is noted that "[t]he 'I' of the book is a neurotic man of letters, who destroys his mistress in the act of portraying her" (121).[40] Assuming that the narrator is Ivan Vaughan, this sentence raises many ambiguities. Is his statement derived from the fact that his representation of Flora (as Laura) effectively kills off the original, in that she is not "true" to herself through his description? Or is it perhaps signalled where the two identities start to mix?[41]

Boyd argues that Nabokov "shows the narrator *effacing* himself, and *deleting* Laura as he (before killing her off fictively later in *My Laura*) portrays her mentioning her husband as 'a writer of sorts,' whose 'mysterious manuscript' itself recounts how he *erases* himself, in another doomed attempt at transcending, or expunging, the self."[42] Given the paradoxical mixture of "annihilation" and "portrayal," it appears that it is the *act* of writing that can effectively kill. Wild seems to equate the erasure of imagination with the erasure of life: "I let the smudge start its evolution and, drawing on an imagined mitten, I simply rubbed out the beast. Three or four times it appeared again in my dreams but now I welcomed its growing shape and gleefully erased it. Finally it gave up – as some day life will give up – bothering me" (253).

Many critics have read Nabokov's prose style in *Laura* as detrimental to the text's overall effect. Simon argues that the turgid word choice hinders our overall take on the narrative – "More offensive to me is the ferreting out of abstruse synonyms and excogitations of gratuitous neologisms."[43] Does the use, for example, of "omnoplates" rather than shoulder blades hinder our ability to imaginatively create the character in question because of the "distant" medical terminology? Regarding the use of esoteric words in *Pale Fire*, Boyd argues that Nabokov is keen on sending readers to their "fattest dictionary to locate the explosive surprise waiting in each word."[44] This abstruseness seems also to be at work in *Laura* – indeed, Nabokov is often self-referential in addressing this difficulty: "[the] spare prose of the author with its pruning of rich adjectives" (123). The equivalence of life and writing is articulated most vocally in the last page of the novel, where Nabokov's lapidary inclusion of the words "efface, expunge, erase, delete, rub out, wipe out, obliterate" (275) effectively serve as his epitaph. As Sam Anderson notes, it is as if Nabokov leaves the world "pulling his pencil in behind him."[45]

The extent to which writing can be seen as commensurate with death is arguably most intriguing in its relationship to Flora's grandfather, Lev Lind, who "emigrated in 1920 from Moscow to New York with his wife Eva and son Adam" (41). It is difficult not to equate Lev Linde the painter with Vladimir Nabokov the writer, given that the latter emigrated to New York with his wife Vera and son Dmitri in 1940. The section describing Lev Linde includes an interesting passage that hybridizes the themes of death and writing explicitly: "What can be sadder than a discouraged artist dying not from his own commonplace maladies, but from the cancer of oblivion invading his once famous pictures such as 'April in Yalta' or 'The Old Bridge[']? Let us not dwell on the choice of the wrong place of exile. Let us not linger at that pityful [sic] bedside" (43–5).

The issue of a *roman à clef* in *Laura* seems difficult to ignore. Not only is the term mentioned in the novel, but the extent to which *Laura* relates to Nabokov is undeniably strong. Wyllie argues that Nabokov "is palpably present. He gives Philip Wild his age, his painful feet and prostate problem; he gives Flora his Russian, his love of chess to Hubert, and extends the authorial impulse to all the novel's writers."[46] The novel also includes a section describing "information demanded by the Russian professor of Russian Literature" (93) and, somewhat eerily, allows Ivan Vaughan to voice his concern that "My <u>Laura</u> was begun very soon after the end of the love affair that it depicts ... and [was] promptly torn apart by a book reviewer in a leading newspaper" (117). In an interview conducted with *The New York Times* not long before his death, Nabokov described that his "audience [for the novel] consisted of peacocks, pigeons, my long-dead parents, two cypresses, several young nurses crouching around, and a family doctor so old as to be almost invisible."[47] Although we must try not to conflate authors' personal views with their fiction, Nabokov's lyrical description of the writing of *Laura* echoes Zarathustra's declaration that "[t]he man consummating his life dies his death triumphantly, surrounded by men filled with hope and making solemn vows."[48] What is arguably most important about this section, though, is the presence of the phrase "cancer of oblivion." Rather than the artist dying from failing health, it is argued that a sadder fate awaits those who suffer from a "lack of interest." The metaphorical death, in which a lack of words is equated with death, once again correlates writing with life – even the "rave reviews of nonentities" (47) constitute a life-affirming interest (despite their authors). Could Nabokov himself be alluding to the amount of published criticism that he felt he deserved in the later years of his life? In this regard, Linde's "April in Yalta" seems to be a highly suggestive pictorial version of Nabokov's "Spring in Fialta" (1936).

As we approach the end of *Laura*, we simultaneously approach the end of *My Laura*. Once again, the allusion to "voluntary death" can help to explain what is occurring. An important issue raised by the novel-in-a-novel form is the mirroring of Laura (Flora) and Philip Wild. Where Wild conducts a bizarre quest to obliterate himself from the toes upwards, Winny (the wife of Mr Carr from the second section) informs Flora of her bizarre death in *My Laura*: "Oh you must! said Winnie, it is, of course, fictionalized and all that but you'll come face to face with yourself at every other corner. And there's your wonderful death. Let me show you your wonderful death. ... Oh, but I simply must find that passage for you. It's not quite at the end. You'll scream with laughter. It's the craziest death in the world" (225–7).

The passage above is humorous in its detailing of Winny's belief that Flora's death (in *My Laura*) is the "craziest death in the world" given that we have just been witness to Wild's experiments. Having already described how Ivan Vaughan "destroys his mistress in the act of portraying her" (121), it could be argued that the act of portrayal – specifically, the "execution" of writing – is what killed her. Ironically, Flora's "crazy death" is mentioned but not described in *Laura* yet it *is* contained in *My Laura*. Suddenly, the bizarreness of Wild's attempted death seems to have met its match in Flora's "fictional" death-by-writing. This seemingly nonsensical act (given the life-giving quality of creativity) is arguably as "crazy" as the illogicality of being able to will oneself away voluntarily.

CONCLUSION

Nabokov's preoccupation with death in *Laura* (coupled with his own failing health) suggests his desire to rebel against the abhorrent egalitarianism of death, to live on like *Pale Fire*'s waxwing. He attempts to weaken death by undermining its regularity, wanting to "stand vitality on its head." As Durantaye argues, "Wild wants to delight in death"[49] – his "auto-dissolution," his "willing one's self away," is therefore said to provide the "greatest ecstasy known to man" (171). On the same card as the Nietzsche reference, Nabokov provides us with an imaginary quote from Philip Nikitin (a minor character from *Anna Karenina* [1877]): "The act of suicide may be 'criminal' in the same sense that murder is criminal but in my case it is purified and hallowed by the incredible delight it gives" (265). Both references can be seen to effectively subjugate death to a rung below the aesthetic realm.[50] Although *Laura*'s relationship with writing arguably echoes Stéphane Mallarmé's dictum that "to name is to destroy, to suggest is to create,"[51] it is Nabokov who has ultimate control as to how the concept of death is broached in his fiction. His control of it outside of fiction, unfortunately, was not as successful. As Zarathustra argues, "equally hateful to the fighter as to the victor is your grinning death, which comes creeping up like a thief – and yet comes as master."[52]

Looking for Flora: Deviance and Disclosure in Nabokov's *The Original of Laura*

BARBARA WYLLIE

The Original of Laura is a book of versions, of fictions within a fiction, a narrative of so many voices that what is true, or original, is almost impossible to determine. This dynamic of elusiveness is compounded by the portrayal of the novel's heroine, Flora Wild. Coldly remote, inscrutable and alienating, after the first few chapters she slips out of focus as the narrative gives way to her husband's excruciatingly extravagant, deviant narcissism and his accounts of bizarre experiments in auto-dissolution. Philip Wild's highly unstable, solipsistic perspective conspires with the novel's other narrative voices – Flora's Russian lover, Eric, and the author of *My Laura* – to ensure that Flora, the original of her famously fictionalized counterpart, remains "safely solipsized."[1] But why does Flora suffer this effacement? Merely to satisfy her various lovers' grievances? Meanwhile, the text both seduces and repels the reader. Its narrators sustain a fragile balance between sympathy and spite, tragedy and bathos, comedy and irony, serving to conceal the ultimate banality of their worlds but also to distract the reader's attention from the significant details of the text. Considered in light of Nabokov's other, deeply fraudulent narratives, the reader's response can only be one of cautious scepticism. The narrative's obfuscating facade is at once undermined by resistance, exposing the text's significant details which indicate the presence of a distinct perspective, that of Nabokov's "gliding eye,"[2] whose principal interest is to reveal the true Flora.

The novel's fugitive quality is established in its opening scene, in which Flora drunkenly negotiates a room full of strangers at a friend's party. The action is described by the narrator of the first sixty or so cards,[3] Flora's yet-to-be but now former Russian lover, who is perhaps the Ivan Vaughan of Nabokov's Chapter [Five].[4] Since only Flora's speech is reported, the reader is forced to deduce her audience's responses: the scene begins with Flora answering a question about her husband, and it quickly becomes apparent that she is attending the party without him. This narrowed perspective focuses exclusively on Flora and her point of view, in turn generating a magnified sense of her estrangement and vulnerability, and her acute isolation under the gaze of the "sober eyes staring at her with nasty compassion from every corner" of the room (5). The scene is thus reduced from a conventional three-dimensional aspect to a single, pivotal perspective. Such narrative absence, or elision, is a key device that fixes Flora at the absolute centre of the reader's vision while simultaneously denying access to her. The reader is offered the occasional glimpse of her marvellous, defeatist cynicism when she replies "I'll drug him next time" (7) as she tries to explain her antisocial husband, or her reaction of quiet acknowledgment on hearing her lover speak Russian – "eyebrows went up, eyes opened and closed again, she didn't meet Russians often" (17–19) – but the implication that this is reliably Flora's story is highly deceptive. The narrative's deceitfulness is another of her Russian lover's calculations, a fraudulence compounded by omission, exclusion, and subtle shifts in perspective, such that the only Flora the reader sees is a heartless, promiscuous, dissolute decadent.

As the novel's opening scene progresses, Flora's request to "be taken home or preferably to some cool quiet place with a clean bed and room service" (3) is answered by her host, Mrs Carr, whose nephew, Anthony, has an empty flat available. A subtly disrupted sequence of action, reminiscent of the "dazzling succession of gaps" in Sebastian Knight's prose,[5] leads the reader to assume that Flora knows the apartment and is directing the seduction of her anonymous companion but, in fact, *he* is the "friend" to whom Anthony and Winny Carr have *already* lent their flat (7), for it is *his* things in the "damned valise" waiting for him "in the vestibule closet" when he and (a not too sober) Flora arrive (11). Establishing the narrator's relationship to the Carrs here is crucial in accounting for his privileged ability to report the encounter between Winny and Flora on the station platform at Sex, where Flora resists all attempts at persuasion by Winny to read the "story of [her] life" and particularly the account of her "wonderful death" (225) – the "craziest death in the world" (227). Winny Carr's light-hearted tone coalesces with that of Flora's Russian lover and the gappy, or sketchy, quality of his text, elements that conspire to present Flora's world as casual, ephemeral, and insignificant, but which belie the reality of loss and pain beneath the novel's surface.

The first five chapters of *The Original of Laura* essentially enact the narrator's contention that "everything about [Flora] is bound to remain blurry, even her name which seems to have been made expressly to have another one modelled upon it by a fantastically lucky artist" (85). This image of a negated, effaced Flora complements the self-erasing purpose of Philip Wild's experiments, ever-dissolving like the vertical white line on the plum-coloured underside of his eyelids (131). At the same time, Flora's Russian narrator remains as elusive as his heroine. Over and above the tone of neutral disinterest he maintains across much of his text, he further distances himself from the reader's gaze by adopting an alternative identity at the end of Chapter One. Appearing in the guise of a "messenger," he refers to himself obliquely in the third person as "the beaming bum" (39), the "shabby" blond "courier" who delivers Flora's flowers and is taken by her housemaid for a Frenchman (37). Despite such artful manipulations, however, the narrator proves himself unable to sustain this distance. Most overtly, he allows the benign surface of his narrative to be shattered by a violent lapse, exposing his festering hatred of Flora who, as has become apparent in the present tense of his writing, is no longer his lover.

Chapter Three is interrupted by an aside, a passing comment about Flora. She has been called cruel before (27), and a "philistine" (25), and portrayed as vacuous and emotionally frigid – "A tear of no particular meaning gemmed the hard top of her cheek" (17). Here, however, the narrator wields a devastating blow: "This is Flora of the close-set dark-blue eyes and cruel mouth recollecting in her midtwenties fragments of her past, with details lost or put back in the wrong order, TAIL betwe[e]n DELTA and SLIT, on dusty dim shelves, this is she" (85).

In a "knight's move" – a chess term that denotes "a sudden swerve to one or the other side of the board" which Nabokov used to describe Fanny's "chequered emotions" in *Mansfield Park*[6] – Flora's narrator turns on her. The by now familiar tone of gentle reproach, here for her poor memory and faulty recall, swerves into an open and visceral attack that he attempts to disguise, unsuccessfully, with a weak metaphor. Not only is it scathingly derogatory, insinuating that sex is *all* that Flora is about, but it is also highly offensive, as he ensures that the reader cannot fail but register those three key capitalized words – "TAIL," "DELTA," and "SLIT" – in the series of her life. This crude allusion to the three points of her sexual anatomy suggests that they are the only things of importance to her. That they are placed in the "wrong order" serves to magnify the insult, the implication being that she is not merely a nymphomaniac but a *stupid* nymphomaniac. Not satisfied to stop there, he then accuses her of not even realizing their significance as she consigns them to near oblivion, as she has presumably consigned him, along with all her other discarded lovers, to the "dusty dim shelves" of a neglected library. With this outburst, the narrator's mask of objective observer and recorder is suddenly lifted and the reader's response to him is fundamentally and permanently altered. Flora's narrator has revealed something in the "scrambled picture" of his text that, until now, has remained unseen – something, however, that the "finder" now "cannot unsee"[7] – and the reader is compelled to return to the narrative with renewed scepticism, to seek out the "second" "main" story that lies so tantalizingly close to the novel's "semitransparent" surface.[8]

The narrator's account of Flora's childhood in Chapter Two, of a "gray home life marked by ill health, and boredom" (55) seems, initially, to be faithful to what Flora had probably told him, and yet there are contradictions, anomalies and omissions in the details that expose its inherent deviance. The narrator sensitively depicts the awkwardness and sadness in Flora's relationship with Hubert H. Hubert, her mother's lover, vacillating between sympathy and repulsion. Hubert is "kindly," but "smelly" and "pushing" (57), the pathetic victim of an "abominable tragedy" in the loss of his daughter (61), but sinister in his "prowling" pursuit of Flora, his attempts to reincarnate his dead daughter through her, his tactile proximity, his requests to stroke her hair with his lips (59). That Flora is profoundly threatened by this man is indicated by her "nightly dreams of erotic torture" (55). Curiously, the narrator deflects the reader's attention away from this critical piece of information by waiting until the end of the following chapter to mention that "at eleven she had read A quoi revent les enfants, by a certain Dr Freud, a madman" (89). This comment, in itself, communicates the degree to which Flora has been affected, emotionally and psychologically, by her experiences with Hubert, to an extent that, at such a young age, she is forced to seek out her own means of therapy (no matter how futile). The narrator's defamation of Freud wryly echoes Nabokov's own opinion of the "Viennese quack [whose] interpretation of dreams [was] one of the greatest pieces of charlatanic, and satanic, nonsense imposed on a gullible public."[9] In one stroke, the "gullible" Flora is neatly dismissed along with her psychoanalyst, but her reasons for turning to him still resonate. Meanwhile, the disruption this comment causes to the chronological sequence of the narrative qualifies it, ironically, as a detail "lost or put back in the wrong order," but its displacement here is deliberately calculated to undermine its impact. Flora may know "where to kick an enterprising gentleman" (63) but she is, nevertheless, a child, trapped in her mother's house with an "elderly but still vigorous Englishm[a]n" (53) until he either chooses to leave or dies. It is not until the end of Chapter Two, its conclusion reminiscent of the final, obtusely blithe paragraphs of *Ada*, in which Lucette's "tragic destiny" is cited as "one of the highlights of this delightful book,"[10] that the reader's suspicions are fully alerted: "There is little to add about the incidental, but not unattractive Mr Hubert H. Hubert. He lodged for another happy year in that cosy house and died of a stroke in a hotel lift after a business dinner. Going up, one would like to surmise" (75).

Although the Hubert episode takes up two-thirds of the account of Flora's childhood (twelve of Chapter Two's eighteen cards), his apparent significance is abruptly undermined by the narrator's admission that he is only, after all, an "incidental" character. Equally, the notion that Hubert is "not unattractive" jars with the narrator's previous portrayal of a bald, middle-aged, weeping, fumbling, quietly grotesque figure, but when the reader looks again at his descriptions, it becomes apparent that the sympathy expressed in these concluding lines is more like an affinity, that despite the revolting "fourfold smell [of] tobacco, sweat, rum and bad teeth [which] emanated from poor old … Mr Hubert," the narrator believes him to be truly "harmless" (67). At the same time, the narrator's assertion of the erotic connotations of the miniature chess set which Hubert presents to Flora, with its "pin-sized pawns [that] penetrated easily, [and] the slightly larger noblemen [which] had to be forced in with an ennervating joggle" (65), suggests that he is complicit in Hubert's perverse sexualization of the child. This affinity extends further to an assimilation of Hubert's point of view in the incongruous depiction of Flora's sickly gray home as "happy" and "cosy," while the narrator's ultimate allegiance to Hubert is confirmed by the notion of his "going up," presumably to Heaven, all his transgressions conveniently forgiven.[11]

This latent approval of Hubert's behaviour further compromises the narrator's objectivity. He has revealed a bias that allies him with every man who has been romantically involved with Flora, who has been rejected and discarded by her, even someone who could be deemed a pedophile. His inability to appreciate Flora's childhood predicament and her declared discomfort in Hubert's presence renders him incapable of understanding or honestly recounting her subsequent behaviour. It is only when Nabokov begins to emerge as a discreet and involute presence, as the "gliding eye implied throughout" the narrative,[12] that the extent of his blindness to the reality of Flora's situation becomes palpable.

Across his fiction, Nabokov's distinct but highly discreet presence is signalled by barely discernible, fugitive details. Occasionally he would make a rare entry, stepping into his texts in surrogate form – in his "visits of inspection" in *King, Queen, Knave*,[13] as the university professor N. in *Pnin* or the writer 'N' in *Look at the Harlequins!*, for example. At the same time, he granted his protagonists facets of his own experience or aspects of his artistic credo – "people tend to underestimate the power of my imagination and my capacity of evolving serial selves in my writings," he once commented.[14] These "serial selves" he reconfigured to guard his personal autonomy and maintain his distance, ensuring his safe position at the very outer limits of his fictional worlds. In *The Original of Laura* he is dismantled and scattered across the text, and donates elements of himself to his various protagonists. Philip Wild has his age and prostate problem,[15] Flora his Russian, and Hubert his love of chess, while his authorial impulse is extended to all of the novel's writers – the Russian narrator (who also despises Freud), Philip Wild, the anonymous author of *My Laura* and, potentially, Eric.[16] Although his artistic purpose in all this remains obscure, buried deep within a surreptitious and oblique patterning of imagery and allusion, his presence is palpable, and declared to the reader in an explicit gesture early in the narrative.

In the scene toward the end of Chapter One, when Flora's new Russian lover arrives at her house pretending to be the florist's delivery man, he presents her with "a banal bevy of bird-of-paradise flowers" (35–7). At the very beginning of his career, Nabokov chose the bird of paradise, or *sirin*, the "fabulous fowl" from Russian folklore, as his pseudonym and artistic emblem, describing it as "the very soul of Russian art."[17] Nabokov "routinely encod[ed] this pen name throughout his oeuvre" and although he seemed to "abandon it in his 'American years,'"[18] its emergence here is given additional emphasis through a repeated allusion contained in a reference to "strelitzias" (39), the flower's botanical name. Flora dismisses them along with her maid and, to cover his humiliation, her Russian narrator quickly dismisses them too – "hateful blooms, regalized bananas, really" (39). Oblivious to their significance, he abolishes them as an embarrassing mistake, and yet they serve as an emphatic sign of Nabokov's presence in the text. A less explicit, but by no means inconsequential Nabokovian manifestation can also be found in Chapter One, in the figure of Flora's pyjama-clad lover. His shock and dismay at being telephoned in the middle of the night to be told their affair is over is conveyed through the colour of his pyjamas, which the narrator imagines changing, "in the spectrum of his surprise and distress, from heliotrope to a sickly gray" (29). Here Nabokov embeds another auto-allusion, this time in the colour "heliotrope" (a shade of violet, but also indicative of a flower that turns its face to the sun, suggestive of inspiration and enlightenment). Nabokov deployed the colour throughout his fiction as a signature motif, most evocatively in his first English novel, *The Real Life of Sebastian Knight*.[19] This same pyjama-clad lover reappears as Flora arrives home, standing in vigil "in the shadows of a side alley," his now white pyjamas covered by a mackintosh (33). His desolation is expressed once again by the colour of his pyjamas, their whiteness symptomatic of emotional and spiritual death,[20] and yet his haunting presence also seems to imply something else, something other than simply a stark dramatization of the hurt Flora has inflicted. In his lecture on James Joyce's *Ulysses*, Nabokov identified the incidental Man in the Brown Mackintosh as Joyce, "setting his face in a dark corner of his canvas."[21] Here, Nabokov sets his face in, what is literally, a dark corner of his canvas via this anonymous, desolate man in a mackintosh, whose original violet cast defines him as a Nabokovian artist, and perhaps even the "neurotic and hesitant man of letters, who destroys his mistress in the act of portraying her," "the 'I' of the book" "begun very soon after the end of the love affair it depicts" (121, 117). Associations generated initially through the colour violet resonate, therefore, with other seemingly arbitrary details that have the potential to reveal the true identity of the mysterious author of the fictionalized version of Flora's life, *My Laura*.

Once registered, these "subliminal coordinates"[22] gradually disclose a patterning of autobiographical allusion that further reinforces the presence of Nabokov's "gliding eye." In Chapter Two the narrator describes Flora's grandfather, the artist Lev Linde, and his "once famous pictures," "April in Yalta" and "The Old Bridge" (45). Linde's romanticized images of pre-Revolutionary Russia recall a country and a time now lost to the old man and to Nabokov but, even more specifically, Nabokov's exile in the Crimea (1917–1919), and the bridge that connected the Batovo and Rozhdestveno mansions on the Nabokov family's country estate. The mention of these paintings reveals yet another "interesting shade and underwater pattern"[23] that connects "April in Yalta" with Heine Street, where the Wilds live, for Nabokov translated several poems by the nineteenth-century German poet, famously set to music by Robert Schumann, for a Russian singer in Yalta in the Spring of 1918. "Though his German was poor, Vladimir acquitted himself so well that ... both the singer and the translator received ovations. ... His version of 'Ich grolle nicht' was particularly successful."[24] Coincidentally, of the sixteen poems in Schumann's *Dichterliebe* taken from Heine's 1827 *Lyrisches Intermezzo*, it was "Ich grolle nicht" that Nabokov remembered in a 1971 interview.[25] The poem eloquently articulates the antagonism between pity and spite expressed by Flora's Russian lover and the destructive impulse of the vengeful *My Laura*. In the case of Philip Wild, for whom Flora is "an object of terror and tenderness" (151), the poem's opening line is appropriately free of irony, while its closing line chillingly echoes the pathetic last vision of Flora, living in "eccentric solitude" in the shadow of a Central European convent (239):

Ich grolle nicht und wenn das Herz auch bricht.
Ewig verlor'nes Lieb, ich grolle nicht.
Wie du auch strahlst in Diamantenpracht,
es fällt kein Strahl in deines Herzens Nacht.

Das weiß ich längst. Ich sah dich ja im Traume,
Und sah die Nacht in deines Herzens Raume,

Und sah die Schlang', die dir am Herzen frißt,
Ich sah, mein Lieb, wie sehr du elend bist.

[I bear no grudge, even though my heart may break,
eternally lost love, I bear no grudge.
You may shine in diamond splendour,
but no ray falls on your heart's night.

I've long known this. I saw you in my dreams,
and saw the night in your heart's chamber,
and saw the snake that feeds on your heart,
I saw, my love, how very wretched you are.][26]

Nabokov's presence in the "dark corners" of his text, no matter how disparate or discreet, serves as a major revelationary dynamic that alerts the reader to the novel's "secret points," the "nerves"[27] that ultimately disclose, if only incompletely in such an unfinished work, its true imperative. The most crucial "nerve" of Flora's story is in the first part of Chapter Three, which describes her teenage excursions to a "romantic refuge" in the "Blue Fountain Forest" just outside Paris, where she and her friends play games of blindman's buff "in the buff" (83). In the same way that the significance of the bird-of-paradise flowers is dismissed by Flora's Russian narrator, so the allusions in the reference to "an earlier period of literature," to "a sparkle of broken glass or a lace-edged rag on moss," are quickly passed over, allusions that are further disguised by the narrator's analogous corruption of the forest's actual location. "Blue Fountain" alludes onomatopoeically to Fontainebleau which, correctly translated, means "the fountain of beautiful water." The narrator's deviance here denies the reader the opportunity to register the potential importance of this place, particularly its role in an "earlier period of literature," a role that proves critical in revealing the truth of Flora's past – the forest of Fontainebleau provided the setting for one of the pivotal scenes in Flaubert's 1869 novel, *L'Education sentimentale* (*A Sentimental Education*), in which a young woman confesses her childhood rape by an older man.

For Flaubert's hero, Frédéric Moreau, and his courtesan lover, Rosanette (Rose-Annette) Bron,[28] the Fontainebleau forest is also a "romantic refuge," an idyllic, secluded place where they experience an emotional intimacy that provokes Rosanette to tell Frédéric about how her mother sold her to a stranger under the pretence that she was "a lucky girl" who would "get a lovely present."[29] Rosanette is only able to recount her story up until the moment the man enters the hot, oppressive room where she has been waiting for him alone and wakes her from her sleep. Frédéric is horrified. "How dreadful it must have been for you, my poor darling," he exclaims. "More dreadful than you think," she answers. "So much so that I tried to put an end to it all, but they pulled me out of the water."[30] Not only does the experience lead her to attempt suicide, but it also seals her fate as a prostitute. Most telling in her story, however, is that she merely alludes to its most traumatic events, and her deliberate omission of key details leaves Frédéric to wonder "about all the things she hadn't told him."[31] The parallels with Flora's childhood predicament are plain – her pursuit by an older man, her mother's negligence and oblivious endorsement of her lover's actions – compounded by the echoes of other episodes across Nabokov's fiction that feature compromised children, in *Lolita* and *The Enchanter* most obviously, but also in *Look at the Harlequins!*, *The Gift* and "A Nursery Tale."[32] At the same time, Rosanette's omissions complement the elisions in Flora's Russian lover's narrative. In light of this, the reader also begins to wonder whether there were aspects of Flora's encounters with Hubert H. Hubert that she chose not to relate to her Russian lover, details that indicate that she too suffered a similar trauma. Ironically, the absence of possibly crucial details in Flora's account explains how easy it is for her narrator, a man evidently lacking the imagination of Frédéric Moreau, to conclude that Hubert was ultimately "harmless."

Meanwhile, the affinities between Rosanette Bron and Flora Wild extend to their promiscuity in adult life and their perfunctory attitude toward sexual relations. For Rosanette, as a kept woman, sex is business, a practicality, a means to an end. Flora, similarly, enjoys a stream of lovers whom she treats with brusque impatience, deflecting all superfluous physical contact and preferring, like her forebear Lolita – who considered "all caresses except kisses on the mouth or the stark act of love either 'romantic slosh' or 'abnormal'"[33] – "dry" kisses (19). Flora's lack of emotional engagement also echoes Lolita's. While Flora is able to summarily destroy a man with a mere phone call, Lolita, when faced with a scene of violence and devastation remains coolly indifferent: "[We] silently stared, with other motorists and their children, at some smashed, blood-bespattered car with a young woman's shoe in the ditch (Lo, as we drove on: "That was the exact type of moccasin I was trying to describe to that jerk in the store").[34]

Both Nabokov's heroines exhibit forms of deviance that betray the degree of emotional damage inflicted by their dysfunctional childhood relationships.[35] Set against her predecessor's fate, Flora's story is that of the girl who survived. In terms of her counterpart from "an earlier period of literature" who, despite her circumstances is, nevertheless, still able to fall in love, there is also a suggestion that there was someone she too loved and lost. Flora's equivalent of Frédéric Moreau – the stranger with whom she regularly exchanges "tender letters" and meets again after a "three-year separation" toward the end of her story (239) – was, it seems, someone she parted with shortly before marrying Philip Wild.[36] The insinuation of loss in this scene instills a dimension of pain in Flora's story which serves, crucially, to humanize her, at the same time exposing the element of self-serving spite that motivates the novel's dominant narrative voices.

The Blue Fountain Forest episode is a key component in Nabokov's "underwater pattern" that combines with other "subliminal coordinates," specifically the chess scene in Chapter Two and the descriptions of *My Laura* from Chapter [Five], in which Flora's husband, Philip Wild, is "sympathetically depicted as a co[n]ventional 'great scientist' ... under the name of Philidor Sauvage" (125). Once again, the distortion of a name generates distinct Nabokovian associations. While "sauvage" is simply French for "wild," the mutation of Philip to Philidor initiates allusions to a particular eighteenth-century chess grandmaster renowned for playing blindfolded – François-André Philidor – featured in two of Nabokov's early chess poems.[37] The act of blindfolding recalls Flora's games of blindman's buff in Chapter Three, its implications of vulnerability and isolation deflected by the narrator's emphasis, through a rather cumbersome double entendre, on the game having been played in the nude, which simultaneously reasserts his overriding preoccupation with Flora's sexuality. Meanwhile, Philidor's famous contention that pawns were "the soul of chess"[38] directs the allusion back to the image of "pin-sized pawns" in the miniature chess set Hubert brings to Flora's sick-bed in Chapter Two

(65). In light of this championing of pawns, Hubert's chess game becomes a means of establishing an explicit link between Flora and his daughter Daisy. Both girls "know the moves" (65, 69), especially "the en passant trick" often used to get out of stalemate in which "a ghost of a pawn can be captured on the square it has crossed" (69). The pawn's tactics of deflection and defence are expressive of the strategy that Flora – and, by implication, Daisy too – is forced to deploy against Hubert's unwanted attentions. It is through this combination of diffuse yet interconnected details that the fact of Flora's abuse becomes unnervingly likely, a revelation that suggests not only Flora's, but also Daisy's subjection to Hubert's deviant proclivities.[39]

The apprehension of these textual "nerves" allows the novel's "second" "main" story to emerge through its "semitransparent" surface, uncorrupted by the ulterior perspectives of its many narrators, reconfiguring, irrevocably, the reader's vision of Flora. Far from being manipulative and acquisitive, cold and cruel, she is transformed from a simple cipher into an opaque and complex figure, revealed as yet another of Nabokov's victims. Profoundly damaged, resolutely solitary, and enduringly unhappy, she uses anything and anyone as an urgent means, no matter how shallow or transitory, of necessary distraction. The revelation of Flora's "original" world in turn generates a sustained ironic dynamic, supported by embedded details that remain unseen by the novel's Russian narrator who, like *Pale Fire*'s John Shade, "lacks the artist's gift of making connections."[40] Shade fails to notice the "subliminal coordinates" of his own poem – Hazel's invocation of T.S. Eliot's *Four Quartets*, or a fateful allusion to Pushkin's *Feast During the Plague*, for example[41] – details that disclose the operation of other dimensions that filter in through textual "cracks" and fissures,[42] dimensions that, in *The Original of Laura*, subvert its narrators' efforts to efface their heroine. Meanwhile, through oblique allusion and the manipulation of signature motifs, Nabokov asserts his "sovereignty [as] authentic creator [of] his character[s'] discourse."[43] In this light, the "unattainable"[44] figure that Flora's narrators conspire to depict proves far from degenerative, and can be considered, rather, in her tantalizingly enigmatic incarnation, as Nabokov's most eloquent expression of "the isolation, and the strangeness, of so-called reality."[45] His contention that "you can get nearer and nearer, so to speak, to reality; but you never get near enough"[46] becomes both Flora's imperative and that of the novel, each in their fictional and actual disintegration leaving the reader with nothing more than traces, glimpses of an intriguing yet palpable "elsewhere"[47] that would remain briefly yet compellingly visible before "all doors close again" (263).

Reading the Posthumous Postmodern: *Laura*'s Productive Fragments

PAUL ARDOIN

The question of whether and how to publish incomplete posthumous works generates controversy because, despite confident critical claims about the figurative death of the author, we still seem to be flummoxed by the literal death of the author. With each controversial new posthumous publication, we are forced to confront issues ranging from the author's *intent* (the vision of the text we will never see) and *intentions* (desires regarding the fate of incomplete works), to the question of whether we really believe that authorial intent is meaningless in the face of individual reader response and experience.

It is my contention that *The Original of Laura* can and should be read together with the controversy surrounding its publication. In this article, I propose ways of reading the fragmented manuscript of *Laura* that suggest a fragmented reading experience is not only parallel to the thematic elements in the book, but also corresponds to the disruptions to critical reception that, I will argue, Nabokov intended. Diegetic fragmentation, instability, and openings draw focus toward *Laura*'s intra- and intertextuality and ultimately direct us to the book's engagement with worlds outside its own textual boundaries. This allows *Laura* to evolve from simply being a part of Nabokov's body of work and thus enter into the critical conversation *about* that body of work. *The Original of Laura*, like the character Flora/Laura/FLaura, has no stable original, but this is not simply a matter of the manuscript's incompleteness or its published form. Rather, its published form is an appropriate embodiment for a work that uses its own fragmentation to disrupt entrenched critical views of Nabokov's canon.

Reading with an eye toward what the book has to tell us about Nabokov's overall intent is critical to understanding what *Laura* is about and is trying to do. Just as Nabokov's swipes at Freud seem to demand a Freudian reading of his works, Nabokov's claims that "the reader will never be able to crack all the novel's secrets without his help, that he is or has the final key that can open all the doors" cry out for an authorless reading through Barthes.[1] To reconcile the presence of well-read readers with the intent of authors, I attempt to chart the most useful path between "death of the author" theories and the position of omnipotence that Nabokov lays claim to in his essay "Good Readers and Good Writers." This also allows room for Nabokov's reports that he envisioned his works, including *Laura*, in their totality before completing their manuscripts.

READING THE PARATEXT

The controversy surrounding *Laura*'s publication, and the ensuing statements of scores of scholars, reviewers, and other fiction writers, are well documented.[2] The overwhelming hesitancy demonstrated by these authors – among them, Winterson, Stoppard, and Amis – is worth revisiting through the lens of another fiction writer, Zadie Smith. Her lecture, "Rereading Barthes and Nabokov," published prior to the publication of *Laura*, describes "a vocational need to believe in Nabokov's vision of total control." As a writer, she needs to believe that it is the author-God who steers not just the creation of the literary work but the reader's experience of that work, and it is safe to suspect that Nabokov himself would agree with that description of his role. "Maybe every author," Smith suggests, "needs to keep faith with Nabokov, and every reader with Barthes."[3] The agreement among Stoppard, Amis, and Winterson that *Laura* should not have seen publication indicates that the alignment of authors in the Nabokov camp goes beyond mere support of the shaping power and "total control" of the author's finished works, to a desire to protect the omnipotent position of the author figure even after death. Any posthumous publication that reveals something about Nabokov, in a way, reveals something about all authors, particularly those who have been so outspoken in this debate and who share with Nabokov a type of fiction that makes use of postmodern elements while remaining essentially modernist in its loyalty to the power and ramifications of art and reading. If a reader can punch out the note cards of *Laura* and rearrange them at a whim, what is to stop that reader from deciding all literature is open for rearranging? This published form of *Laura* does not do much to allay those fears: one imagines the all-powerful author-Gods cringing at all the new possibilities for appropriation and misappropriation when a temptingly perforated text is published with crossed-out words and ideas-in-progress still included. If *Laura* lays bare the devices behind the magic of Nabokov's fiction-making, does it not do the same to Winterson's well-orchestrated *Sexing the Cherry* and Smith's symphonic *White Teeth*?[4] Smith, Winterson, and Stoppard have a vested interest in preserving the hallowed position of the author – a position that has been a source of anxiety since long before literary theory killed the author.

Benjamin decries the loss of an "aura" surrounding art: it used to be, he explains, that "a small number of writers were confronted by many thousands of readers." Then the means to become a writer became available to everyone. Nowadays, Benjamin complains, "there is hardly a gainfully employed European who could not, in principle, find an opportunity to publish somewhere or other comments on his work, grievances, documentary reports, or that sort of thing." If, in his time, "[t]he distinction between author and public [was] about to lose its basic character," then in our post-wide-web world, the line is surely even fuzzier. "Hold the line," cry Nabokov's fellow artists.[5]

This is not to say that authors are the only ones with a stake in the outcome of a controversy like the one surrounding *Laura*. The publisher and the estate obviously have their reasons for wanting to see Nabokov's draft in print as a book.[6] What is at stake for readers is a bit more difficult to discern. Literary critics, for example, move from the act of reading a work toward a kind of rewriting. If writers depend upon a godlike status for the author, rewriters make careers of explaining, interpreting, and debunking. But "If one begins with a readymade generalization" about a book, Nabokov warns, "one begins at the wrong end and travels away from the book before one has started to understand it."[7] This backwards reader might approach a book "with the preconceived notion that it is a denunciation of the bourgeoisie," or the reader might find Nabokov, as the male author, complicit in and responsible for Humbert's wilful erasure of the real Dolores in *Lolita*.[8] Dangerously tempting for readers, the published form of *Laura* seems designed to encourage those who might relish the degree of editorial power the index cards offer.

Before I rearrange the cards a bit myself, it is worth examining this power a little more closely. The conflict between a reader like Barthes (who resists the idea of an authorial figure or proxy who might limit the readings of a text) and a writer like Nabokov (who makes no secret of his desire to limit not just the readings of a text but also the definition of that text's "good" reader) is not resolved for *The Original of Laura* by the death of its author. Like the unfinished poem in *Pale Fire* or Nabokov's heavily annotated translation of *Eugene Onegin*, *Laura* replaces the absent author not with liberation for the reader, but with new restraints. With *Laura*, the reader may simply have exchanged the tyranny of Vladimir Nabokov for that of the editor, Dmitri Nabokov, or the publisher.[9]

Publishers, cover artists, typeface designers, writers of introductions, and many others have long exerted some influence on the texts they present. Genette examines the large role that the elements surrounding a text – whether included by the author, the publisher, or someone else – have in the reader's experience of it.[10] With *Laura* especially, and many posthumous works in general, this mediation of the text is additionally complicated by the absence of a literal author to whom readers can attribute final responsibility. Knopf and Dmitri Nabokov seem to step in to fill the role of the author in numerous ways, among them creating a new list of acknowledgments and providing an initial selection and arrangement of the cards the reader can then potentially rearrange. Even that initial selection, though, exerts authority over the reader.

The first sign of this dilemma is Vladimir Nabokov's striking list of near-synonyms that appears immediately after the title and copyright pages: "efface expunge erase delete rub out wipe out obliterate" (275).[11] The card on which this list appears is not numbered. In fact, it is a different type of note card entirely, printed with a grid rather than lines. We might conclude from this that Nabokov did not consider this card part of the more authoritative, "whole" stack of cards but, in our edition of *Laura*, the card is not only included but emphasized. It appears again as the last page of the manuscript, taking advantage of the convenient finality that such a list of words might provide; in this way, *Laura*'s editor seals the unfinished work. The reader is left not just with an authoritative arrangement of the cards (with a standardized sense of order, regardless of the option to rearrange the cards) but with a deceptive "beginning" and "ending" that moves toward a kind of closure that obscures the truly unfinished nature of the book: one official arranger-interpreter has simply replaced another. The same list serves as the front cover art, beneath the dust jacket, again drawing attention toward and generating meaning from an element that does not seem a likely ingredient in the finished *Laura* to which we will never have access.

There is more work of this sort worth doing here. Certainly, the reading experience of *Laura* is shaped in large degree by the book's published form. Moreover, the book's published form is less flexible than the perforated lines would indicate: no doubt the reader has the opportunity to rearrange *Laura*, but this is not the likeliest of scenarios. To begin with, there is the overwhelming finality of the current arrangement, attributable to that list. There is also some degree of ordering on the cards: most are numbered or categorized by the author himself. Even if a reader feels the current arrangement can be improved upon, that feeling is not likely to be strong enough to permanently alter the structure of the book – those perforations cannot be made whole again once punched – and many readers are likely to consider removing the cards an act of destruction. The Nabokovian good reader (and, in fact, most readers) will be restrained by a book's publication format and paratextual apparatus and will restrain herself further in response, and seemingly by choice. This may or may not indicate an unspoken need for authorities to limit our readings: it would certainly seem to indicate a desire for the determination of finality to rest in another's hands.

The physical nature of the cards, moreover, contributes visual and tactile roles to the task of interpretation. The colour reproduction of the note cards renders the contrast of Nabokov's handwritten words against the white background of the cards more striking than that of the black type that reproduces his text against a gray background below the cards. Additionally, Nabokov's handwriting itself draws attention: it carries the innate implications of personality that all handwritings do, and offers curves and curls that contrast with the typed text. The words on the cards are certainly text, but they are also a picture. Readers are invited, by the colour reproduction of the cards and the typed transcriptions below, to receive the cards as illustrations, rather than the primary source of verbal communication. This surely adds to the pressures against punching the cards out: the typeset text below carries the weight of an authoritative interpretation and primary source in and of itself, and dissuades readers from challenging the work the editors have already done. Note, for example, the lack of perforation around the typed portions of the text. Do what we will with the cards, the official, authoritative interpretation of *The Original of Laura* stays intact.

While the competing texts on the page reinforce the authority of the publisher and editors, the cards also interject the presence of Vladimir Nabokov onto every page of the book. In fact, the personal presence of the author through his handwriting offers a way for him to be more alive in this book than he can seem in any of his finished works. On each page, we see a handwritten note, the most personal of communications, from the author himself.

The interpretative (and artistic) potential of that handwriting, along with the reproduced cards, is an example of "what happens to reading when images overpower the verbal texts with which they share the page," or perhaps what happens when both separately overpower the reader. Here, there is a curious split: the typed text carries the logocentric authority on each page, but the placement, colour, and pictorial character of the cards carry their own authority as evidence of Nabokov's presence. I cite Kenneth Clay Smith above because of his discussion of the paratextual role of pictures; conveniently, though, he approaches that discussion through the work of Aubrey Beardsley, the Victorian artist and illustrator whom Kuzmanovich, Vries and Johnson, and others cite as the inspiration for Beardsley College in *Lolita*.[12] Smith argues that, as an illustrator, Beardsley was not just concerned with "complementing texts, he was commenting on them and competing with them," a fitting parallel to Nabokov's dissatisfaction with simply providing texts for others to critique.[13]

This paratextual apparatus means that, despite the apparent editorial authority allotted to readers of *Laura*, we have, in reality, a text most readers will not challenge, and will, in fact, consider final, if not complete. It is not, though, a text Nabokov would have considered finished. There is no way, then, to entirely fulfill the role of the "good reader," but let us consider how to read what we have.

READING THE FRAGMENTS OF THE TEXT

Most notable in what we have of *The Original of Laura* are not just the multiple narratives and narrators of the book but the attempts by those narrators to reach out from their different diegetic levels to their various audiences of readers. Without drawing conclusions about the exact number of competing narratives, we are able to determine that some of the audiences are directly addressed by the narrators, such as the "I" who addresses us as "readers" and directs us to a "book – on a very high shelf, in a very bad light" (23). Others are not. We get our first hint of an identifiable narrator in the story when Flora turns toward her lover after hanging up the phone: "'That's done,['] she said," referring to ending her relationship with another lover. "Was I game now for another round, she wanted to know" (29). The "I" here is but one narrator, the first, whose primacy will be challenged soon enough.

The narrator of these scenes seems to be the author of *My Laura*: we are his audience, and he soon lets us in on that secret. While describing Flora and her family, he mentions, as an aside, "certainly for no earthly reason does this passage ressemble [sic] in r[h]ythm another novel, <u>My Laura</u>, where the mother appears as 'Maya Umanskaya,' a fabricated film actress" (101–3). That novel, of which we see an excerpt at the beginning of Chapter Five and which introduces the name "Laura," has its own audience of readers, readers within the fictional world of *Laura*.

This is complex enough, to be sure, but it is additionally complicated by a few possible variations. Flora has more than one lover, and this one's narrative may not be the same as that of the author of *My Laura*. When the narrator writes that his passage (if he is a "he") may "resemble" one from the other novel, he may mean that he is imitating the previous lover's writing (just as he imitates his affair) as a sort of mockery of or homage to his predecessor, or he may mean that he is "re*a*ssembling" the predecessor's story of and with Flora.

And the introduction of "Laura" in Chapter Five, though it appears, for the reason of its position, to be an excerpt from *My Laura*, seems instead a sort of conflation of that novel with a continuation of its author's earlier narration. This conflation becomes literal with the curiously capitalized "FLaura" (111), but from the very start of Chapter Five there are more ambiguous examples: Laura's husband, for example, is given the same name as Flora's husband, Dr Phillip Wild, who, we are told later, was portrayed in the book *My Laura* "under the name of Philidor Sauvage" (125). Some of this confusion can be attributed to *Laura*'s unfinished state, but certainly not all. Narratives and narrators all compete for a lover/character and an audience.

We see, then, that aside from the book's incomplete nature, even the original of *The Original of Laura* is indeed a novel in fragments. Flora (or Laura, or FLaura) is never a stable original; she is presented to us only through narrators, each of whom pieces together a sketch of a woman through personal experience and the portrayals of others. Indeed, we learn in a description of her childhood that Laura can be rendered only "by identifying her with an unwritten, half-written, rewritten difficult book" (21). There is a parallel here with what Genette calls the epitext of a book, in this case the controversy surrounding the decision to publish *Laura*.[14] Elements of the book's readership chime into the debate, and the readership ultimately fragments as it weaves its own narratives of the publication. Above, I break this down in terms of readers, critics, authors, and publishers, but one could easily imagine a wholly different arrangement. In an unexpected way, the book enacts the very fragmentation it depicts of its title character.

Lara Delage-Toriel locates the earliest versions of Laura (perhaps Nabokov's inspiration, she suggests) in Giorgione's Renaissance-era painting of *Laura* and Titian's of *Flora*, both of which are themselves "variations on the theme of Petrarch's Laura." Delage-Toriel writes, "the manuscript's involuted plot expands upon the ambivalence of the sign inscribed within its title. The referential indetermination of 'original' and 'Laura' is indeed refracted by a complex *matrioshka*-type of narrative in which pictorial and literary representations appear to mirror each other and thus unhinge the classical foundations of mimesis."[15]

The most obvious of these versions is the book-within-a-book *My Laura*, of which we learn, "The 'I' of the book is a neurotic and hesitant man of letters, who destroys his mistress in the act of portraying her" (121). This is perhaps a crime of which all Flora's lovers are guilty, and it is an echo of Barthes's assessment that writing destroys both its author and its subject, contrary to the belief of many of Flora's lovers and even the younger Nabokov of *Speak, Memory*, who believes he can preserve his family in his memoir: "Everything is as it should be, nothing will ever change, nobody will ever die."[16] But Flora is not as she should be; she is destroyed as early as when a narrator first depicts her on the first card. All we have left is a distorted palimpsest viewed through a kaleidoscope and the echoes of portray-and-destroy we find in Phillip's self-annihilation and Adam Lind(e)'s artistic suicide (49).

Again, parallels with the published form of *Laura* are obvious: the final card ("efface, expunge," etc.) is without a doubt Nabokov's card, but it is not as it should be or would have been. The real *Laura* can now be viewed only in fragments, and even those are mediated through the eyes of authoritative publishers and editors. Even within those fragments, though, there are glimpses recognizable to the Nabokovian good reader.

READING NABOKOV

In our search for Flora, we join together the competing narrative views of her, only to find that there is no original. Conveniently, and probably accidentally, the published form of *Laura* parallels that frustrating struggle. *Pale Fire* has already proven itself among commentators to be a convenient analogue to the controversy surrounding *Laura*. Charles Kinbote abuses his role as posthumous editor of the supposedly unfinished work of poet John Shade, in the process more firmly disguising both the work and its author (and revealing more than he intends of himself). Couturier points out in *Pale Fire* the competing presence of numerous "narrative contracts ... so cleverly combined that it is difficult, often impossible, to pinpoint the exact moment when a shift is made." As a result, this "metatextual novel ... is a highly daunting text which forces the reader to enter its black box and compels him to try and recompose or refigure it in an attempt to free himself from it."[17] *Pale Fire* foregrounds that struggle by its very form, just as *Laura* accidentally does, by its very incompleteness, but also by its foregrounding of the portrayal-making process and by its multiple narratives existing on multiple levels.

Flora's possession of *My Laura* (itself only one version, the soft cover, of at least two editions) offers the most illustrative example of this: She holds a book of her life as depicted by someone else. The book has already been read by someone else – Flora's friend Winny. Winny becomes excited by the possibility of showing her own version of the book's highlights (her interpretation of someone else's depiction) to Flora, who passes up the opportunity to have the presentation of her own "wonderful death" presented to her. Her response is deceptively simple: "Please, let me have my book" (227). In the larger context of *Laura*, though, it is difficult not to read several meanings in her plea. Winny has a hold of the book that has a hold of Flora. Like Nabokov's most famous title character, FLaura has no control over her own book.

Lolita famously masks its protagonist behind Humbert's veil and, many claim, Nabokov's; we see this latter criticism almost from the date of the book's publication to the present day. The horrifying subject matter of *Lolita* diverts many readers from the implications of the fact that Dolores "exists only as Humbert's representation"; that is, Dolores does not exist in the book at all.[18] In *Laura*, Nabokov enters into that conversation. Here, the title character is not just the object of multiple affections (as Dolores is for Humbert, Quilty, and her eventual husband) but of multiple narrations. Perhaps as a reference to the Dolores/Lolita conflation of *Lolita*, Nabokov titled his *The Original of Laura* as not just a reference to the *My Laura* that first disguised Flora's name, but as a pun: the original Laura is fLaura.

Instead of giving critics an opportunity to discuss Flora's absence from the book, Nabokov makes her absence the subject of the book. One suitor after another tries and fails to capture her by constructing his own version of Flora; each literally inscribes her into the boundaries of his own work. The truth here, as with *Lolita*, is that we never meet the book's namesake: we only meet facsimiles of her, never the original. She is simultaneously the subject of the book and effaced, erased, expunged from that book. Just like Dolores Haze, Laura variously resists attempts to pin her down. Similarly, *Laura* transgresses attempts to pin any of Nabokov's works down. The numerous intertextual elements in the small part we have of the book support the resistance of such boundaries. Hubert Hubert moves in with Flora and her mother, resembling the Humbert of *Lolita* not only in name but also in desires. He brings Flora presents that would be familiar to any reader of *Lolita* and tries to seduce her (65, 71).

Intertextual references to other books in Nabokov's oeuvre are not unique to *Laura*; Pnin, after all, pops up in *Pale Fire*, and Vadim Vadimovich offers us a comical inundation of Nabokov references in *Look at the Harlequins!*[19] *The Original of Laura*, though, does not just expect us to pick up on the intertextual references; it *tells us* that it expects us to pick up on the intertextual references. We are introduced to the character of Hubert in *Laura* as follows: "His name, no doubt assumed, was Hubert H. Hubert" (53). This not only mirrors the name of *Lolita*'s protagonist but his narrative style: in that text, Humbert uses a near-identical phrase to teasingly withhold Quilty's name, "the name that the astute reader had guessed long ago."[20] Most important, though, is that the diegetic breach in *The Original of Laura* assumes its reader's knowledge of a *different* book from itself.

Here we have a diegetic breach more severe than even the ending of *Invitation to a Beheading*,[21] and whoever the narrator is at the time, he or she wants to make sure we notice it. By the time we reach a later reference such as Wild's memories of Aurora Lee (201), we cannot avoid thinking of Annabel Lee in *Lolita*, even on our way to that earlier book's own intertextual relationship with Poe's poem of the same name. Now we are chasing from level to level both within and across books.[22]

What Nabokov is up to here with *Laura* is reminiscent of Beckett's French trilogy, translated as *Molloy*, *Malone Dies*, and *The Unnamable*. The borders between the three books share a certain type of permeability, with later narrators taking credit for the creation of earlier narrators, and early narrators sensing their own impending narrative replacement.[23] While *The Unnamable* aims for the exterior borders of the entire trilogy, its narrator taking credit for all of Beckett's canon, or "at least from Murphy on,"[24] the publication of *The Original of Laura* complicates the existing scholarly canon *surrounding* Nabokov's earlier work. Nabokov does not purport to change the authorship or diegetic reality of his earlier works, only to comment on and continue the conversations they started.

Nabokov warns us in "Good Readers and Good Writers" not to approach a book with a motive to find "connection with the worlds we already know," but in *Laura* he not only gives us permission to see connections but also insists that we make use of those "links."[25] There can be no mistake that we are being referred to worlds outside the text when we have "no doubt assumed" Hubert's identity. Nabokov's insistence allows *Laura* to evolve from representing a part of his body of work to entering into the critical conversation *about* that body of work. The destruction of Flora through others' portrayals of her is not, then, simply similar to *Lolita*, it is about *Lolita*. This time Nabokov has not simply stirred up controversy; he has not merely complicated our critical conversation, but rather has co-opted it.

That Nabokov would nominate *Lolita* for further discussion is surprising, considering the degree of attention the book has (and had by the time of *Laura*'s composition) already received. But Nabokov's intertextuality points at a project still in progress.[26] This project is something larger than simply rewarding the constant reader. In interviews, he famously criticized books he accused of that type of posturing, holding up *Finnegans Wake* as a "most aggravating" example, "nothing but a formless and dull mass of phony folklore, a cold pudding of a book, a persistent snore in the next room."[27] He echoes this criticism in *Invitation to a Beheading* when Cincinnatus reads a novel that "was unquestionably the best that his age had produced; yet he ... plodded through the pages with dull distress," not feeling overwhelmingly transported by "a paragraph a page and a half long in which all the words began with 'p'" or any of the author's other clever tricks.[28] Rather, Cincinnatus begins to muse about the inevitability and necessity of the figurative and literal death of the author, a consideration that continues to echo throughout Nabokov's canon, including and following *The Original of Laura*.

The first of Flora's many authors, her father Adam Lind, whose chosen medium of portraying his subjects is photography, documents his own death "from different angles" (49). The "pictures did not come out to[o] well," but that does not stop Flora's mother from callously marketing those final works (50–1). Wild, another creator of the Flora we know, mirrors this process as he slowly erases himself, authoring his own attempted destruction and multiple partial deaths and documenting the process in his notes. Nabokov's intratextual play with authorial figures here parallels his intertextual play with characters such as Hubert Hubert and the extratextual complications that arise not only from a posthumous publication but from one that challenges the reception of and conversation surrounding earlier texts. Ultimately, this is an insistence on the right of an authorial authority to not simply create a work but to comment on critical responses even as we concoct them.

The various pieces of Nabokov's canon, then, are no more ours to recklessly reinterpret and rearrange than the index cards of *Laura*, if we are to meet the author's definition of a "good" reader. What we have of the novel is fragmented, but it is also indisputably *about* fragmentation. We are constrained by the arrangement of the text and our desire to be good readers, but we are also constrained by its nature and its conversation with Nabokov's other works.[29] This intertextuality becomes one more restraint, one more stand-in for the supposedly absent author. It ensures that we cannot disentangle *Laura* from the works it engages.

The fears of Zadie Smith and those with her vocational need should be allayed: Nabokov's good reader will stop *herself* from rearranging at a whim, and Nabokov will continue to steer *Laura* and the reader's experience of its universe, even when that universe is perforated or incomplete. In the case of *Laura*, the intratextuality of the book itself is its most useful perforation, revealing an intertextuality that determines our understanding of *Laura* and what came before.[30]

Critical Reception

Dimitri Nabokov's playful admission ("Why not make some money on the damn thing?") has sparked controversy: some critics called the publication of *The Original of Laura* "a money-spinner" (Jonathan Bate, *The Telegraph*). (Photograph © 2011 Yuri Leving)

The Problem with Nabokov[I]

MARTIN AMIS

Language leads a double life – and so does the novelist. You chat with family and friends, you attend to your correspondence, you consult menus and shopping lists, you observe road signs (LOOK LEFT), and so on. Then you enter your study, where language exists in quite another form – as the stuff of patterned artifice. Most writers, I think, would want to go along with Vladimir Nabokov, when he reminisced in 1974: "I regarded Paris, with its gray-toned days and charcoal nights, merely as the chance setting for the most authentic and faithful joys of my life: the coloured phrase in my mind under the drizzle, the white page under the desk lamp awaiting me in my humble home."

Well, the creative joy is authentic; and yet it isn't faithful (in common with pretty well the entire cast of Nabokov's fictional women, creative joy, in the end, is sadistically fickle). Writing remains a very interesting job, but destiny, or "fat Fate," as Humbert Humbert calls it, has arranged a very interesting retribution. Writers lead a double life. And they die doubly, too. This is modern literature's dirty little secret. Writers die twice: once when the body dies, and once when the talent dies.

Nabokov composed *The Original of Laura*, or what we have of it, against the clock of doom (a series of sickening falls, then hospital infections, then bronchial collapse). It is not "A novel in fragments," as the cover states; it is immediately recognizable as a longish short story struggling to become a novella. In this palatial edition, every left-hand page is blank, and every right-hand page reproduces Nabokov's manuscript (with its robust handwriting and fragile spelling – "bycycle," "stomack," "suprize"), plus the text in typed print (and infested with square brackets).

It is nice, I dare say, to see those world-famous index cards up close; but in truth there is little in *Laura* that reverberates in the mind. "Auroral rumbles and bangs had begun jolting the cold misty city": in this we hear an echo of the Nabokovian music. And in the following we glimpse the funny and fearless Nabokovian disdain for our "abject physicality": "I loathe my belly, that trunkful of bowels, which I have to carry around, and everything connected with it – the wrong food, heartburn, constipation's leaden load, or else indigestion with a first installment of hot filth pouring out of me in a public toilet."

Otherwise and in general *Laura* is somewhere between larva and pupa (to use a lepidopteral metaphor), and very far from the finished imago.

Apart from a welcome flurry of interest in the work, the only thing this relic will effect, I fear, is the slight exacerbation of what is already a problem from hell. It is infernal, for me, because I bow to no one in my love for this great and greatly inspiring genius. And yet Nabokov, in his decline, imposes on even the keenest reader a horrible brew of piety, literal-mindedness, vulgarity and philistinism. Nothing much, in *Laura*, qualifies as a theme (i.e., as a structural or at least a recurring motif). But we do notice the appearance of a certain Hubert H Hubert (a reeking Englishman who slobbers over a pre-teen's bed), we do notice the 24-year-old vamp with 12-year-old breasts ("pale squinty nipples and firm form"), and we do notice the fevered dream about a juvenile love ("her little bottom, so smooth, so moonlit"). In other words, *Laura* joins *The Enchanter* (1939), *Lolita* (1955), *Ada* (1970), *Transparent Things* (1972), and *Look at the Harlequins!* (1974) in unignorably concerning itself with the sexual despoliation of very young girls.

Six fictions: six fictions, two or perhaps three of which are spectacular masterpieces. You will, I hope, admit that the hellish problem is at least Nabokovian in its complexity and ticklishness. For no human being in the history of the world has done more to vivify the cruelty, the violence, and the dismal squalor of this particular crime. The problem, which turns out to be an aesthetic problem, and not quite a moral one, has to do with the intimate malice of age.

The word we want is not the legalistic "paedophilia," which in any case deceitfully translates as "fondness for children." The word we want is "nympholepsy," which doesn't quite mean what you think it means.

It means "frenzy caused by desire for the unattainable," and is rightly characterized by my *Concise Oxford Dictionary* as *literary*. As such, nympholepsy is a legitimate, indeed an almost inevitable subject for this very singular talent. "Nabokov's is really an amorous style," John Updike lucidly observed: "It yearns to clasp diaphanous exactitude into its hairy arms." With the later Nabokov, though, nympholepsy crumbles into its etymology – "from Gk *numpholeptos* 'caught by nymphs,' on the pattern of EPILEPSY"; "from Gk *epilepsia*, from *epilambanein* = 'seize, attack'."

Dreamed up in 1930s Berlin (with Hitler's voice spluttering out from the rooftop loudspeakers), and written in Paris (post-*Kristallnacht*, at the start of the Nabokovs' frenetic flight from Europe), *The Enchanter* is a vicious triumph, brilliantly and almost osmotically translated from the Russian by Dmitri Nabokov in 1987, 10 years after his father's death. As a narrative it is logistically identical to the first half of *Lolita*: the rapist will marry – and perhaps murder – the mother, and then negotiate the child. Unlike the redoubtable Charlotte Haze ("she of the noble nipple and massive thigh"), the nameless widow in *The Enchanter* is already promisingly frail, her large body warped out of symmetry by hospitalizations and surgeons' knives. And this is why her suitor reluctantly rejects the idea of poison: "Besides, they'll inevitably open her up, out of sheer habit."

The wedding takes place, and so does the wedding night: "and it was perfectly clear that he (little Gulliver)" would be physically unable to tackle "those multiple caverns" and "the repulsively listing conformation of her ponderous pelvis." But "in the middle of his farewell speeches about his migraine," things take an unexpected turn, "so that, after the fact, it was with astonishment that he discovered the corpse of the miraculously vanquished giantess and gazed at the moiré girdle that almost totally concealed her scar."

Soon the mother is dead for real, and the enchanter is alone with his 12-year-old. "The lone wolf was getting ready to don Granny's nightcap."

In *Lolita*, Humbert has "strenuous sexual intercourse" with his nymphet at least twice a day for two years. In *The Enchanter* there is a single delectation – non-invasive, voyeuristic, masturbatory. In the hotel room the girl is asleep, and naked; "he began passing his magic wand above her body," measuring her "with an enchanted yardstick." She awakes, she looks at "his rearing nudity," and she screams. With his obsession now reduced to a cooling smear on the raincoat he throws on, our enchanter runs out into the street, seeking to rid himself, by any means, of a world "already-looked-at" and "no-longer-needed." A tramcar grinds into sight, and under "this growing, grinning, megathundering mass, this instantaneous cinema of dismemberment – that's it, drag me under, tear at my frailty – I'm travelling flattened, on my smacked-down face ... don't rip me to pieces – you're shredding me, I've had enough ... Zigzag gymnastics of lightning, spectogram of a thunderbolt's split seconds – and the film of life had burst."

In moral terms *The Enchanter* is sulphurously direct. *Lolita*, by contrast, is delicately cumulative; but in its judgment of Humbert's abomination it is, if anything, the more severe. To establish this it is necessary to adduce only two key points. First, the fate of its tragic heroine. No unprepared reader could be expected to notice that Lolita meets a terrible end on page two of the novel that bears her name: "Mrs 'Richard F Schiller' died in childbed," says the "editor" in his Foreword, "giving birth to a still-born girl ... in Gray Star, a settlement in the remotest Northwest"; and the novel is almost over by the time Mrs Richard F Schiller (i.e., Lo) briefly appears. Thus we note, with a parenthetical gasp, the size of Nabokov's gamble on greatness. "Curiously enough, one cannot read a book," he once announced (at the lectern), "one can only reread it." Nabokov *knew* that *Lolita* would be reread, and re-reread. He knew that we would eventually absorb Lolita's fate – her stolen childhood, her stolen womanhood. Gray Star, he wrote, is "the capital town of the book." The shifting half-tone – gray star, pale fire, torpid smoke: this is the Nabokovian crux.

The second fundamental point is the description of a recurring dream that shadows Humbert after Lolita has flown (she absconds with the cynically carnal Quilty). It is also proof of the fact that style, that prose itself, can control morality. Who would want to do something that gave them dreams like these?

> [S]he did haunt my sleep but she appeared there in strange and ludicrous disguises as Valeria or Charlotte [his ex-wives], or a cross between them. That complex ghost would come to me, shedding shift after shift, in an atmosphere of great melancholy and disgust, and would recline in dull invitation on some narrow board or hard

settee, with flesh ajar like the rubber valve of a soccer ball's bladder. I would find myself, dentures fractured or hopelessly misplaced, in horrible *chambres garnies*, where I would be entertained at tedious vivisecting parties that generally ended with Charlotte or Valeria weeping in my bleeding arms and being tenderly kissed by my brotherly lips in a dream disorder of auctioneered Viennese bric-a-brac, pity, impotence and the brown wigs of tragic old women who had just been gassed.

That final phrase, with its clear allusion, reminds us of the painful and tender diffidence with which Nabokov wrote about the century's terminal crime. His father, the distinguished liberal statesman (whom Trotsky loathed), was shot dead by a fascist thug in Berlin; and Nabokov's homosexual brother, Sergey, was murdered in a Nazi concentration camp ("What a joy you are well, alive, in good spirits," Nabokov wrote to his sister Elena, from the US to the USSR, in November 1945. "Poor, poor Seryozha ...!"). Nabokov's wife, Véra, was Jewish, and so, therefore, was their son (born in 1934); and there is a strong likelihood that if the Nabokovs had failed to escape from France when they did (in May 1940, with the *Wehrmacht* 70 miles from Paris), they would have joined the scores of thousands of undesirables delivered by Vichy to the Reich.

In his fiction, to my knowledge, Nabokov wrote about the Holocaust at paragraph length only once – in the incomparable *Pnin* (1957). Other references, as in *Lolita*, are glancing. Take, for example, this one-sentence demonstration of genius from the insanely inspired six-page short story "Signs and Symbols" (it is a description of a Jewish matriarch): "Aunt Rosa, a fussy, angular, wild-eyed old lady, who had lived in a tremulous world of bad news, bankruptcies, train accidents, cancerous growths – until the Germans put her to death, together with all the people she had worried about."

Pnin goes further. At an *émigré* house party in rural America a Madam Shpolyanski mentions her cousin, Mira, and asks Timofey Pnin if he has heard of her "terrible end." "Indeed, I have," Pnin answers. Gentle Timofey sits on alone in the twilight. Then Nabokov gives us this:

What chatty Madam Shpolyanski mentioned had conjured up Mira's image with unusual force. This was disturbing. Only in the

> detachment of an incurable complaint, in the sanity of near death, could one cope with this for a moment. In order to exist rationally, Pnin had taught himself ... never to remember Mira Belochkin – not because ... the evocation of a youthful love affair, banal and brief, threatened his peace of mind ... but because, if one were quite sincere with oneself, no conscience, and hence no consciousness, could be expected to subsist in a world where such things as Mira's death were possible. One had to forget – because one could not live with the thought that this graceful, fragile, tender young woman with those eyes, that smile, those gardens and snows in the background, had been brought in a cattle car and killed by an injection of phenol into the heart, into the gentle heart one had heard beating under one's lips in the dusk of the past.

How resonantly this passage chimes with Primo Levi's crucial observation that we cannot, we *must not*, "understand what happened." Because to "understand" it would be to "contain" it. "What happened" was "non-human," or "counter-human," and remains incomprehensible to human beings.

By linking Humbert Humbert's crime to the Shoah, and to "those whom the wind of death has scattered" (Paul Celan), Nabokov pushes out to the very limits of the moral universe. Like *The Enchanter*, *Lolita* is airtight, intact and entire. The frenzy of the unattainable desire is confronted, and framed, with stupendous courage and cunning. And so matters might have rested. But then came the meltdown of artistic self-possession – tumultuously announced, in 1970, by the arrival of *Ada*. When a writer starts to come off the rails, you expect skidmarks and broken glass; with Nabokov, naturally, the eruption is on the scale of a nuclear accident.

I have read at least half a dozen Nabokov novels at least half a dozen times. And at least half a dozen times I have tried, and promptly failed, to read *Ada* ("Or Ardor: A Family Chronicle"). My first attempt took place about three decades ago. I put it down after the first chapter, with a curious sensation, a kind of negative tingle. Every five years or so (this became the pattern), I picked it up again; and after a while I began to articulate the difficulty: "But this is dead," I said to myself. The curious sensation, the negative tingle, is of course miserably familiar to me now: it is the reader's response to what seems to happen to all writers as they overstep the biblical span. The radiance, the life-giving power, begins to fade. Last summer I went away with *Ada* and locked myself up with it. And I was right. At 600 pages, two or three times Nabokov's usual fighting-weight, the novel is what homicide detectives call "a burster." It is a waterlogged corpse at the stage of maximal bloat.

When *Finnegans Wake* appeared, in 1939, it was greeted with wary respect – or with "terror-stricken praise," in the words of Jorge Luis Borges. *Ada* garnered plenty of terror-stricken praise; and the similarities between the two *magna opera* are in fact profound. Nabokov nominated *Ulysses* as his novel of the century, but he described *Finnegans Wake* as, variously, "formless and dull," "a cold pudding of a book," "a tragic failure," and "a frightful bore." Both novels seek to make a virtue of unbounded self-indulgence; they turn away, so to speak, and fold in on themselves. Literary talent has several ways of dying. With Joyce and Nabokov, we see a decisive loss of love for the reader – a loss of comity, of courtesy. The pleasures of writing, Nabokov said, "correspond exactly to the pleasures of reading"; and the two activities are in some sense indivisible. In *Ada*, that bond loosens and frays.

There is a weakness in Nabokov for "patricianism," as Saul Bellow called it (Nabokov the classic *émigré*, Bellow the classic immigrant). In the former's purely "Russian" novels (I mean the novels written in Russian that Nabokov did not himself translate), the male characters, in particular, have a self-magnifying quality: they are larger and louder than life. They don't walk – they "march" or "stride"; they don't eat and drink – they "munch" and "gulp"; they don't laugh – they "roar." They are very far from being the furtive, hesitant neurasthenics of mainstream anglophone fiction: they are brawny (and gifted) heart-throbs, who win all the fights and win all the girls. Pride, for them, is not a deadly sin but a cardinal virtue. Of course, we cannot do without this vein in Nabokov: it gives us, elsewhere, his magnificently comic *hauteur*. In *Lolita*, the superbity is meant to be funny; elsewhere, it is a trait that irony does not protect.

In *Ada* nabobism disastrously combines with a nympholepsy that is lavishly, monotonously, and frictionlessly gratified. Ada herself, at the outset, is 12; and Van Veen, her cousin (and half-sibling) is 14.[2] As Ada starts to age, in adolescence, her tiny sister Lucette is also on hand to enliven their "strenuous trysts." On top of this, there is a running quasi-fantasy about an international chain of elite bordellos where girls as young as 11 can be "fondled and fouled." And Van's 60-year-old father (incidentally but typically) has a mistress who is barely out of single figures: she is 10. This interminable book is written in dense, erudite, alliterative, punsome, pore-clogging prose; and every character, without exception, sounds like late Henry James.

In common with *Finnegans Wake*, *Ada* probably does "work out" and "measure up" – the multilingual decoder, given enough time and nothing better to do, might eventually disentangle its toiling systems and symmetries, its lonely and comfortless labyrinths, and its glutinous *nostalgies*. What both novels signally lack, however, is any hint of narrative traction: they slip and they slide; they just can't hold the road. And then, too, with Ada, there is something altogether alien – a sense of monstrous entitlement, of unbridled, head-in-air seigneurism. Morally, this is the world for which the twisted Humbert thirsts: a world where "nothing matters," and "everything is allowed."

This leaves us with *Transparent Things* and *Look at the Harlequins!* – as well as the more or less negligible volume under review. "*LATH!*," as the author called it, just as he called *The Original of Laura* "TOOL," is the Nabokov swansong. It has some wonderful rumbles, and glimmers of unearthly colour, but it is hard-of-hearing and rheumy-eyed; and the little-girl theme is by now hardly more than a logo – part of the Nabokovian furniture, like mirrors, doubles, chess, butterflies. There is a visit to a motel called Lolita Lodge; there is a brief impersonation of Dumbert Dumbert. More centrally, the narrator, Vadim Vadimovich, suddenly finds himself in sole charge of his seldom-seen daughter, Bel, who, inexorably, is twelve years old.

Now, where does this thread lead?

> I was still deliriously happy, still seeing nothing wrong or dangerous, or absurd or downright cretinous, in the relationship between my daughter and me. Save for a few insignificant lapses – a few hot drops of overflowing tenderness, a gasp masked by a cough and that sort of stuff – my relations with her remained essentially innocent.

Well, the dismaying answer is that this thread leads nowhere. The only repercussion, thematic or otherwise, is that Vadim ends up marrying one of Bel's classmates, who is 43 years his junior. And that is all.

Between the hysterical *Ada* and the doddery *Look at the Harlequins!* comes the mysterious, sinister, and beautifully melancholic novella, *Transparent Things*: Nabokov's remission. Our hero, Hugh Person, a middle-grade American publisher, is an endearing misfit and sexual loser, like Timofey Pnin (Pnin regularly dines at a shabby little restaurant called The Egg and We, which he frequents out of "sheer sympathy with failure"). Four visits to Switzerland provide the cornerstones of this expert little piece, as Hugh shyly courts the exasperating flirt, Armande, and also monitors an aged, portly, decadent, and forbiddingly highbrow novelist called "Mr R."

Mr R is said to have debauched his stepdaughter (a friend of Armande's) when she was a child or at any rate a minor. The nympholeptic theme thus hovers over the story, and is reinforced, in one extraordinary scene, by the disclosure of Hugh's latent yearnings. A pitiful bumbler, with a treacherous libido (wiltings and premature ejaculations mark his "mediocre potency"), Hugh calls on Armande's villa, and her mother diverts him, while he waits, with some family snapshots. He comes across a photo of a naked Armande, aged 10:

> The visitor constructed a pile of albums to screen the flame of his interest ... and returned several times to the pictures of little Armande in her bath, pressing a proboscidate rubber toy to her shiny stomach or standing up, dimple-bottomed, to be lathered. Another revelation of impuberal softness (its middle line just distinguishable from the less vertical grass-blade next to it) was afforded by a photo of her in which she sat in the buff on the grass, combing her sun-shot hair and spreading wide, in false perspective, the lovely legs of a giantess.
>
> He heard a toilet flush upstairs and with a guilty wince slapped the thick book shut. His retractile heart moodily withdrew, its throbs quietened.

At first this passage seems shockingly anomalous. But then we reflect that Hugh's unconscious thoughts, his dreams, his insomnias ("night is always a giant"), are saturated with inarticulate dreads:

> He could not believe that decent people had the sort of obscene and absurd nightmares which shattered his night and continued to tingle throughout the day. Neither the incidental accounts of bad dreams reported by friends nor the case histories in Freudian dream books, with their hilarious elucidations, presented anything like the complicated vileness of his almost nightly experience.

Hugh marries Armande and then, years later, strangles her *in his sleep*. So it may be that Nabokov identifies the paedophiliac prompting as an urge towards violence and self-obliteration. Hugh Person's subliminal churning extracts a terrible revenge, in pathos and isolation (prison, madhouse), and demands the ultimate purgation: he is burnt to death in one of the most ravishing conflagrations in all literature. The torched hotel:

> Now flames were mounting the stairs, in pairs, in trios, in redskin file, hand in hand, tongue after tongue, conversing and humming happily. It was not, though, the heat of their flicker, but the acrid dark smoke that caused Person to retreat back into the room; excuse me, said a polite flamelet holding open the door he was vainly trying to close. The window banged with such force that its panes broke into a torrent of rubies ... At last suffocation made him try to get out by climbing out and down, but there were no ledges or balconies on that side of the roaring house. As he reached the window a long lavender-tipped flame danced up to stop him with a graceful gesture of its gloved hand. Crumbling partitions of plaster and wood allowed human cries to reach him, and one of his last wrong ideas was that those were the shouts of people anxious to help him, and not the howls of fellow men.

Left to themselves, *The Enchanter*, *Lolita*, and *Transparent Things* might have formed a lustrous and utterly unnerving trilogy. But they are not left to themselves; by sheer weight of numbers, by sheer iteration, the nympholepsy novels begin to infect one another – they cross-contaminate. We gratefully take all we can from them; and yet ... Where else in the canon do we find such wayward fixity? In the awful itch of Lawrence, maybe, or in the murky sexual transpositions of Proust? No: you would need to venture to the very fringes of literature – Lewis Carroll, William

Burroughs, the Marquis de Sade – to find an equivalent emphasis: an emphasis on activities we rightly and eternally hold to be unforgivable.

In fiction, of course, nobody ever gets hurt; the flaw, as I said, is not moral but aesthetic. And I intend no innuendo by pointing out that Nabokov's obsession with nymphets has a parallel: the ponderous intrusiveness of his obsession with Freud – "the vulgar, shabby, fundamentally medieval world" of "the Viennese quack," with "its bitter little embryos, spying, from their natural nooks, upon the love life of their parents." Nabokov cherished the anarchy of the inner life, and Freud is excoriated because he sought to systematize it. Is there something rivalrous in this hatred? Well, in the end it is Nabokov, and not Freud, who emerges as our supreme poet of dreams (with Kafka), and our supreme poet of madness.

One commonsensical caveat persists, for all our literary-critical impartiality: writers like to write about the things they like to think about. And, to put it at its sternest, Nabokov's mind, during his last period, insufficiently honoured the innocence – insufficiently honoured the honour – of twelve-year-old girls. In the three novels mentioned above he prepotently defends the emphasis; in *Ada* (that incontinent splurge), in *Look at the Harlequins!*, and now in *The Original of Laura*, he does not defend it. This leaves a faint but visible scar on the leviathan of his corpus.

"Now, *soyons raisonnable*," says Quilty, staring down the barrel of Humbert's revolver. "You will only wound me hideously and then rot in jail while I recuperate in a tropical setting." All right, let us be reasonable. In his book about Updike, Nicholson Baker refers to an order of literary achievement that he calls "Prousto-Nabokovian." Yes, Prousto-Nabokovian, or Joyceo-Borgesian, or, for the Americans, Jameso-Bellovian. And it is at the highest table that Vladimir Nabokov coolly takes his place.

Lolita, *Pnin*, *Despair* (1936; translated by the author in 1966), and four or five short stories are immortal. *King, Queen, Knave* (1928, 1968), *Laughter in the Dark* (1932, 1936), *The Enchanter*, *The Eye* (1930), *Bend Sinister* (1947), *Pale Fire* (1962), and *Transparent Things* are ferociously accomplished; and little *Mary* (1925), his first novel, is a little beauty. *Lectures on Literature* (1980), *Lectures on Russian Literature* (1981), and *Lectures on Don Quixote* (1983), together with *Strong Opinions* (1973), constitute the shining record of a pre-eminent artist-critic. And the *Selected Letters* (1989), the *Nabokov–Wilson Letters* (1979), and that marshlight of an autobiography, *Speak, Memory* (1967), give us a four-dimensional portrait of a delightful and honourable man. The vice Nabokov most frequently reviled was "cruelty." And his gentleness of nature is most clearly seen in the loving attentiveness with which, in his fiction, he writes about animals. A minute's thought gives me the cat in *King, Queen, Knave* (washing itself with one hindleg raised "like a shouldered club"), the charming dogs and monkeys in *Lolita*, the shadow-tailed squirrel and the unforgettable ant in *Pnin*, and the sick bat in *Pale Fire* – creeping past "like a cripple with a broken umbrella."

They call it a "shimmer" – a glint, a glitter, a glisten. The Nabokovian essence is a miraculously fertile instability, where without warning the words detach themselves from the everyday and streak off like flares in a night sky, illuminating hidden *versts* of longing and terror. From *Lolita*, as the fateful cohabitation begins (*nous connûmes*, a Flaubertian intonation, means "we came to know"):

> *Nous connûmes* the various types of motor court operators, the reformed criminal, the retired teacher, and the business flop, among the males; and the motherly, pseudo-ladylike and madamic variants among the females. And sometimes trains would cry in the monstrously hot and humid night with heartrending and ominous plangency, mingling power and hysteria in one desperate scream.

Trump Cards[1]

JOHN BANVILLE

Aptly, we may begin with the title. The dust jacket has it as *The Original of Laura: A novel in fragments*, while the title page varies this to *The Original of Laura (Dying Is Fun)*. However, the author himself, at the top of the first of the 138 file cards on which the novel – let us call it a novel, for now – is composed, calls the book merely *The Original of Laura*. The subtitle *A novel in fragments* is easily accepted as an editor's addendum, since the book is published posthumously, but where did *(Dying Is Fun)* come from? Nabokov biographer Brian Boyd tells us that *The Original of Laura: Dying Is Fun* was "a first tentative title" that Nabokov noted in his diary in December 1974, three years before his death. *Dying Is Fun* has an appropriately jaunty, Nabokovian ring to it, but did the author himself, or his son, decide that it should be part of the finished title? The book comes to us out of a nebulous region, and any clear glimpse through the mist would be welcome.

That Nabokov left behind an incomplete novel has been known since his death in a Swiss hospital in 1977; known, too, his instruction to his wife, Véra Nabokov – that if he died before finishing the book the draft was to be destroyed. His directive was disobeyed, as such directives frequently are – one thinks of Virgil and the *Aeneid* and, of course, of Kafka and Max Brod. The latter precedent is specifically evoked by Dmitri Nabokov in his introduction to *The Original of Laura*. Brod, according to Nabokov fils, never had any intention of destroying Kafka's work, and Kafka knew it; Vladimir Nabokov "exercised similar reasoning when he assigned *Laura*'s annihilation to my mother." Véra's failure to carry out the grim task was, according to her son, "rooted in procrastination –

procrastination due to age, weakness, and immeasurable love." This is not the first of her husband's novels to survive thanks to her. In his 1956 afterword to *Lolita*, its author recounts how on more than one occasion he had carried an unfinished draft to the incinerator but "was stopped by the thought that the ghost of the destroyed book would haunt my files for the rest of my life." It had to wait for later biographers to point out that it was not the fear of ghosts alone that stayed Nabokov's hand but the intervention of his wife, who would not allow him to burn the manuscript. Writers' wives are like that.

For all that, though, the inevitable question arises: If Nabokov said he wanted the draft of *The Original of Laura* destroyed, and in this instance his wife would not have moved to save the thing, why now, thirty-two years later, has their son decided to publish and risk being damned?

It is not a nice thing to have to say in the circumstances, but Dmitri Nabokov's introduction is a lamentable performance, stridently defensive, slippery on particulars, and frequently repellent in tone. Aping Nabokov père at his aristocratically disdainful worst, he makes jibes at "half-literate journalists," dismisses someone's "asinine electronic biography" of his father, and wearily deplores the "lesser minds" whom it has been his misfortune to encounter over the years when he was debating whether to publish or not. Reading these introductory pages is like being trapped in an airless room with a priggish adolescent dressed up in his father's outsize clothes – tails, white tie, spats, and all – who expatiates on the awfulness of the masters at his school while puffing on one of Daddy's finest cigars and turning slowly green.

As to the justifications he offers for publishing the book, it is worth allowing him a good long piece of rope:

> I have said and written more than once that, to me, my parents, in a sense, had never died but lived on, looking over my shoulder in a kind of virtual limbo, available to offer a thought or counsel to assist me with a vital decision, whether a crucial mot juste or a more mundane concern. I did not need to borrow my "*ton bon*" (thus deliberately garbled) from the titles of fashionable morons but had it from the source. If it pleases an adventurous commentator to liken the case to mystical phenomena, so be it. I decided at this juncture that, in putative retrospect, Nabokov would not have wanted me to become

his Person from Porlock or allow little Juanita Dark – for that was the name of an early Lolita, destined for cremation – to burn like a latter-day Jeanne d'Arc.[2]

Over the page, and in conclusion, he abruptly drops the lordly manner and says he decided to publish the book because "I am a nice guy, and having noticed that people the world over find themselves on a first-name basis with me as they empathize with 'Dmitri's dilemma,' I felt it would be kind to alleviate their sufferings."[3] Let us give him the benefit of the doubt.

Ever since word got out that publication of the book was being seriously contemplated, opinions have been canvassed on the matter and have differed widely. Aside from the ethical question of whether the express wish of a dying man should be accepted or ignored, it seemed, to some of us at least, that the sole criterion was whether the novel was in a state close enough to completion to justify its being published. Nabokov was a famously meticulous stylist – none more so, surely, among his contemporaries – and would have died before he would have let work appear that had not been polished to the highest finish. Well, he did die, and the work has been published. Polished it is not, fragmented it is. What we have, in fact, is little more than a blurred outline, a preliminary shiver of a novel. And yet.

This edition is a triumph of the book-maker's art, and the design, by the Nabokovianly named Chip Kidd, is masterly. There will be those who will deplore the production as gimmicky, but the greatest magicians depend on gimmicks for their most elegant illusions. And Knopf's *The Original of Laura* is magic right through, from the dust jacket, in sideways-fading white on black with just the merest flicks of gules, past the cloth cover that reproduces the last words of Nabokov the novelist, to the heavy gray pages divided between, on the top half, photographic reproductions of the 138 file cards, front and back, and, on the bottom half, the text in print, including misspellings, slips of the pen, blank spaces, all.

A quibble, or perhaps more than a quibble. The reproductions of the file cards are perforated around the edges, so that, as a "Note on the Text" informs us, they "can be removed and rearranged, as the author likely did when he was writing the novel." This seems dubious, for the reason that most of the cards have run-over text, and to take them out of the pages and shuffle them would make nonsense of the plot, slight and elusive though it is. And what reader would be so wanton as to remove the very vitals of the book and leave a rectangular hole running through from page 1 to page 275? There will be disputes, dear me, yes, there will be hot disputes.

And the fiction? It is a flux; even the names of the characters are not fixed. The protagonist, if we may call her that, the eponymous original herself, is Flora Wild née Lind, the daughter of a famous and, it would seem, homosexual photographer, and a faded Russian ballerina. The period is hard to pin down, but the milieu seems to be that of the novels Nabokov wrote in his European exile and of short stories from the time such as the masterpiece "Spring in Fialta": interwar and international, brittle, debonair and dazzlingly superficial. One realizes again what an artistic blessing in disguise it was that the exigencies of the times forced Nabokov relentlessly westward, for America was the biggest and best gift a writer such as he could have received, given his inclination toward mere cleverness and the dandyism of the boulevard. In the great works of his American years, especially *Lolita*, with its unrelenting background buzz of anguish, we put up with the tedium of wrestling with his puns and his puzzles because we see in them the desperate diversions – yes, the alliteration is catching of a narrator writhing in spiritual pain. Nabokov's return to Europe after the great success of *Lolita* and *Pale Fire* (1962) saw a falling off, or at least a falling back into the bad old prewar ways. Like *Transparent Things* (1972) and *Look at the Harlequins!* (1974) – oh, that exclamation mark! – *The Original of Laura* is altogether too knowing for its own good, and the tone grates on the ear and the nerves, so that one feels that one has been buttonholed by a relentlessly garrulous flaneur.

Still, the book is deeply interesting, not so much for what it thinks itself to be as for what we know it is: a master's final work. The flickering narrative of Flora – there are many teasing allusions to Lolita, including a character called Hubert H. Hubert – and her pathetically corpulent but brilliant and rich husband, her anonymous lover who is our occasional first-person narrator, her shadowy friends and the unfriendly shadows through which she moves, gives way gradually to the account of a fat man (it seems to be Flora's husband, Philip Wild) conducting a thought experiment on himself that, if he has his way, will end in his erasing himself from life, starting with his toes and working upward. It is a nice conceit, and desperately sad, especially as Dmitri Nabokov has informed us of the agonies his father suffered in his final months from inflammation of the toenails. It is a piece of information we could probably have done without. As the son's account of the father's last days attests, and as the father's final novel shows, in contradiction of VN's subtitle, dying is most definitely not fun.

In the Cards, a Last Hand[1]

ALEXANDER THEROUX

Before his death in 1977, Vladimir Nabokov instructed his wife, Véra, to burn the unfinished draft of a novel called *The Original of Laura* – a handwritten mélange of notes on 138 index cards. Vera ignored the instruction. Instead, she temporized for 16 years about whether to publish the book in its incomplete form, and never did. When she died in 1991, the cards were still locked in a Swiss bank vault. Dmitri Nabokov, the novelist's 75-year-old son, has now liberated them. Indeed, they are displayed for all to see, precisely duplicated on detachable cards – one per page, with printed transcriptions underneath – in the first published edition of *The Original of Laura*. Should we be glad for this posthumous novel, however incomplete?

The first effect of reading *The Original of Laura* gives less pleasure than a certain squeamishness. The bony, tentative hand of illness can be found on the cards themselves. The lineaments of a serious literary undertaking are obvious, too, but in only a few places can one discern even a hint of the technical brilliance, the penchant for parody, the irresistible flippancy that we would recognize as the work of the author of *Lolita*, *Pale Fire*, and *Ada*. *The Original of Laura* shows us the writer's version of a great athlete in decline: not, so to speak, the glorious Lou Gehrig of 1927, but the feeble shadow of the same man, retiring at midseason in 1939.

The novel's plot is a simple one: A flighty adventuress named Flora, the daughter of an artistic couple, becomes, as the years pass, the subject of a scandalous novel, "My Laura." It has been written, we are told, "by a neurotic and hesitant man of letters" (a former lover, it is suggested). Young Flora experiences sex early, not excluding a groping encounter at age twelve with a lecher named (drum roll) Hubert H. Hubert, a paramour of Flora's own flighty mother. Years later, she marries fat, wealthy Philip Wild, another older man, with whom after three years she becomes bored – then faithless.

That a child molester named Hubert H. Hubert should show up in a late Nabokov novel is hard to comprehend artistically, even parodically. Hubert's appearance seems less a final salute to *Lolita* – where, two decades before, Humbert Humbert had done the lusting – than a lapse in judgment. It is charming, up to a point, that a great novelist in his last years remains so beguiled by nubile females that he must lavish his gifts upon them yet again, but it is not a cause for literary celebration.

More fitting to Nabokov's older self are the novel's portraits of Hubert and Wild, both intensely unattractive men. They allow Nabokov to sketch the shipwreck of old age, the humiliations of desire in a spent, decrepit body. After one Wild-ean mating session with Laura, described in sad and eloquent detail, Nabokov writes: "Like toads or tortoises neither saw each other's faces." Philip Wild catalogues his weakening extremities and imagines his own death by "auto dissolution" – and Hubert himself dies of a stroke.

Reflections on disease, mortality and impotence, not to mention a Swiftian disgust with the human body, figure prominently in *The Original of Laura*. On one card we find a reference to Wild's "stomack ailment": "I loathe my belly, that trunkful of bowels, which I have to carry around, and everything connected with it – the wrong food, heartburn, constipation's leaden load." One can't help thinking that such passages capture the author's own musings: The novel was begun in 1975, two years before Nabokov's death. Its deadpan subtitle: "Dying is fun."

It is not all about dying. There are witty Nabokovian moments as well. The virtuoso Nabokov parentheses are in evidence. "First of all she dismissed Cora with the strelitzias (hateful blooms, regalized bananas, really)." One remembers the early passage from *Lolita*: "My very photogenic mother died in a freak accident (picnic, lightning) when I was three."

Nabokov wrote most of his novels, including *Lolita* and *Pale Fire*, on index cards, a portable strategy that allowed him to compose in the car while his wife drove the devoted lepidopterist on butterfly expeditions. The cards could be shuffled around and often were. Nabokov always wrote in pencil and non-linearly, a mode he preferred since 1940s. His novel *Ada* incorporated over 2000 cards. One may recall that his fictional poet John Shade in *Pale Fire* also composed his 999-line poem on index cards, a mode, incidentally, also favored by the philosopher Ludwig Wittgenstein – he repeatedly rearranged his *Philosophical Investigations* – as well as Marcel Duchamp (green cards were his favourite) and John F. Kennedy who used them for his famous "*Ich bin ein Berliner*" speech.[2] Knopf's choice to reproduce the originals on perforated cards, easily lifted out of the book and ready to be shuffled by the reader, gives us a book with pages as stiff and strong as cardboard.

So are we to assume that *The Original of Laura* is also a play-kit? As if Nabokov *shuffled* his index cards serendipitously to discern the arc of the plot! I recall Nabokov wittily once suggested that his ideal reader buy two copies of his novel, *Pale Fire*, keeping one copy intact while using the other to scissor out Kinbot's commentary the easier to compare it side-by-side with John Shade's poem! Was his father's comically exaggerated ruse to try to sell two copies to each reader recapitulated in Dmitri's nutty suggestion that someone actually *remove and rearrange these cards* for sense?

It is of course always a treat to be able to see a work in progress, never mind Nabokov's handwriting (chalked slants and serifs on a Parisian blackboard menu, I first saw his lepidoptery notes when I was teaching at Harvard in the late 1970s, at the Museum of Comparative Zoology), many of them the author's emendations on the fly – erasures, ballooned additions, line-outs, inserted words, afterthoughts, the scrupulous appendage of an *OED* definition, one blast of an idea superimposed by another. (Six cards used in Nabokov's writing for *Look at the Harlequins!* a few years ago were on display at the "Nabokov Under Glass" exhibit at the New York Public Library.) In *The Original of Laura* we see words inserted, memos to himself, marginal afterthoughts, typesetting directions ("no quotes") and copy-editing symbols dot the cards. On card Ex (1) we find him entering a self-suggestion: "invent tradename [for a medicine], e.g., cephalopium." At a certain point the novel noticeably weakens; the prose, ever more hallucinatory and random, nods off.

It is no surprise to discover an author in failing health losing his writerly powers. For son Dmitri, there is no such excuse. He claims English to be his "favorite and most flexible means of expression" – Dmitri, you see, is multilingual – but his introduction is nonsensical, snobbish, and cruel and reads as if it has been translated from the Albanian. Of his father's medical treatment: "The tests continued; a succession of doctors rubbed their chins as their bedside manner edged toward the graveside."

"Nabokov would not have wanted me to become his Person from Porlock," Dmitri says, in a typically ham-fisted reference to the figure who intruded on Coleridge's great poem "Kubla Khan" before it was finished. But his preface lacks an appropriately chastened quality (after all, he defied his father's wishes). Instead, Dmitri airs old grievances. He complains of a customs inspector stealing a flask of cognac from the family (in 1940) and then of his own personal loss (in 1948) of an inscribed first edition of *Lolita*. He guiltily attacks those who would fault his decision to publish *The Original of Laura* as "half-literate journalists" and "lesser minds" and "individuals of limited imagination."

The last card of *The Original of Laura* is a poignant list of synonyms for "efface" – *expunge, erase, delete, rub out, wipe out, obliterate*. Although we might hope that Nabokov was on his way to a great book, it is a pity that his instructions were ignored and the novel survived in such a form. English professors may assign *The Original of Laura* to their students someday, but it is really better suited to a college ethics class.

A Generous Gift to Readers[1]

HELLER MCALPIN

When Vladimir Nabokov died in Switzerland in 1977, he left explicit instructions for his heirs to destroy the pencilled index cards that made up his work to date on his unfinished 18th novel, *The Original of Laura (Dying is Fun)*. Véra, his loyal wife and amanuensis, who died in 1991, couldn't bring herself to do it. And, fortunately, after much debate, neither could their son, Dmitri.

Of course, it's one thing not to burn the partial draft, and another to publish it. But, although Nabokov may be squirming in his grave, Nabokov fans and scholars have reason to thank Dmitri for his brave parental defiance in publishing this invaluable glimpse into the way his brilliant father worked.

All too often, publications of half-cooked literary fragments are not just disappointing in literary terms, but seem motivated as much by greed as by the heirs' desire to keep their famous forebearer alive in print. But whatever one thinks of Nabokov's emphatically unfinished book – and we'll get to that – it certainly hasn't been rushed into print in an unseemly fashion. Thirty-two years after Nabokov's death at 78, its publication feels more like a generous gift to readers than a ploy for fame or fortune.

This is in great part due to the dazzlingly clever presentation of the material. By reproducing facsimiles of Nabokov's 138 penciled index cards at the top of each page and printing typeset transcriptions with minimal editorial changes and notes below, Chip Kidd, associate art director at Knopf, has designed a format that reminds us forcefully, in graphic terms, that *The Original of Laura* is a work in progress and not an ordinary manuscript. The photographed cards are perforated, to encourage us to stack and shuffle them – as Nabokov apparently did – into an order that might make more sense. Nabokov's neat handwriting is punctuated by eraser smudges, inserted phrases, and emphatically crossed-out or scribbled-over words.

But it becomes fainter, sketchier, and more sparse as he races against time and illness in a Lausanne hospital, trying to net ideas and pin down a draft, a goal as elusive as some of the butterflies he chased and collected around the globe.

Although Nabokov's last novel is especially intriguing to his devotees, readers whose familiarity with Nabokov's work is limited to his most famous novel, *Lolita* (1955), will also find plenty of interest. The story – such as it is – involves "an extravagantly slender girl," Flora, whom we meet at age 24 in the act of cheating on her older husband. Her current lover is a writer who, shortly after their affair ends, writes a critically attacked but bestselling novel (as was *Lolita*) about her, called "My Laura."

Flora – thus the original of Laura – is the daughter of a ballerina named Lanskaya (as in land and sky) and, probably, her husband Adam Lind, a photographer also of Russian extraction who shoots himself over a jilted homosexual love. Raised by her flighty mother in Paris, lovely 12-year-old Flora is pestered by the too-close attentions of her mother's creepy older English lover, Hubert B. Hubert – a clear echo of Lolita's Humbert Humbert.

Flora's cuckolded husband is an obese, brilliant neurologist and lecturer named Philip Wild. Flora is "mesmerized by his fame and fortune" but otherwise indifferent to his wit and accomplishments.

Despite its limited word count – each card contains barely a paragraph or two of prose – the book is filled with sly wit and memorable images, many of which evoke Flora's girlish body, in sharp contrast with her hard, emotional detachment. A lover "pinafores" her stomach with kisses, a phone rings "ecstatically," and during sex, "A tear of no particular meaning gemmed the hard top of her cheek."

The manuscript gets stranger and more fitfully elliptical in the second half, which largely concerns Wild's description of his weird psychological experiments. These involve putting himself into a trance and willing the dissolution of various parts of his body, beginning with his painful toes – "suicide made a pleasure."

Wild dreams of a high school crush, Aurora Lee, whose "cold gaze" reminds him of his wife (and whose name evokes Flora, Laura, and Poe's Annabel Lee). But he confesses wistfully to loving "only one girl in my life, an object of terror and tenderness."

Perhaps Wild's desire to "think away thought" and himself and make dying fun by "auto-dissolution" stems from a broken heart over wayward Flora. But it isn't a stretch to imagine a wretched Nabokov in his Lausanne hospital bed, wishing to "efface/expunge/erase/delete/rub out/wipe out/obliterate" his offending body parts. These are the words listed on the last card of this tantalizing, fascinating, occasionally perplexing manuscript. Pity he didn't get to finish it. Fortunate we get to see it at all.

The Nabokov Mess[I]

NATHANIEL RICH

Let's come clean – $35 is at stake, after all. Vladimir Nabokov's posthumously published *The Original of Laura (Dying Is Fun)*, despite its considerable width (nearly 2 inches) and heft (2 pounds, 11 ounces), its publisher's description ("a novel in fragments"), and its advance praise ("a fascinating novel" says biographer Brian Boyd), is not a novel. Not remotely. It is not to be confused with Truman Capote's *Answered Prayers*, Ralph Ellison's *Juneteenth*, or Italo Svevo's *Further Confessions of Zeno* – unfinished novels that contain long, continuous sections of writing, from which it is possible to apprehend the larger work's subject matter, scope, and ambition, however imperfect the execution. To describe *The Original of Laura* as a novel would be like mistaking a construction site for a cathedral. Yes, the blueprints might call for flying buttresses and oriel windows, but for now it is only a mess of wheelbarrows, uncut limestone, and piles of sand.

These pages are the embryonic jottings made in preparation for a novel – long before it's certain there's even a novel to be written. There are notes to self ("What kind of folklore preceded poetry in Rus?; speak a little of Lom. and Derzh."); marooned sentence fragments, some of them striking ("The orange awnings of southern summers" and a reference to death's "tempting emptiness"); and incomplete scenes haunted by faintly drawn characters. Many of the scenes deal with the grim obsessions of old age: sexual futility, corporeal decrepitude, and death. There is also wordplay ("He brought from the favorite florist of fashionable girls a banal bevy of bird-of-paradise flowers"), misspellings (what the Note on Text charitably refers to as "nonstandard" spellings), and unveiled references to Nabokov's own earlier stories and novels, *Lolita* especially. This may indicate some self-referential design; the allusions also might have been private jokes that Nabokov never intended to publish. Who knows?

"I have decided that my father, with a wry and fond smile, might well have contradicted himself upon seeing me in my present situation and said ... Say or do what you like, but why not make some money on the damn thing?"

I've read summaries of the plot in other publications, but I couldn't for the life of me offer my own. At one point in the three-year public debate that preceded *Laura*'s publication, different Nabokov scholars, who had been granted access to the secret manuscript, offered different plot summaries. One talked about a character named Philip Wild, an enormously corpulent scholar, who marries a much younger, wildly promiscuous woman called Flora. In the other version, Flora is the heroine and the model for "Laura," a character in a novel written by her lover; Laura and Flora then engage in some sort of meta-fictional battle. Nabokovians wanted to know – which plot summary was correct? As it turns out, both describe sections that do appear in *The Original of Laura*. But that doesn't mean any of it makes sense.

What is evident, however, is that the furious controversy over the manuscript's publication was waged on false grounds. The question was whether Dmitri Nabokov, Vladimir's heir and literary executive, should publish *Laura* and defy his father's wish to burn the manuscript upon his death. Ron Rosenbaum, John Banville, Tom Stoppard, and newspaper book reporters the world over joined the debate. Dmitri raised the stakes by declaring *Laura* "the most concentrated distillation" of his father's creativity. Now that *Laura* has been revealed to be little more than a collection of notes, the debate seems silly, meretricious.

It would be unfair to fault Dmitri, who is now 75 and reportedly quite ill, for choosing to publish. Despite its flaws, *Laura* is not embarrassing to his father because it doesn't come close to resembling a finished work. In Dmitri's introduction to the book, he takes a darkly mystical tone when justifying his decision: *Laura* is described as existing in a "penumbra," a "disturbing specter" shrouded in "gloom"; he says he doesn't think "my father or my father's shade would have opposed the release of *Laura* once *Laura* had survived the hum of time this long" and describes being finally overcome by "an otherforce I could not resist." Otherforce, indeed: Besides a contract with Knopf, there was an excerpt in *Playboy* ("we've never paid this much for a book excerpt, ever," acknowledged the magazine's literary editor), and the day before the book's publication, Dmitri announced he would auction off the very note cards on which *Laura* is composed (Christie's estimates a take of $400,000–$600,000). Given these developments, a different comment by Dmitri comes to mind: "I have decided that my father, with a wry and fond smile, might well have contradicted himself upon seeing me in my present situation and said ... Say or do what you like, but why not make some money on the damn thing?"

More power to him, though readers may be surprised to find that the giant hardcover of *Laura* has a text of just 9,000 words (i.e., 25 to 30 standard book pages). The $35 retail price is achieved by an expensive, and impeccable, design, featuring perforated reproductions of Nabokov's index cards. The publisher's note advises that the cards can be "removed and rearranged, as the author likely did when he was writing the novel." It is a shrewd marketing strategy, not because anyone will follow this advice (they won't), but because it justifies the use of heavyweight paper and the decision to leave every other page blank, thus resulting in a 280-page hardcover and what the industry calls a higher "price point."

What's gone missing in the hubbub about *Laura* is a basic understanding of what makes Nabokov the master he is. It is not his puns, tricks, or allusions, though his high-wire gamesmanship is often thrilling. Nor is it his unusual method of writing notes and early drafts of his novels on index cards; cards written in preparation for other novels can easily be viewed at the New York Public Library and other archives. The publication of *Laura* makes a fetish out of the obscure and the unknowable, but Nabokov is not that kind of writer at all. He is a genius of clarity, of the surprising detail that illuminates a universe. Take, for instance, his description in *Lolita* of the "cesspoolful of rotting monsters behind [Humbert Humbert's] slow boyish smile"; or, in *Speak, Memory*, the way his childhood nanny would react when a fly settled on her "stern forehead and its three wrinkles would instantly leap up all together like three runners over three hurdles." There are thousands of additional examples, so this one, from his story "A Guide to Berlin," will have to stand for all the rest: "Here lies the sense of literary creation: to portray ordinary objects as they will be reflected in the kindly mirrors of future times ... the times when a man who might put on the most ordinary jacket of today will be dressed up for an elegant masquerade."

Vladimir Nabokov, Reduced to Notes[1]

MICHAEL DIRDA

Should this book have been published? Certainly all the work of a great writer like Vladimir Nabokov ought to be available to scholars and interested readers. To my mind, Dmitri Nabokov was clearly right to ignore his dying father's request that he destroy these fragments of an unfinished novel. But that doesn't mean *The Original of Laura* actually deserves the attention of anyone but the most rabid Nabokov fanatic. Apart from a few enchanting phrases – "the orange awnings of southern summers" – there's just not much here.

But first a little background.

When Nabokov died in Switzerland at the age of 78, he left behind an extraordinary artistic legacy. During the first half of his life, he produced a series of important novels in his native Russian, including at least one masterpiece, *The Gift*. He was, arguably, the leading writer among those Russians who, having fled the Bolshevik Revolution, were then living in exile in Germany and France. But when Hitler's forces began to overwhelm Europe, Nabokov, his wife, Véra, and their little son, Dmitri, fled to the United States. Here the writer found teaching jobs, most notably at Cornell University, while he began to create – in English – technically dazzling and deeply moving books, among them *The Real Life of Sebastian Knight*, *Pnin* and the exquisite memoir *Speak, Memory*.

Wonderful as these books were (and are), none sold particularly well – and none quite prepared the world for the one that opens: "Lolita, light of my life, fire of my loins. My sin, my soul." Originally brought out in Paris by a publisher who specialized in erotica, Nabokov's *Lolita* (1955) is now considered by many readers to be the most beautifully composed novel of the mid-20th century.

The story of Humbert Humbert and poor Dolores Haze was followed, a few years later, by *Pale Fire* (1962), the most formally intricate and playful of Nabokov's books. It consists of John Shade's long, rather traditional poem of that title, edited with extensive annotation by his erstwhile colleague Prof. Charles Kinbote. Its opening couplet is another of Nabokov's striking first lines: "I was the shadow of the waxwing slain / By the false azure in the windowpane." But *Pale Fire*, as interpreted by Kinbote, turns out to be something far richer and stranger than a simple elegy for the poet's dead daughter: As one consults the editor's notes and commentary, the astonished reader gradually learns that the poem actually traces the secret history of the deposed prince of a country called Zembla, a prince who, to escape assassins, has changed his name to... Charles Kinbote. As it happens, Nabokov wrote this marvelous send-up of literary criticism on index cards, which were later acquired by the Library of Congress. I went to see them when I first came to Washington 30 years ago.

At the time of Nabokov's death, *The Original of Laura* also existed as a series of index cards, more than a hundred of them, in no obvious order. This Knopf edition consists of photographs of his miscellaneous handwritten cards, with a printed transcription of their text below, in a tentative order determined by Dmitri Nabokov.

The cards themselves may be detached from the book and, if desired, rearranged by the reader. This gimmick, I feel, may give a false impression. Unlike experimental works by B.S. Johnson and Marc Saporta, which were published as loose pages in boxes, *The Original of Laura* was never intended to be shuffled into any sequence whatsoever. As we have it, the novel revolves around two characters: The promiscuous Flora and her obese husband, Dr. Philip Wild, "a brilliant neurologist, a renowned lecturer [and] a gentleman of independent means." One of Flora's lovers, we discover, has written a roman à clef about her entitled "Laura." He is described as "a neurotic and hesitant man of letters, who destroys his mistress in the act of portraying her." We also learn that in her girlhood the young Flora was pursued by her stepfather, a Mr. Hubert H. Hubert:

> She was often alone in the house with Mr. Hubert, who constantly "prowled" (*rodait*) around her, humming a monotonous tune and sort of mesmerizing her, enveloping her, so to speak in some sticky invisible substance and coming closer and closer no matter what way she turned. For instance she did not dare to let her arms hang

> aimlessly lest her knuckles came into contact with some horrible part of that kindly but smelly and "pushing" old male.

In the sections dealing with Wild, the scientist tells us that he has taken to playing a game in which he imagines various parts of his body dying and dropping away. According to Wild, such "auto-dissolution afforded the greatest ecstasy known to man." Hence this novel's subtitle: "Dying Is Fun."

In many of Nabokov's late works, he seems to be reflecting on his own life and earlier fiction. For instance, in his last completed novel, *Look at the Harlequins!*, he focused on a writer whose bibliography closely resembled his own. Nabokov appears to be playing a similar game here, offering riffs on *Lolita* and his somewhat underappreciated novel about literary biography, *The Real Life of Sebastian Knight*. One passage even recalls the wistful, haunted tone of the famous short story "Spring in Fialta":

> Every now and then she would turn up for a few moments between trains, between planes, between lovers. My morning sleep would be interrupted by heartrending sounds – a window opening, a little bustle downstairs, a trunk coming, a trunk going, distant telephone conversations that seemed to be conducted in conspiratorial whispers. If shivering in my nightshirt I dared to waylay her all she said would be "you really ought to lose some weight" or "I hope you transferred that money as I indicated" – and all doors closed again.

That's quite beautiful, but, alas, there aren't many such pages in *The Original of Laura*. Where the action was intended to go remains elusive, and without any serious editorial apparatus it's difficult even to speculate. In consequence, this book remains only a posthumous collection of rough drafts and authorial notes, more novelty than anything else. *The Original of Laura* is for Nabokov completists only.

An Earnest Proposal to Dmitri Nabokov[1]

AMELIA GLASER

The damage, I fear, has been done. Dmitri Nabokov, after years of teasing his father's readers, has announced the imminent publication of Vladimir Nabokov's unfinished last manuscript, *The Original of Laura*, which has been sitting, we are told, in a Swiss safety deposit box, hostage to filial indecision. Early this year it seemed that Dmitri was close to carrying out Vladimir Nabokov's deathbed wishes, thus spiting the maxim uttered by Mikhail Bulgakov's devilish Woland in *Master and Margarita* that "manuscripts don't burn." The suspense story, as it has been narrated by bloggers, scholars and journalists for the past couple of months, has continued to shift the devil from the shoulder inclined to burn the text to the shoulder inclined to capitalize on it.

Those who have weighed in on *Laura* have gleefully changed their minds time and again. Vladimir Nabokov's biographer Brian Boyd, who has seen the novel and initially advised burning, publicly changed his mind. He recently told *The Times* reporter Stephanie Marsh, "It is very fragmentary, people shouldn't expect to be swept away. He is doing some very brilliant things with the prose, the story just flashes by, the characters are rather unappealing. It seems a technical tour de force, just as Shakespeare's later works where he is extending his own technique in very, very concentrated ways."[2] A more skeptical Vladimir Meskin, docent at the Moscow State Pedagogical University, told Viktor Borzenko of *Novye Izvestiia* on April 28, 2008: "Once the author made his request, that meant that the publication of the text would ruin the overall system of his life's work." The Swiss safe, Meskin concludes, is the best possible place for the unfinished work.

Making *Laura* widely available would mean subjecting Nabokov to a new wave of imperfect criticism. Dmitri hinted at his apprehension about Nabokov critics in an interview with Suellen Stringer-Hye for the *Nabokov Online Journal*, "Of course, one of the most offensive critical cracks was that of certain dour post-Soviet pundits affirming that Lolita and other writings of Nabokov's suggest a malignant contempt for America and all things American. Nothing could be further from the truth."

One is apt to be reminded of the final scene in *Pale Fire*, in which the critic and madman Kinbote snatches John Shade's manuscript, and the latter is shot down, leaving the fate of his last masterpiece in imperfect hands. "My commentary to this poem," Kinbote writes, "now in the hands of my readers, represents an attempt to sort out those echoes and wavelets of fire, and pale phosphorescent hints, and all the many subliminal debts to me."[3] The text that remains might be the work of a maniac, a genius, or some collaboration between the two, John Shades' ghost (or the ghost of his child) reappearing to dictate changes to the text. Nabokov's ghost, or the shadow of it, has also conversed with Dmitri. In a February 15, 2008, instalment of the Australian Broadcasting Corporation's "Book Talk," the host, Ramona Koval, cited an apparent change of heart:

> "To wit, and quite independently of any words anyone might have wanted to put in my mouth or thoughts into my brain, I have decided that my father, with a wry and fond smile, might well have contradicted himself upon seeing me in my present situation and said, 'Well, why don't you mix the useful with the pleasurable? That is, say or do what you like but why not make some money on the damn thing?'"[4]

But wait, Dmitri Vladimirovich – before you dash our hopes for *Laura* by publishing her, consider a proposal that would both adhere to the letter of your father's request, and give his readers a taste of the last moments of his creativity. My solution, I believe, allows for both, throwing in a bit of healthy rebellion to boot. I say, translate the text (into whatever language you please). That is, change every word of the original without burning its content. Let translation save *Laura* and its mystery, not so much from the furnace, as from the kind of criticism that plagued your father at the end of his life. Precisely the uncertainty of translation – its invitation to doubt accuracy and meaning – would offer a glimpse of Nabokov's poetic narrative, and an excuse for the failings of an unfinished plot.

Dmitri Nabokov, upon graduating cum laude from Harvard, became an opera singer. His musical career did not eliminate his responsibility to a close-knit literary family, which included working with his father on a series of Russian–English translations – both his father's works and samples from the Russian literary canon. "Nabokov naturally preferred his son to any other translator," Boyd tells us in *The American Years*. "Dmitri accepted his father's principle of literality and knew that an undulating or knobby Russian phrase should not be flattened into plain English. Where other translators often felt Nabokov's exacting corrections and innumerable rephrasings a threat to their professional competence, Dmitri could simply welcome the improvements."[5] Four years ago, at an auction in Geneva, Dmitri, the last heir to Vladimir Nabokov's estate and legacy, was forced to sell his family's library. According to a May 6, 2004 *New York Times* article, among these was a copy of *Despair*, inscribed: "For Dmitri. From translator to translator. With love. Vladimir Nabokov. Papa. Montreux. 1966."[6]

Ironically, it seems to have been translation, in part, that kept Vladimir Nabokov from finishing Laura. Boyd tells us,

> Early in October, Nabokov began translating for the last volume of his Russian stories, *Details of a Sunset*. Dmitri had prepared draft translations of some stories, while his father tackled others on his own. But the chief task facing him for the winter was the remainder of the harrowing French *Ada*. He knew he had to rid himself of all his translation before settling down to the new novel "that keeps adding nightly a couple of hours to my habitual insomnias."

The burden of translation indeed weighed heavily in Nabokov's life, absorbing, delaying, but perhaps, at times, accounting for, the author's genius. Walter Benjamin, who, in his 1923 "The Task of the Translator" set the tone for theories of translation that would dominate the past century, suggests that a translation adds to our understanding of the concept behind the original text, issuing out of a work's afterlife: "For a translation comes later than the original, and since the important works of world literature never find their chosen translators at the time of their origin, their translation marks their stage of continued life."[7]

Which returns me to my plea: If it has been so painful to give *Laura* life, why not go straight for an afterlife? Lose the text in translation. Or rather, let us find it there. After all, as Boyd informs us, a provisional title for the novel was *The Original of Laura: Dying is Fun*.

Solomonic wisdom? The Modern Hebrew poet Chaim Nachman Bialik has famously compared reading a translation to kissing a bride through her veil. Generations of readers would never know how thick the fabric is through which they are kissing Laura. But speculation would also force those critics who, driven by referential mania, have attempted to blend Nabokov's past with his fiction, to take a step back, to consider the possibility of a translator's faulty wording. Students of Nabokov would wonder whether Dmitri (or whoever has done the deed) has missed something, added something of his own, tricked them. Mystics would enjoy the possibility that Nabokov, appearing in dreams, dictated the translation himself. Hungry fans would read this book differently from the others, humbled by their obscured view. Granted, the translator may be left with nightmares of inadequacy, haunted by Nabokov's compendium of criticism of his fellow translators. (Found in his posthumous *Selected Letters*: "I can do nothing with Constance Garnett's dry shit."[8] "Paraphrases are related to the original text as dreams are to reality, and Miss Deutsche's version is little more than a nightmare."[9])

But in compensation for a daunting translator's task, this rendition will never be compared to an original. To relieve the burden of responsibility, why not commission two translations, or three, or seventy-two?

Once this is done, Dmitri Vladimirovich, burn *Laura* in good faith. Or tell us you did.

TWO YEARS LATER[10]

The dedication to *The Original of Laura, or, Dying is Fun*, is in Dmitri Nabokov's hand: "To all the worldwide contributors of opinion, comment, and advice, of whatever its stripe, who imagined that their views, sometimes deftly expressed, might somehow change mine."[11]

For the last few years Mr. Nabokov, son of the literary giant, has been on the receiving end of much eccentric, unsolicited advice. Should his father's unfinished final novel be burned, as the author had requested before his death in 1977, or should the ailing author's instructions, like the words of Kafka and Gogol before him, be ignored and his work spared? I too had my say, and *Open Letters* indulgently published it. My Solomonic two cents – publish a translation of the novel but burn the original – were intended to comment less upon the Nabokov estate than on a useful potential of translation. The semi-transparent veil of translation, I argued, might protect the deceased from ruthless misinterpretation.

Two years later I am grateful to Dmitri Vladimirovich for his decision not only to publish *Laura*, but to publish it in just the form in which his father had abandoned it: in note-cards, facsimiles of the author's stained originals, perforated for easy removal, reshuffling and contemplation. These cards are deciphered in typed footnotes so that, like the reader of *Pale Fire*, *Laura*'s reader must choose whether to begin with the upper or lower portion of each page. Reading *Laura* from start to finish (admittedly, the typed lower half), I was surprised at how captivated I became by the story, disjointed and confusing though it often is. And should a disgruntled Vladimir Nabokov return from the dead he could hardly rebuke his son, who has been careful to discourage misinterpretation, not by obscuring *Laura*, but by publishing it in what could never be mistaken for a final draft. The book practically shouts, "interpret away, but you'll never know how it ends."

Laura braids three narratives, the first of which chronicles the life of Flora, daughter of a photographer and a dancer, desired in childhood by one "incidental, but not unattractive" Hubert H. Hubert. (Unlike her distant cousin Lolita, who wanders into Humbert's trap, Flora kicks Hubert in the groin, putting an early end to his advances.) The grown-up Flora is somewhat fickle and annoying. Her lover, the impressively fat, eminent neurologist Dr. Philip Wild, invents a fictional version of her named Laura, who flows seamlessly from Flora: "Her exquisite bone structure immediately slipped into a novel–became in fact the secret structure of that novel, besides supporting a number of poems." The creation of Laura, however, marks the disappearance of Flora. Wild, like his near-namesake Wilde's foppish Dorian Gray, must choose between a portrait and its original: "The 'I' of the book is a neurotic and hesitant man of letters, who destroys his mistress in the act of portraying her." The third, most poignant, strip of narrative finds an author studying self-erasure, attempting to psychologically master death by visualizing his own slow disappearance. This author is Dr. Wild, presumably, though it's impossible not to envision Nabokov. The chapter heading "Settling for a single line" teases the reader with an allusion to the Greek artist Apelles' famous determination to go "no day without painting a line." But Nabokov's narrator refers to a single vertical line, which represents the protagonist's body: "[A] simple vertical line across my field of inner vision could be chalked in an instant, and what is more I could mark lightly by transverse marks the three divisions of my physical self: legs, torso, and head" (137).

The novel is heavy with sexual innuendo, from Flora's conception, childhood, and translation into Laura, to the sheer physicality in Wild's experimental self-erasure. If he cannot control the growth and disappearance of his flesh, Dr. Wild aims to at least preserve his carnal desire, through *Laura, ad aeternum*. By preserving Laura, he preserves "the mouth she made automatically while using that towel to wipe her thighs after the promised withdrawal" (25).

If Philip Wild's book is about sex, Nabokov's *Original* is about art. It is about which gifts are preserved, and the artist's loss of any say in the matter. Most of the characters in *The Original of Laura* are artists, and a great many have misplaced, miscalculated or misinterpreted their artistic gifts. The most famous Nabokovian signposts appear on these cards. Devoted readers will appreciate the trademark wordplay, recognize the sophisticated pedophile, the game of chess, and Pushkin's *Onegin*. Annabel Lee, who haunts Humbert Humbert's memory in *Lolita*, is transformed into *Aurora* Lee, a reminder of the Baltic Sea Cruiser, *Avrora*, from Nabokov's native Petersburg, and a rhyming triplet with our doubled heroin FLaura. Annabel is, of course, on loan from Poe:

> For the moon never beams without bringing me dreams
> Of the beautiful Annabel Lee;
> And the stars never rise but I feel the bright eyes
> Of the beautiful Annabel Lee;
> And so, all the night-tide, I lie down by the side
> Of my darling – my darling – my life and my bride,
> In the sepulchre there by the sea,
> In her tomb by the sounding sea.[12]

Dr. Philip Wild, too, has a moon-lit dream in which Aurora reveals her ambiguous sex: "At the height of your guarded ecstasy I thrust my cupped hand from behind between your consenting thighs and felt the sweat-stuck folds of a long scrotum and then, further in front, the droop of a short member" (203–5).

The unexpected male organ (which may shock the reader into discomfort, titillation, or confusion), beyond muddying the protagonist's sexuality, hints at his oddly masturbatory pleasure in studying his own body. Lover and self, *fille* and phallus, become one and the same. Nabokov and Poe scholars will no doubt observe that Dr. Wild's doubled muse, like Poe's Annabel, is not "*wife* and bride" but "life and bride."

When confronted with Dr. Wild's novel, Flora cannot bring herself to open it. An acquaintance insists, "Oh, but I simply must find that passage for you. It's not quite at the end. You'll scream with laughter. It's the craziest death in the world" (227).

Vladimir Nabokov's death, too, comes not quite at the end. As he wrote in his autobiography, "Initially, I was unaware that time, so boundless at first blush, was a prison." But if the walls of time closed for Nabokov in 1977, the gift of his note-cards to his survivors comes remarkably close to the kind of echo from the other side Nabokov's characters strained to make heard – a deceased author narrates *Transparent Things*; the departed Humbert Humbert narrates *Lolita* through a diary; Cincinnatus C. leaves the arena following his own beheading.

When I removed the cards (surely you didn't expect me to leave them on their pages?), I'll admit I was unable to glean much meaning beyond what I had gotten from their more legible, typed shadows. The odd spelling patterns, the Cyrilloid handwriting and many blotted out words distracted me from the sense of the novel. (However, the cavity left by the dislodged note-cards is a delightful little casket, a hiding place for a Fabergé egg or a resting place for a butterfly.) Shuffling the cards did little for the already charmingly fragmented plot. Having reached the limits of my imagination I solicited the help of 34 smart undergraduates who had only a few days earlier signed up for ten weeks' worth of Nabokov (not including *Laura*). Passing out the cards I asked how they would read them. Their answers were lucid and, unlike the referential mania[13] I contracted in reading this book from front to back, showed fresh insight into Nabokov's last lines.

Genius Erased[1]

MICHAEL ANTMAN

Here, at last, is *Laura*. The most eagerly awaited literary novel of this fledgling century is the posthumous and fragmentary work of the greatest writer of the second half of the last century, Vladimir Nabokov, who specified that it be burned if left uncompleted at his death.

Nonetheless, though it's as unfinished as any book that calls itself a "book" could possibly be – and after considerable controversy and quarrel about whether to give greater weight to Nabokov's wishes or those of his ardent fans – it is here.

From *Ada* to Zembla, Nabokov's oeuvre is distinctly uneven, though that is like asserting that the Alps are uneven. His peaks – *Pale Fire*; *Pnin*; *Lolita*; his classic memoir *Speak, Memory*; many of his short stories; and portions of his Russian-language novels *Glory* and *The Gift* – are works of empyrean brilliance, and even his lesser productions (except, maybe, for the unreadable *Ada*) range far above those of nearly all of his rivals.

What little of *The Original of Laura* that Nabokov was able to complete before his death in 1977 in Lausanne, Switzerland is not anywhere near these high points of English and Russian literature, and, it is likely, never would have been, even had he lived for another decade. In the book's introduction, Nabokov's son Dmitri, who edited this volume, describes *The Original of Laura* as "an embryonic masterpiece whose pockets of genius were beginning to pupate here and there on his ever-present index cards."[2] But it is no disrespect to either the elder or younger Nabokov to note that the "embryonic" part of this formulation is infinitely more apropos than the "masterpiece" part.

Would *Laura* ever have soared? The book's very themes argue strongly against it.

The Original of Laura's parenthetical subtitle, *Dying is Fun*, would likely not have survived Nabokov's final draft, but it does hint at one of the odd and off-putting preoccupations of this novel, self-obliteration, if not exactly suicide, that takes the unlikely form of apotemnophilia (deliberate self-amputation of healthy limbs), here implausibly accomplished through self-hypnosis. Indeed, the haunting final words of this book, in Nabokov's own handwriting, are "efface," "expunge," "erase," "delete," "rub out," "wipe out," and, lastly, "obliterate." The words gave me a chill, but perhaps for extra-literary reasons; it isn't hard to see them as Nabokov's own half-relieved and half-embittered ruminations as this most alive of all writers sensed his time on earth fading away.

Dmitri confirms in the introduction that "[d]uring the last months of his life in the Lausanne hospital, Nabokov was working feverishly on the book, impervious to ... his own suffering ... [including] incessant inflammations under and around his toenails. At times, he felt almost as if he would rather be rid of them altogether than undergo tentative pedicures from the nurses, and the compulsion to correct them and seek relief by painfully digging at the digits himself. We shall recognize, in *Laura*, some echoes of these torments" (xvi).

In *The Original of Laura*, Nabokov *père* introduces this theme with a bit of wry Proustian foolery:

> I was enjoying a petit-beurre with my noontime tea when the droll configuration of that particular bisquit's margins set into motion a train of thought that may have occurred to the reader even before it occurred to me. He knows already how much I disliked my toes. An ingrown nail on one foot and a corn on the other were now pestering me. Would it no[t] be a brilliant move, thought I, to get rid of my toes by sacrificing them to an experiment that only cowardness [sic] kept postponing? ... I dipped a last petit-beurre in my tea, swallowed the sweet mush and resolutely started to work on my wretched flesh. (157–8)

Later, the tone turns even stranger; the narrator writes that "the process of dying by auto-dissolution afforded the greatest ecstasy known to man."

The plot of *The Original of Laura* is a little hard to follow, which is not at all surprising, and not at all the fault of V. Nabokov, given that these handwritten notes, which he didn't want published at all, constitute far less than even a first draft – no more than an hour or two of reading in all. Much of the writing is beautiful, but the overall effect of reading this holograph, with its elisions and eerie allusions and frequent vaguenesses, makes it seem less like notes for a novel than the accurate transcription of a dream. [...] The whole dirty ball of wax created by Nabokov's conflation of Humbert Humbert and Hubert Hubert and Philip Wild and other ugly adult males – possibly, in Nabokov's mind, including himself in his latter years – creates a self-referential narrative structure with very little light or air. Other, that is, than the very depictions of youthful female beauty that so obsessed Nabokov in *Lolita*, in his short proto-*Lolita* novella *The Enchanter*, and here: "She was an extravagantly slender girl. Her ribs showed. The conspicuous knobs of her hipbones framed a hollowed abdomen, so flat as to belie the notion of "belly"... The cup-sized breasts of that 24-year-old impatient beauty seemed a dozen years younger than she, with those pale squinty nipples and fine form" (14–15).

Flora becomes the subject of a fictional novel (if you know what I mean) called *My Laura*, whose narrator is "a neurotic and hesitant man of letters, who destroys his mistress in the act of portraying her. Statically – if one can put it that way – the portrait is a faithful one. Such fixed details as her trick of opening her mouth when toweling her inguen or of closing her eyes when smelling an inodorous rose are absolutely true to the original" (121).

This, then, is the "original of Laura." And the self-referentialism, at which Nabokov excelled, eventually begins to shade into self-disgust, as every attempt by the "author" of *My Laura*, and of *The Original of Laura*, to depict the beauty of female adolescence inevitably and simultaneously creates a portrait of ugly male obsession. *Lolita*, in spite of its inherently distasteful male protagonist and subject matter, was a miraculous act of conjuring; it is hard to believe that this attempted repeat performance could ever have been the same.

The fictional *My Laura*, Nabokov writes, "was promptly torn apart by a book reviewer in a leading newspaper. It grimly survived and to the accompaniment of muffled grunts on the part of the librarious fates, its invisible hoisters, it wriggled up to the top of the bestsellers' list then started to slip, but stopped at a midway step in the vertical ice" (117)." That may have been Nabokov's fictionalized rendering of the fate of *Lolita* (which was in fact a big bestseller in its time), or it may have been his forecast, probably more accurate, for *The Original of Laura*.

The Original of Laura is published in an unusual form. The top portion of each page contains a scored reproduction of one of the hundred-and-a-handful index cards that Nabokov used to compose the partial first draft, so that we can see his own handwriting. Underneath each index card is a typeset transcription, though Nabokov's writing is rarely hard to read.

The scoring is employed so that the reader can remove and shuffle the cards, according to a note on the text, "as the author likely did when he was writing the novel." This seems pointless, even if one is in the mood to play a game of po-mo 52 pick-up. Nabokov did intend the book to ultimately have shape and form, and even numbered the index cards, so that the order of the pages in the present manuscript would seem to be the best guess as to the novel's ultimate shape and form, however incomplete it may be.

On the other hand, removing all the cards makes the book a lot lighter without rendering it any less readable. And, at the same time, it creates a nifty rectangular cavity for smuggling an actual deck of playing cards inside the book, although into where, and for whom, isn't easy to say.

Ultimately, I believe it would take a heroic effort of rationalization and cognitive dissonance to represent this assemblage of notes and odd obsessions as a masterwork, or as a satisfying culmination of Nabokov's incredible career.

But Dmitri Nabokov's eventual decision to publish these notes, abetted by a long and intelligently argued campaign by the author Ron Rosenbaum, was ultimately a good one.

It is, after all, Nabokov.

This is not an easy book to rate. As a reminder of a great writer's genius and obsessions, for its historical value, for its fragments of beautiful prose, and as a paper *objet d'art* utterly unreplicable by any flat slab of plastic, *The Original of Laura* is a ten. As an actual work of literature, it's no more than a four.

Hence, after averaging, seven. As a posthumous gift, that is more than enough.

A Curiosity for Nabokov's Fans[1]

JAMES MARCUS

In the fall of 1976, a newspaper contacted Vladimir Nabokov in his Swiss refuge and asked him which books he had recently read. He responded with three typical titles: Dante's *Inferno* (in Charles Singleton's deliciously literal translation), a big, fat book about butterflies, and his own work-in-progress, *The Original of Laura.*

The latter project had preoccupied him over the summer, despite a serious illness. It was, he told his correspondent, "completed in my mind." The revisions went on while he was confined to a hospital bed, a febrile process he describes in some detail in his *Selected Letters*: "I must have gone through it some fifty times and in my diurnal delirium kept reading it aloud to a small dream audience in a walled garden. My audience consisted of peacocks, pigeons, my long dead parents, two cypresses, several young nurses crouching around, and a family doctor so old as to be almost invisible."[2]

Here was a description to whet the appetite of every Nabokov fanatic. If that's how he discussed the book, the actual product had to be beyond imagining. Alas, the author died of congestive bronchitis in July 1977. And although he may have completed *The Original of Laura* in his mind, he had managed to transcribe only a small portion of the book onto index cards.

Those elegantly scribbled cards went into a Swiss vault, and then a long tug of war began. Nabokov had asked for the sketchy product to be burned after his death. His wife, Véra, who died in 1991, couldn't bring herself to destroy his final work. Nor could his son, Dmitri, who eventually let drop a few stray comments about the book to interviewers. This dutiful son was vague about his father's last effort, but he did allow that it was "the most concentrated distillation of [Nabokov's] creativity."

Increasingly, readers wondered whether this Holy Grail would ever be shared with the public. The answer arrived at by Dmitri Nabokov, after many years of agonized dithering, turns out to be yes. A 5,000-word excerpt appears in *Playboy* (a venue hotly defended by Dmitri, who noted that his father always enjoyed the skin magazine's cartoons).

And now we have *The Original of Laura* in its entirety – not so much a book as a devotional object, which photographically reproduces every single index card and even allows the reader to punch out these perforated simulacra and shuffle through them, just as the author did.[3]

And what about, you know, the book? To be honest, the lavish packaging is more than a little disproportionate. *The Original of Laura* begins in the speedy, sexy, impressionistic vein of Nabokov's late work. The heroine, Flora, is at a party, whose brittle atmosphere the author nails in a single sentence: "The party seemed to have degenerated into a lot of sober eyes staring at her with nasty compassion from every corner, every cushion and ashtray, and even from the hills of the spring night framed in the open french window" (5).

Flora is married to an older, fatter and considerably unhappier neurologist named Philip Wild, who has given the party a miss. Unencumbered by her fun-hating husband, Flora scurries over to a borrowed apartment and has a sexual encounter with a partner not worth describing – or possibly with no partner at all.

At once we are given to understand that Flora, with her protective carapace of contempt, is not only the heart of the work but is also herself a walking, talking, fornicating metaphor. "Her exquisite bone structure," we read, "immediately slipped into a novel – became in fact the secret structure of that novel, besides supporting a number of poems" (15). No doubt we are encountering the original of *The Original of Laura*, who the enchanting author will now put through her metafictional paces.

Wrong. Nabokov zips through the early history of his heroine, complete with a sticky-fingered stepfather named Hubert H. Hubert (surely that rings a bell). But then, about halfway through his stack of index cards, he veers off in a new direction. Delectable, damaged Flora is rudely discarded.

Instead, the focus switches to Philip Wild, who is determined to kill himself. What he has in mind is a strange process of subtraction: He imagines himself as a kind of stick figure on a mental blackboard, then slowly erases parts of his body, starting with his toes. Dying, he imagines, will be fun, since "auto-dissolution afforded the greatest ecstasy known to man" (171).

Nabokov was seventy-seven years old and in failing health when he wrote those words. It is understandable that death suddenly struck him as a more urgent topic than Flora's sexual betrayals and metaphoric malleability. He was staring at the end himself. The problem is that Wild's portion of the narrative consists largely of jotted notes. Some cards include just a few words, while others seem to be bits and bobs copied out of the *Oxford English Dictionary* or other reference books. Of course, they give us some precious insight into Nabokov's compositional methods. And there are glimpses, here and there, of his own physical trials, all the more moving for being unvarnished. But their scholarly interest far outweighs their value as art.

To be blunt: As a novel – even as the sketch of a novel, with operating instructions enclosed – *The Original of Laura* is largely an exercise in frustration. There are enough Nabokovian touches, at least in the earlier section, to tantalize any devotee of the English language. But if you want to see the author truly reckon with the joys of dissolution, turn to the last page of *Transparent Things*, in which he addresses "not the crude anguish of physical death but the incomparable pangs of the mysterious mental manoeuvre needed to pass from one state of being to another." It doesn't get more original than that.

Deaths of the Authors[1]

THOMAS KARSHAN

This November [of 2009], Vladimir Nabokov will have a new novel out. It's quite an achievement, you might have thought, for someone who died 32 years ago. But then Nabokov died and reinvented himself many times, and one could be forgiven for wondering if he just staged his death in 1977, and slipped off into another identity, like Elvis in the popular imagination; or like Sebastian Knight, John Shade, or any of the other escape artists who populate Nabokov's own novels. And perhaps *The Original of Laura*, the novel that he left unfinished, when his heart supposedly gave out, is not really unfinished at all, but a non finito, that is, an art work that feigns incompletion. And so, perhaps to justify its aesthetic, Nabokov had to pretend to die. After all, ... *Laura* is subtitled "Dying is Fun," and tells the story of an ageing novelist, Philip Wild, who is trying to erase himself, using the rubber at the end of his pencil, starting from his toes and working upwards. To call ... *Laura*, as Penguin are doing, "A novel in fragments" may be to do more than state the dull fact that it is unfinished.

Such thoughts are absurd, but no less attractive for that – and considerably more Nabokovian than the boring old ethical debate provoked by the decision made by Nabokov's son Dmitri to publish *Laura*'s dying fragments, against his father's explicit wish that they should be burned. The interesting issue, to my mind, is not ethical, but theoretical. As every humanities undergraduate now knows, Roland Barthes, in his famous 1967 essay "The Death of the Author," declared that writing is a kind of self-annihilation or death – not an act of self-discovery or self-expression, not a covenant with immortality: "Writing is that neutral, composite, oblique space where our subject slips away, the negative where all identity is lost, starting with the very identity of the body writing. [... T]he voice loses its origin, the author enters into his own death, writing begins."[2] Or to put it in Nabokov's terms, one writes oneself not with the graphite at the nub of one's pencil, but with the eraser at the other end.

For Nabokov, being a writer involved many deaths. He had died once, in the late 1930s, when he killed off Sirin, the pen-name under which he had written his Russian works. But the death of Sirin is only the apex of a long series of authorial deaths in Nabokov's writing of the late 1930s and early 1940s. In "The Paris Poem" (1943), for instance, Nabokov imagines how "now and then / one's heart starts clamouring: Author! Author!," only to receive the reply, "He is not in the house, gentlemen." In the 1939 story "Vasiliy Shishkov," Nabokov imagines meeting an author who wants to compose "A Survey of Pain and Vulgarity," only to leave a manuscript in the author's hands and vanish. In the accompanying poem, "The Poets," signed Vasiliy Shishkov, the Russian poets announce their departure from the world: "into a region – name it as you please: / wilderness, death, disavowal of language, / or maybe simpler: the silence of love." The death of the author is here one link in a chain of metaphors, a point Nabokov develops at the end of his 1947 novel *Bend Sinister*, where the author, having saved the hero Krug, concedes that "the immortality I had conferred on the poor fellow was a slippery sophism, a play upon words," adding, "But the very last lap of his life has been happy and it had been proven to him that death was but a question of style."

Nabokov was only one of several great Modernists who in the late 1930s were thinking about the question of style embodied by the death of the author. In Jorge Luis Borges' 1939 story, "Pierre Menard, Author of *Don Quixote*," the title character decides to copy out several chapters of Miguel de Cervantes' *Don Quixote* (1605–15). Word for word, Menard's Quixote is identical to the original, but it is a different book, since the same phrases mean something completely different when written in the 1930s to what they meant when written in the Spanish Golden Age; or also to someone who reads them while bearing their original linguistic context in mind. The meaning of a text is given neither by author nor words alone, but by both in enigmatic combination with the reader's expectations and the assumptions of the linguistic context in which one reads it. In *Finnegans Wake* (1939), James Joyce repeatedly imagines the author as a mere forger, claiming authority for words not his own, and the book as "an epical forged cheque on the public."

Barthes, Michel Foucault and other French post-Structuralist thinkers [in] the late 1960s, were, then, reporting on a death that had taken place 30 years earlier – a death first foreseen in the 19th century by the poet Stéphane Mallarmé, who wrote in "Crisis in Poetry" (1895), "if the poem is to be pure, the poet's voice must be stilled and the initiative taken by the words themselves, which will be set in motion as they meet unequally in collision," so that "the poet will be absent." Barthes is clear about Mallarmé's importance; Borges' Menard is a devotee of Mallarmé and his Symbolist followers; Joyce and Nabokov were both Mallarméans.

So was Marcel Duchamp, whose apparent disavowal of art-making for chess must rank as the most famous disappearing act of 20th-century art. Duchamp's ready-mades take to its limit Mallarmé's principle that the poet or artist should withdraw from the scene. Art no longer inheres in the will and craft of the deep-souled artist but in the multi-hued flow of possible thoughts that the infinity of possible viewers can bring to the piece – just as in chess an almost unlimited number of games can be played on the fixed system of 64 squares and 32 pieces. That is why Duchamp, like Nabokov, loved chess. It was the perfect model for an art whose appeal, as Duchamp liked to say, would be no longer "retinal," but intellectual. "I am sick," he said, "of the expression *bête comme un peintre* – stupid as a painter." Duchamp meant his most famous work, *The Bride Stripped Bare by her Bachelors, Even* (1915–23), to consist not only of *The Large Glass*, the art-object, but also of the accompanying notes, entitled *The Green Box*.

The road from here to Conceptualism and high theory seems clear. As Kazimir Malevich said, "The artist who wants to develop art beyond its painting possibilities is forced to theory and logic," a comment the Conceptual artist Joseph Kosuth liked to quote. Still, a view of Duchamp's legacy which understands its roots in Mallarmé's poetry and which sees how that poetry developed into Modernist literature might see a different path out of Duchamp to the no-exit motorway that finishes with Conceptualism. Yes, the craft-object evanesces in Duchamp. Painting or etching on glass, as he does in *The Bride Stripped Bare*, Duchamp lets in air, light, emptiness, like Mallarmé, who wanted a "matchless nothingness," and said that the poet "writes upon our minds or upon pure space" so that it is not “the paper-knife” but “our consciousness alone” which “gives us possession” of the poem. Yet in a magnificently double-edged passage of his magnum opus, *A Throw of the Dice* (1897), Mallarmé wrote that “RIEN [...] N’AURA EU LIEU [...] QUE LE LIEU” [“Nothing will have taken place but the place”]. His verse is nothingness. But that nothingness is a something, not an absence. “The ‘blanks’,” Mallarmé said, “in effect, assume importance and are what is immediately most striking.” It is those blank spaces between words which are the material of Mallarméan art, the art that follows the death of the author. They are hard to see, and we need theories, whether Mallarmé’s or Barthes’, which, like night-vision goggles, can make them perceptible. It is the blanks which assume importance, like the line which runs across the middle of Duchamp’s *The Bride Stripped Bare*, or the white space between the poem and commentary of Nabokov’s 1962 novel *Pale Fire*.

The Critics' *Laura*

MARIJETA BOZOVIC

RECEPTION

On 17 November 2009, Nabokov's posthumous last work, or the long-awaited fragments thereof, was released into the arms of the reading public. To say that a critical feeding frenzy followed would be an understatement; indeed, the pond had begun to froth years in advance.

The reviews and excerpts included in this volume offer a representative slice, but are far from the first (or last) word. Long before the publication of *Laura*, as volume editor Yuri Leving has pointed out,[1] there was already something to talk about. Dmitri Nabokov had ensured continuing public interest in his father's unfinished last manuscript by dropping contradictory hints about its impending fate fairly regularly since the late 1990s. In 2005, *The New York Times* reported that Dmitri had resolved to burn *Laura*, setting off a media campaign led in part by the New York columnist Ron Rosenbaum to save Nabokov's last potential masterpiece. Much debate ensued.

The ethics and aesthetics of "Dmitri's Dilemma," so-called, were deliciously thorny and far more popularly accessible than Nabokov's actual work: to disregard a beloved dying father's last wishes, or to torch the final word of an undisputed genius? Scholars were consulted. Notables were allowed limited access to the file cards. A deluge of public statements, debates, exchanges – and an odd competition in the pages of *The Nabokovian* to identify fragments of authentic never-before-seen Nabokov from the counterfeit of fan pastiche as early as 1999 – all contributed to the furor over *Laura*. Dmitri's gambit brought Nabokov right back into the public eye, more so than the celebrations of *Lolita*'s 50th birthday (in 2005 *and* in 2008, because of that novel's stormy publication history). Today the last of this branch of Nabokovs is gone, but the books, and now the letters, continue selling.

The last five years have seen Nabokov "venerated in exhibitions, prestigious collections, and museums, and validated in record auction prices," as Leving summarizes. Without what amounted to a free publicity campaign, without "interviews on National Public Radio, the British Broadcasting Corporation, the Canadian Broadcasting Corporation, and the Australian Broadcasting Corporation; without Dmitri's infamous ALL-CAPITAL-LETTERED EMAILS; without the extensive blog commentary in respected online publications worldwide," the whole *Laura* dilemma would have amounted to little.[2] It is hard to imagine any comparable uproar – or consumer interest – had Dmitri Nabokov made what many would have considered a gracious and reasonable compromise by allowing the fragments of *Laura* to be published in a modest scholarly journal for the benefit of specialists.

Instead, Dmitri's choices seemed shrewdly calculated to capture the public's imagination and to increase the symbolic value not only of *Laura* but of his father's entire estate. He proved to be a natural at this game. Rosenbaum soon reported his suspicion that he had been a pawn.[3] My own guess is that Dmitri must have intended to publish *Laura* at least as early as the 1990s, and that all shows of public indecision were marketing choices just as clever as the ultimate book design. Certainly, Dmitri's showy and well-advertised decision to deposit the original file cards in a Swiss bank was hardly neutral or motivated by practicality. As Leving notes, the symbolism of depositing the manuscript in a bank, "a place where money or valuables are usually safeguarded," confirmed its value to the public: "The very mention of the storage location – especially with the 'Swiss' bank's clichéd connotations of secrecy and heightened security – imposes on *Laura* a symbolic value quite different from that of a text discovered in grandma's attic."[4]

If the goal was to make a splash, and the working premise that all publicity is good publicity, the manoeuvre paid off. There was so much to talk about that the fuming critics did not particularly need the text of *Laura*: the topoi and tenor of the debate remained much the same after as before the publication. The reviews interrogated ethics, parents' last wishes, respecting and communicating with the dead, and so forth. There were "earnest proposals to Dmitri Nabokov," as in the title of Amelia Glaser's piece for *Open Letters Monthly*; speculation as to his motives (Robert Douglas-Fairhurst quipped by quoting "Mrs. Merton's opening gambit when she interviewed Debbie McGee, 'So, Debbie, what first attracted you to the millionaire Paul Daniels?'"); and unusually personal attacks on the aging heir.[5]

Dmitri noted and commented on the media attention directed his way in the introduction to *Laura.* Responding to an imaginary reporter's question, "But why, Mr. Nabokov, why did you *really* decide to publish *Laura*?" he wrote, "Well, I am a nice guy, and, having noticed that people the world over find themselves on a first-name basis with me as they empathize with 'Dmitri's dilemma,' I felt it would be kind to alleviate their sufferings."[6] Douglas-Fairhurst, a Dickens scholar at Oxford as well as frequent contributor to *The Telegraph*, quips again that only "a wise guy" would give an answer like that.

What is evident and remarkable is the degree of identification, and of ownership, that several generations feel with regard to Vladimir Nabokov and his works. We read it in the genuine expressions of anger and anxiety that Dmitri really did manage to embarrass his brilliant dead father, in part by failing to live up to the older Nabokov ethically or æsthetically. The esteemed John Banville speaks for many when he calls Dmitri's introduction to *Laura* a "lamentable performance, stridently defensive, slippery on particulars, and frequently repellent in tone. Aping Nabokov père at his aristocratically disdainful worst, he makes jibes ... and wearily deplores the 'lesser minds' whom it has been his misfortune to encounter." The Irish novelist's wickedly funny caricature sums up much of the media response to Dmitri throughout the years: "Reading these introductory pages is like being trapped in an airless room with a priggish adolescent dressed up in his father's outsize clothes – tails, white tie, spats, and all – who expatiates on the awfulness of the masters at his school while puffing on one of Daddy's finest cigars and turning slowly green."[7] Douglas-Fairhurst reminds us that the Italian press regularly referred to Dmitri as "Lolito."

One wonders if there isn't a trace of competitiveness with Dmitri in the reactions of some of these (predominantly male) writers, scholars, and journalists, many of whom seem to see themselves in some less (or perhaps more?) direct way as Nabokov's sons. Why should the undeserving blood heir claim his father's mantle? At the very least, the question "Could I have done better in Dmitri's place?" recurs noticeably throughout the debates, statements, and critical reviews. The young Harvard English professor Leland de la Durantaye answers, "When posed the question of what I would do were I in Dmitri's position, I said what I thought then and think now, which is that I like to think that I would have placed family concerns over public ones, would have preferred a dying father's last wish to all others; that I would have chosen fire."[8]

EXPOSURE

The titles alone of the reviews that followed the publication of *The Original of Laura* sum up the rest of the story. Reviewers, journalists, and writers – including such heavyweights as Banville, Martin Amis, and Alexander Theroux – burst out with the following headlines: "The Problem with Nabokov" (Amis, *The Guardian*); "The Nabokov Mess" (Nathaniel Rich, *The Daily Beast)*; "The Master's Sputum" (Arthur Phillips, *Paste Magazine*); "Genius Erased" (Michael Antman, *PopMatters*); the directly accusatory "A Money-spinner" (Jonathan Bate, *The Telegraph*); and the expressly directive "Best to Revisit Old Nabokov than Fragments of the New" (Laura Serrano, *San Francisco Examiner*).

Among such a pile, the rare "A Generous Gift to Readers" by New York–based critic Heller McAlpin (*The Christian Science Monitor*) reads like the exception that proves the rule. Yet even McAlpin, in her very praise, finds herself using the same language as the negative reviewers. She alone appears to see *Laura*'s publication "more like a generous gift to readers than a ploy for fame or fortune," but echoes the accusations against Dmitri when she writes, "All too often, publications of half-cooked literary fragments are not just disappointing in literary terms, but seem motivated as much by greed as by the heirs' desire to keep their famous forbearer alive in print."[9]

So what are the critics criticizing? The majority position holds that the fragments of *Laura* should not have been published; that the half-cooked novella is in fact disappointing (or worse) in literary terms; and that Dmitri's motivation to publish was precisely a ploy for fortune and fame. Underwriting their protests is a sense that Nabokov has been indecently exposed by the one man he should have been able to trust. More than one review grimly includes a variation on the phrase, "the deed is done."[10]

Yet these same reviewers hardly protest, say, the inherent betrayal of publishing Shakespeare's quarto and folio texts, or even the clever recombining of the two practised by most critical editions of the plays – not to mention by theatre companies. Most readers of Kafka or Virgil do not harbour similar resentments against Max Brod or the Roman literary executors halted in their deliberations by Augustus's *deus ex machina* intervention to save the *Aeneid*.[11] Just as few would wish away the great literary fragments of the Romantic and modernist eras, from Coleridge's "Kubla Khan" to Proust's monumental and unfinished *À la recherche du temps perdu*. And Nabokov himself took great pleasure in adding to Pushkin's unfinished 1819 narrative poem "Rusalka."

But some fragments are more literary than others. Durantaye writes, "As Nabokov's century discovered like none before it, fragments have a poetry all their own – from the bits of Sappho found in an Egyptian garbage heap or of Catullus used to bung up a medieval wine cask, to the intentionally fragmentary forms of Ezra Pound, or, more recently, Anne Carson."[12] However, this does not guarantee that *The Original of Laura* will cut it. The sparseness of the existing text, the world's judgment of Dmitri as "dressed-up in his father's outside clothes," and, above all, the enormous profit presumably at stake make the affair resonate very differently from the parallels with Kafka, Virgil, and Coleridge that Dmitri himself suggested in his introduction.

From one reviewer after another comes the rebuttal that *The Original of Laura* is not equivalent to the vast majority of Kafka's oeuvre; that Dmitri (it remains personal) was no Max Brod; and Nabokov hardly Kafka. Nabokov was not "someone who suffered from bouts of depression or was inclined to underestimate his accomplishments. Nabokov was a genius and he knew it," writes Durantaye.[13] By extension, Nabokov would have known – and did know – not to publish *Laura* because it simply was not good enough yet. (Amis, Banville, and Theroux would disagree with Durantaye, at least to the extent that they share reservations about Nabokov's "late period" more generally; but I will save their preoccupation with the figure of the aging writer for last in this section.)

Young American novelist Nathaniel Rich differentiates *Laura* from "unfinished novels that contain long, continuous sections of writing, from which it is possible to apprehend the larger work's subject matter, scope, and ambition, however imperfect the execution." These pages are instead merely "the embryonic jottings made in preparation for a novel – long before it's certain that there's even a novel to be written."[14] Rich argues that the entire ethical debate joined by "newspaper book reporters the world over" has been revealed as silly, and that "the furious controversy over the manuscript's publication was waged on false grounds."[15]

Banville leads the pack in shifting blame from the putative author of the embryonic jottings to the Nabokov who supervised the metamorphosis of *Laura* from notes into book. In even the title, or subtitle, Banville suspects Dmitri's hand: "*Dying is Fun* has an appropriately jaunty, Nabokovian ring to it, but did the author himself, or his son, decide that it should be part of the finished title? The book comes to us out of a nebulous region."[16] Vladimir Nabokov, the ultimate novelist-as-auteur of the twentieth century, finds himself posthumously involved in a glib and glossy collaboration. Academic, writer (and, incidentally, Oxford Provost) Jonathan Bate suggests that the publishing house really invented *Laura*: "Penguin has created an extraordinarily handsome book, in which the index cards are reproduced in perforated form so that deranged Nabokovian readers can press them out and shuffle them into random order ... This is nonsense that would have horrified Nabokov, the supreme craftsman."[17]

In fact, the packaging of *Laura* stirs a mix of admiration and resentment that no reviewer fails to comment on. Banville reserves praise for the "Nabokovianly named" Chip Kidd, who made out of *The Original of Laura* a "triumph of the book-maker's art." He concedes that some "will deplore the production as gimmicky, but the greatest magicians depend on gimmicks for their most elegant illusions."[18] McAlpin, all admiration, calls the entire package a "dazzlingly clever presentation of the material" and suggests that Kidd "has designed a format that reminds us forcefully, in graphic terms, that *The Original of Laura* is a work in progress and not an ordinary manuscript."[19] For McAlpin, the design problem, and Kidd's clever solution, are about remaining true to the material.

American novelist Alexander Theroux, meanwhile, snorts at *Laura* as a play-kit allowing fans to play Nabokov: "As if Nabokov *shuffled* his index cards serendipitously to discern the arc of the plot!"[20] And Douglas-Fairhurst archly suggests that bookshops will be "grateful for the shrink-wrapped plastic cover that guards it from inquisitive fingers." Presumably, he writes, they hope that shrink-wrapping will keep the unwary consumer from noticing "the crafty sleight of hand that involves transforming fragments of a novel into a 'novel in fragments,' which is a little like advertising a bookcase and then delivering a box that contains a couple of saplings and a handful of misshapen screws."[21]

All of this leads to the usually unmentionable money question: *Laura* was clearly published in the hope of turning a profit. The uproar over that fact perhaps reveals less about Nabokov *père* or *fils* than about our own anxieties and delusions about the relation between art and money.

When Nabokov *père* marketed his works, it could be read as charming and funny. Theroux recalls Nabokov's witty suggestion that the ideal reader buy two copies of *Pale Fire* and cut one apart to read Kinbote's commentary next to Shade's poem: "Was his father's comically exaggerated ruse to try to sell two copies to each reader recapitulated in Dmitri's nutty suggestion that someone actually *remove and rearrange these cards* for sense?"[22] Rich unsparingly calls the perforated cards and publisher's note to remove and rearrange a "shrewd marketing strategy, not because anyone will follow this advice (they won't), but because it justifies the use of heavyweight paper and the decision to leave every other page blank, thus resulting in a 280-page hardcover and what the industry calls a higher 'price point.'"[23] Bate likewise does not hesitate to ascribe motive, cause and effect: "Now 75 years old and in need of a few bob, Dmitri has decided to publish the fragments of his father's last and unfinished novel."[24]

Dmitri offered a defensive, or over determined heap of reasons as to why he decided to publish, including an appeal to a mystical "otherforce" he could not resist. Rich snorts in response: "Otherforce, indeed: Besides a contract with Knopf, there was an excerpt in *Playboy* ('we've never paid this much for a book excerpt, ever,' acknowledged the magazine's literary editor), and the day before the book's publication, Dmitri announced he would auction off the very note cards on which *Laura* is composed (Christie's estimates a take of $400,000–$600,000)."[25]

And yet, of course, all novels published with commercial presses look to turn a profit. Dmitri himself links otherworld and financial otherforce when he suggests, in his introduction, that his father's ghost would have told him, with a "wry and fond smile," "Say or do what you like, but why not make some money on the damn thing?" But readers seem less willing to imagine his father saying such a thing.

The most provocative and interesting accusation of all is not that Dmitri has conjured up a *succès de scandale* and made considerably more money from the fragments of *Laura* than it was worth: It is that, by doing so, Dmitri and the Penguin team have seriously and unforgivably betrayed Vladimir Nabokov. (The deed is done.) Douglas-Fairhurst writes, "Tennyson's greatest fear towards the end of his life was not death, but what would happen once the 'ghouls' – biographers, critics, gossip-hounds – descended to pick him apart. He would be 'ripped open like a pig.'"[26] With *Laura,* readers have been invited to rip into Nabokov quite literally.

The violation of parental wishes appears "particularly grievous considering the horror Nabokov expressed at having his incomplete work put on public display,"[27] Durantaye puts it: "More than any great writer of his century, Nabokov was exacting about the presentation of his words and works, from his painstaking translations to his routine destruction, by fire, of preliminary drafts once his novels were complete."[28] Nabokov was perhaps the writer who least wanted to be exposed or analyzed, to relinquish control to the priers. That said, the sense of an unforgivable reveal has to be about something more than exposing the draft, for as Rich points out, the note-cards written in preparation for several Nabokov novels can easily be viewed at the Berg archives at the New York Public Library. Nabokov never gets the last word in the case of *Laura*, but perhaps there is still more at stake.

Laura shows the reader sides of Vladimir Nabokov that are "desperately sad," Banville writes, "especially as Dmitri Nabokov has informed us of the agonies his father suffered in his final months from inflammation of the toenails. It is a piece of information we could probably have done without."[29] The implication is that Dmitri sold his aged, dying father at a time when his son should most have tried to protect and hide him from the world – that *Laura* exposes Nabokov not only because it is unfinished and unpolished, but because of his already diminishing powers at the time of writing: in other words, because of the embarrassment of old age. (It is reputed that the security team keeping a close watch on Nelson Mandela does so in part to make sure that the 94-year-old secular saint does not tarnish his reputation with an impolitic slip.)

And indeed, this is what most seems to bother the most famous writer-critics. Theroux writes that *Laura* shows us "the writer's version of a great athlete in decline."[30] He adds that while it is "no surprise to discover an author in failing health losing his writerly powers. For son Dmitri, there is no such excuse."[31] And yet, Dmitri was 75 at publication and dead a mere three years later, like his father, at the age of 78.

The famously stern Martin Amis is prompted to declare: "Writers die twice: once when the body dies, and once when the talent dies."[32] For Amis, Nabokov's "meltdown of artistic self-possession" began with "that incontinent splurge," the 1969 *Ada* ("what homicide detectives call a 'burster' ... a waterlogged corpse at the stage of maximal bloat").[33] In fact, Amis spends just as much time talking about *Ada* as about *Laura* in his review article. He compares Nabokov's longest novel to *Finnegans Wake* and finds in *Ada* an equivalent moment of "decisive loss of love for the reader – a loss of comity, of courtesy" from which Nabokov never recovered. Then again, Amis writes, "When a writer starts to come off the rails, you expect skidmarks and broken glass; with Nabokov, naturally, the eruption is on the scale of a nuclear accident."[34]

As the title of the piece suggests, Amis's problem is less *The Original of Laura* than with Nabokov himself. The real dilemma from hell is not whether Dmitri should have burned this particular book, but whether we shouldn't chuck the previous three or four as well. In other words, how is one to reconcile a great love for an earlier period that feels exposed and betrayed by the style and plotlines of Nabokov's last novels? Banville, who shares Amis's taste for middle-period Nabokov, suggests that exile to America was "the biggest and best gift" a writer such as Nabokov could have received, "given his inclination toward mere cleverness and the dandyism of the boulevard." It is no surprise that Nabokov's return to Europe saw "a falling off, or at least a falling back into the bad old prewar ways."[35] And according to Bate as well, in his last novels Nabokov "was beginning to become a parody of himself"; in *Laura* the self-indulgence finally becomes "irredeemable."[36]

But the most extreme accusation by far is Amis's, when he more or less claims that Vladimir Nabokov's "little-girl theme" ("by now hardly more than a logo – part of the Nabokovian furniture, like mirrors, doubles, chess, butterflies"[37]) finally crosses the line. The logo is at last too frequent to be an accident, and for the author convincingly to remain interested in nympholepsy only as case-study. "[T]o put it at its sternest," Amis writes, "Nabokov's mind, during his last period, insufficiently honoured the innocence – insufficiently honoured the honour–of twelve-year-old girls ... This leaves a faint but visible scar on the leviathan of his corpus."[38] Theroux, who implies the same, writes with less force and judgment (even somewhat oddly) that "[i]t is charming, up to a point, that a great novelist in his last years remains so beguiled by nubile females that he must lavish his gifts upon them yet again, but it is not a cause for literary celebration."[39]

I will interject briefly that for those of us who tend to read even Nabokov's erotics as hovering between the allegoric and the episodic, the leitmotif of terrible longing for girl-children is less troubling in its recurrence. For me it has always read as a stand-in for universal and anguished desire for immortality, or at least immorality; for the object of love; for youth and desire itself; and (more clearly in *The Enchanter*) for the terrible but equally universal desire to possess, to exclusively own the beloved. This at least has explained to me why I can inhabit Humbert and his agonies with gut-wrenching force. Amis must surely accept this on some level, for he refers to nympholepsy as "'frenzy caused by desire for the unattainable' ... rightly characterized by my *Concise Oxford Dictionary* as *literary*."[40] And yet it is finally too much. *Lolita* contains its own critique, but Amis fails to find that redeeming counterpoint in the later novels. Nabokov lost his balance.

One also cannot but wonder if this triumvirate of writers, Amis, Theroux, Banville – not one under the age of 63 – is exorcising the spectre of old age with fervent wishes that Vladimir Nabokov had known when to stop.

CAPITAL

One of the most striking aspects of this volume on *Laura* is the radically different tone taken by the scholars from the critical response of reviewers. It is logical that there should be a difference: different contractual bonds tie the reviewer and scholar to the book, although both rest on certain near-mystical premises. In his afterword to this volume, Brian Boyd speaks of the trust required to read and understand a text: "For reviewers, their reluctance to trust an inchoate Nabokov text ... was compounded by their suspicion of the rationale for its publication."[41]

The critic focuses on the work itself, and needs to trust (or refuses to believe) that this is an authentic work of art – whatever that may mean. The scholar takes for granted the worth of the source, or sometimes of her own questions. The Nabokovian scholar has implicit faith in everything touched by the genius; the word *genius* itself, which has fallen out of popularity, recurs in pieces both critical and admiring in tone. Every fragment becomes a relic worthy of exegesis. James Marcus calls *Laura* "not so much a book as a devotional object," and at the same time notes that the fragments' "scholarly interest far outweighs their value as art."[42]

In "Interpreting Voids," Leving suggests that we must think about cultural capital when we think about *The Original of Laura*. Perhaps, in the final analysis, *Laura* provides a rich and useful resource for reading the ways that we read – from the frustrated close reading these fragments render impossible, to the distant readings that foreground publication and distribution over the text itself.

In other words, *Laura* calls attention to itself as a material object and consumer product, and forces us to see all those things that Vladimir Nabokov *par excellence* was so remarkably good at obscuring. More than most great modernists, he could trick us into seeing the book as platonic text (manuscripts don't burn), written for a ghost audience and not mediated by materiality, market, or even the medium itself. According to Nabokov, he composed *The Original of Laura* for a "small dream audience in a walled garden. My audience consisted of peacocks, pigeons, my long dead parents, two cypresses, several young nurses crouching around, and a family doctor so old as to be almost invisible."[43] For once, we cannot imagine it. Instead, we think of Dmitri, Penguin, designer Chip Kidd, the scholars and journalists who fought for *Laura*'s preservation, the reviewers who reviled Dmitri's decision: the entire machine of production has been exposed.

My own somewhat mischievous reading is that the critical response amounts to a protest against publishing Houdini's tricks and thereby minimizing the marvel or magic. We would dearly like to believe in genius; we would dearly like to believe in immortality. Thomas Karshan, in "Deaths of the Authors," even writes that "Nabokov died and reinvented himself many times, and one could be forgiven for wondering if he just staged his death in 1977, and slipped off into another identity." He concedes that the thought is "absurd, but no less attractive for that – and considerably more Nabokovian than the boring old ethical debate" over publication.[44]

Self-awareness is the project, one way or another, of cultural studies. *The Original of Laura* may prove a useful tool indeed, forcibly exposing not Nabokov but the book as commodity, tangible object, the product of collaboration, and something with a history and life all its own. I expect that the fragments will not only reinvigorate (or as Leving writes, rebrand) Nabokov's estate, but will also encourage scholars looking backward to apply to Nabokov's works a wider variety of critical approaches than before. Nabokov's own forceful control over interpretation often constrained readers into reading either with him or against him – but there are so many other ways to read.

McAlpin's words in the sole positive review reprinted in this volume initially sounded naive to me: "Nabokov fans and scholars have reason to thank Dmitri for his brave parental defiance in publishing this invaluable glimpse into the way his brilliant father worked."[45] But perhaps Dmitri *has* given us a new tool for Nabokov studies – and also a glimpse into our own readerly practices.

A Toolbox

The cover of the Russian pocket edition. Jacket design by Vadim Pozhidaev. (© 2011 Azbooka-Atticus Publishing Group LLC.)

The cover of the Russian de luxe edition. Jacket design by Vadim Pozhidaev. (© 2011 Azbooka-Atticus Publishing Group LLC.)

Translating *Laura*

GENNADY BARABTARLO (RUSSIAN TRANSLATOR),
MAURICE COUTURIER (FRENCH TRANSLATOR),
ANNA RAFFETTO (ITALIAN TRANSLATOR), RIEN VERHOEF
(DUTCH TRANSLATOR), AND TADASHI WAKASHIMA
(JAPANESE TRANSLATOR)

YURI LEVING: *Brian Boyd predicts that scholars of narrative for centuries will focus on the opening chapter of* The Original of Laura, *saying that its first sentence "wins no prizes as prose – plain diction, and a double concession that weakens the force of the statement – but as storytelling it astounds."*[1] *It should be noted that, for some unknown reason, the same sentence has been mutilated in the* Playboy *version: "Flora's husband ... was a writer ... – at least, after a fashion." Could you please reproduce the opening sentence of Laura in the language of your translation?*

ENGLISH: Her husband, she answered, was a writer, too – at least, after a fashion.

DUTCH: Haar man was ook schrijver, antwoordde ze – in zekere zin, tenminste.

ITALIAN: Suo marito, rispose lei, era anche uno scrittore – per lo meno a modo suo.

JAPANESE: 夫も物書きなの、と彼女は答えた――少なくとも、ある意味で。[Otto mo monokaki nano, to kanojo wa kotaeta – sukunaku tomo, aru imi de.]

FRENCH: Son mari, répondit-elle, était écrivain, lui aussi – d'une certaine façon du moins.

GERMAN: Ihr Ehemann, antwortete sie, war auch Schriftsteller – zumindest in einem gewissen Sinne.

PORTUGUESE: Seu marido, ela respondeu, era escritor rambern – ao menos sub certo aspecto.

RUSSIAN: Ее муж, отвечала она, тоже в некотором роде писатель.

GENNADY BARABTARLO: Card 95 (by the through-numeration), inscribed "First a," carries what may be a variant of the beginning ("Well, a writer of sorts" etc.) – or perhaps a rippling reflection of the beginning of the novel *My Laura*, nestled inside *Laura*.

Playboy was probably afraid that the below-brow reader would be baffled by a text opening on an unattached possessive pronoun.

TADASHI WAKASHIMA: If you translate this back into English, then you get "[My] husband is a writer, too, she answered – at least, after a fashion."

As Monika Fludenik explains, "In Japanese there is no clear syntactic difference between direct and indirect discourse."[2] In usual practice, indirect discourse is translated as direct discourse with quotational suffix 「と」 [*to*]. My translation above follows this rule, with a few exceptions.

If the original sentence is translated literally, then it begins with 「私の夫も. . . 」 [Watashi no otto mo ... (= My husband ...)]. I omitted the possessive adjective 「私の」 [watashi no (= my)]. Both are possible in everyday speech, but we must take the narrative strategies of *Laura* into consideration. In Chapter One, the narrator Ivan Vaughan almost never refers to himself as "I" [watashi], so he is properly called the absent I-narrator. The problem is, can I begin the opening sentence with the forbidden 「私」 [watashi], even if it is uttered by Flora? I am still wondering whether my choice was right or not.

The second point to consider is the ambiguous "too." When we read the opening sentence, we naturally assume that her interlocutor introduced himself as a writer prior to her answer. But still, there is a possibility, however slight it may be, that what she means is "My husband has some main occupation and he writes on the side." I assume that Nabokov intended this ambiguity because on the 95th card he wrote "Yes, he is a lecturer *too*" (italics mine) with the intention of fitting it in with the conversation depicted in the opening scene. Whatever the case may be, the reader is delayed in arriving at the right conclusion that the absent I-narrator is a writer. And, as we know well enough, such withholding of information is a typical Nabokovian strategy.

This innocent-looking "too" is a real killer for a Japanese translator. Perhaps there is no way to handle this in Japanese, and my translation unfortunately erases the ambiguity.

YURI LEVING: *Could you share your personal experience and past projects related to translating Nabokov?*

RIEN VERHOEF: In the early 1990s I made new translations of *Speak, Memory* (*Geheugen, spreek*, 1992), *King, Queen, Knave* (*Heer, vrouw, boer*, 1993), and *Lolita* (1994). They were published by the Dutch publishing house De Bezige Bij in the "Nabokov Library" (20 volumes). In 2008 I translated a short story "Natasha" ("Natasja") for *Hollands Diep*, a Dutch magazine.

TADASHI WAKASHIMA: My translations of Nabokov's works are, in the order of publication, *The Defense*, *Transparent Things* (with Akiko Nakata), *The Nabokov–Wilson Letters* (with Noichi Nakamura) and *Lolita*.

During the process of translating *Lolita*, I locked myself in my office and never went out, seven days in a row. I really felt like a "galley slave." I finished my translation on 5 August 2005 (it took two months) and suddenly realized that it was exactly fifty years after the date of John Ray Jr.'s foreword. It certainly was a strange coincidence.

ANNA RAFFETTO: My experience with Nabokov's works is twofold: as a literary editor of some Italian translations and as a professional translator.

In my editorial work since 2000 (when I started working for Adelphi publishing house), I have been attending to *Zashchita Luzhina* (*The Defense*), *Invitation to a Beheading*, *Despair*, *The Stories*, and the first volume of *Nabokov's Selected Works*, and my main task was to offer the reader a faithful translation of the definitive edition of each novel.

In the first case – *Zashchita Luzhina* – the translation, very good indeed, initially showed some contaminations between the original Russian version and the English translation by Michael Scammell; therefore I corrected some passages which did not match the Russian text by checking the Italian translation word by word. As to *Invitation*, my task was still more serious because the translator had decided to follow "mainly" the Russian version of 1934 instead of the new and final one by Dmitri and Vladimir Nabokov published in 1959, as Dmitri Nabokov and Adelphi had requested. In short, I had to retranslate the book. For *Despair*, my intervention concerned the stylistic rendering of the third edition (1965), which is considered wholly valid since the author himself had revised it. One of my most recent works is the *Stories* translated and edited by Dmitri Nabokov, and I cooperated with him in this splendid enterprise.

As a translator, I worked on *Pale Fire* (translating the poem and editing the Commentary), the short story "Christmas," and lately *Speak, Memory* and *The Original of Laura*.

Both as a translator and editor, I can say that the essential requirement to translate Nabokov successfully is to adhere to his texts with a very deep respect, making use of the ductility of the target language as much as possible, because Nabokov always describes circumstances, psychologies, and feelings with the highest accuracy of terms. He maps out the route, and the translator has only to follow it.

GENNADY BARABTARLO: I am not a professional translator. At first, while still in Moscow, I was making rather clumsy renditions of his prose for training purposes: to improve my command of literary English and Russian (I did my own imaginative writing). My translation of *Pnin*, begun in Moscow, in part during a long stay at a hospital, was finished in Urbana, Illinois, where I was doing doctoral studies, and in Montreux, where Véra Nabokov and I had daily editing sessions. It was published by Ardis in 1983. Mrs Nabokov then asked me to translate VN's prefaces to the English editions of his Russian novels, for the collected works that Ardis was about to launch. She also suggested that I try *Ada* but did not like the samples I showed her, concluding that the work had better be left untranslated. Later I russified, again with the benefit of her consultation, Nabokov's English short stories and published some of them in émigré periodicals, and much later collected all of them in *Byl' i ubyl'* (St Petersburg: Amphora 2000).

When three years ago Azbooka Classics, a St Petersburg publishing house, started an authorized series of Nabokov's collected works, I was asked by his estate to take part in the enterprise. I redid my translation of *Pnin*, its publication timed to the book's 50th anniversary; it came out with my introduction and a long interpretative essay. I then translated *The Real Life of Sebastian Knight,* again with an introduction and an essay. And I revised my old versions of VN's English prefaces for the Russian novels, which were published, by a queer editorial decision, as *afterwords.*

MAURICE COUTURIER: I started translating Nabokov in the early 1980s. When I published my first book on Nabokov in 1979, I included my translation of "Details of a Sunset," which was endorsed by Véra Nabokov. She later asked the French publisher to approach me to translate *Glory*, as well as two collections of short prose, *Details of a Sunset*, and *Nabokov's Dozen.* We exchanged a number of letters while I was doing it. At the time, I was working with my wife. We also did the *Lolita* screenplay for Gallimard, before I did my own translation of *Lolita*, and lately of *The Original of Laura.*

Translating David Lodge's books was a difficult task (my wife and I have translated six of his books) but, of course, it was nothing compared to doing the Nabokov translations, a more daunting and more pleasurable task. *Glory*, for example, was particularly demanding. When I was translating *Lolita* I frequently consulted Nabokov's Russian translation; whenever there was some ambiguity in the English original, I checked the author's Russian-language version to see how he had interpreted his own text.

YURI LEVING: *How were you approached to translate* Laura*? Did you contemplate it as a possibility at any point, prior to receiving an invitation, during the years of public debate surrounding the fate of* Laura*? What was your initial response to this commission, considering the great amount of controversy and secrecy surrounding the issue of publication?*

GENNADY BARABTARLO: I think "years of public debate" is an exaggeration. In March 2008 I was asked by the Estate to join a tight circle of specialists to read the text and advise Dmitri Nabokov on the question of whether it ought to be published. When it became clear that a decision to publish had been reached, I suggested to Dmitri, whom I had known since the early 1980s, that I do the Russian edition so as to prevent, as much as I could, a ham version in the Soviet newspeak that Nabokov abhorred so much. It turned out that he already had me in mind for the task, and I started at once. So there was no "commission" as such.

MAURICE COUTURIER: By the time the invitation came through, I had been the official translator of Vladimir Nabokov with Les Éditions

Gallimard for over ten years. I guess there was no question of somebody else doing it, so I was contacted immediately. Dmitri Nabokov asked that I be sent the manuscript of *Laura* at the time when he was reaching a decision.

TADASHI WAKASHIMA: Sakuhinsha (a publisher in Tokyo) has published the Japanese translations of *The Stories of Vladimir Nabokov* and *The Nabokov–Wilson Letters* as well as my monograph on *Lolita*, and was very enthusiastic about publishing *Laura* from the beginning. I could not imagine myself as a Japanese translator of *Laura* because I was working on a new translation of *Ada* at that time (and still am now). Moreover, I could foresee that several difficult problems in translating *Laura* would await me if I accepted the invitation, but after some deliberation I decided to accept the challenge. My translation appeared just after a massive earthquake struck the eastern coast of Japan on 11 March 2011.

ANNA RAFFETTO: Frankly speaking, at the beginning, when Adelphi expressed the wish to entrust me with the task of translating *Laura*, at first I did not agree because I had read the manuscript and realized how difficult it could be to reproduce such a fragmentary text in Italian. But Dmitri Nabokov and Roberto Calasso, the president of Adelphi, insisted on my translating the work and finally I accepted because I did not want to disappoint them.

As for the possibility of receiving an invitation, I would never have thought of being involved in a public debate around *Laura*. Your invitation to participate in this discussion has been a great and unforeseen surprise.

RIEN VERHOEF: By the time I was asked to translate "Natasha," it was known (and announced by the magazine) that *Laura* would be published in the near future. De Bezige Bij could have asked one of the other translators who worked on the Nabokov Library in the 1990s, but they decided to ask me.

In the first place, I was honoured. Second, I'm a professional translator, and the job was quite interesting from a professional point of view. Third, who was I to question a decision someone (i.e., Dmitri Nabokov) struggled with for over thirty years? And finally, if I had declined, one of my colleagues would most certainly have said yes, so *Laura* would not have remained untranslated anyhow.

YURI LEVING: *Michael Scammell, the translator who collaborated with Nabokov, states that his way of thinking at the time of translating* The Gift *and* The Defense *from Russian into English was very close to Nabokov's. Furthermore, he believed it was "the translator's job to follow every twist and turn in the original language, and to try to capture every lexical and cultural nuance on the level of the sentence." Since then, Scammell has altered his views; he believes now that a translation has to capture the larger significance and resonance of images and meanings that transcend a literal rendering, and that this task frequently requires a departure from literalism.*[3] *Could you describe your own preferences in relation to Nabokov's definition of the three kinds of translation (free translation, which he calls paraphrase; word-for-word mechanical transposition, which he calls lexical; and, in the middle of these, his choice – the literal translation)? What role did your own philosophy of translation play in the process of rendering Laura?*

TADASHI WAKASHIMA: My first choice is lexical translation. I try to stick to Nabokov's words. But, as Umberto Eco postulates, translation can be viewed as an act of negotiation.[4] You always have "losses and gains." Lexical translation has its limits, and when it fails I switch to literal translation.

GENNADY BARABTARLO: Nabokov's rather coarse division was meant primarily for translating poetry, with its special technical difficulties of transferring both rhyme and reason into another tongue. I do not think he would extend it to prose. A paraphrastic or clumsy "lexical" translation of prose cannot be justified by the desire for semantic exactness: a minimally fit operator should be able and indeed is expected to be both properly idiomatic and "exact." The choice here is not between liberal and literal but between sloppily and expertly.

I think Scammell nailed it both times: a faithful translator should indeed follow every turn in the original, trying not to miss subtleties of semantics and style, and then find maximally close correspondences in the target idiom. Faithfulness to the original is the goal of every honest translator, but reaching it may require not only departure from verbalism but sometimes recourse to an exegetic translation, in pursuit of finer precision. A longer route here is often the only right way. In his Russian version of *Lolita* Nabokov uses two words to translate "automatic" (as in handgun), three for "glower," four for "jitterbug," and twenty for "cheerleader."[5]

I haven't any philosophy of translation. A translator should be a true philologist (*sensu lato*) and a deep reader. In fact, a good translator is the best reader an author can hope for.

ANNA RAFFETTO: Undoubtedly I have always followed Nabokov's choice: the *literal translation*. Several times I have discussed with Dmitri Nabokov how to render Nabokov's works, and our viewpoints have always turned out to be the same.

RIEN VERHOEF: I don't want my translations to "read as translations" – having said this, I try to stay as close and to be as faithful to the original as I can. This would be quite close to Nabokov's "literal translation," I suppose.

MAURICE COUTURIER: I have spent a great deal of time in my career doing translations. I have always preferred a *literal translation* to a word-by-word translation, but never attempted to rewrite Nabokov, of course. When translating *Lolita,* I found out that Humbert Humbert's syntax was comparatively easy to emulate in French, but the French vocabulary (very poor in many cases) often proved inadequate. I was very careful to keep all the cultural elements intact: not only did I not change the names (leaving Mr and Miss), I also made sure that the French reader would realize that the story was taking place in America and not in France. At the same time, in this and all my other translations, I have always insisted that the text be written in perfect and fluent French, with no indication that it was a translation. The reviewers have always acknowledged that it was the case.

YURI LEVING: *Describe, if possible, your particular methods while working on this translation project (i.e., a linear vs. non-systematic approach, typing vs. handwriting, the use of dictionaries, rereading Nabokov's other texts whether in English or those already existing in the language of your translation, etc.)?*

GENNADY BARABTARLO: On the first run I pencilled in some variants; I drafted the translation sequentially, by hand, on cards larger than the original, and unlined; then I typed out the second draft on-screen; then went over it several times, polishing. I was surrounded, as usual, by stacks of reference books: interpretive English (*OED* and *Webster's II*) and Russian (Dal'-III) lexicons, the three-volume English–Russian dictionary (Mednikov–Apresian), and a number of very specialized Russian ones, such as *A Dictionary of Nabokov's "Lolita," A Dictionary of Seawater Fish,*

A Dictionary of the Winds, and the wistful *The Briton in Russia: Pocket Interpreter Containing Phrases and Travel Talk Etc.*,[6] the last snapshot a foreigner could take of the as-yet-undefiled Russian idiom.

I find rereading Nabokov's Russian prose before and during translation most useful; it restores and refines my sense of proper style.

TADASHI WAKASHIMA: When I translate Nabokov, I usually adopt a mixture of literal and non-systematic approaches, translating chapter by chapter and at the same time jotting down my solution to some nagging local problems in the whole text. I mainly use *Webster's* (second edition, of course) and *OED*, but nowadays googling often helps.

RIEN VERHOEF: I worked more or less the way I do on all my translations. I type, I go over and over my translation to make it "sound right" (including reading it aloud), I look up things in dictionaries and other sources. I did not reread Nabokov's work extensively for *Laura*. Of course, *Laura* posed some additional and specific difficulties: the unfinished sentences, the break in lines continuing on a next card, etc.

MAURICE COUTURIER: Translating *Laura* was a much less exciting experience than doing *Lolita*. The "gappy" nature of the text often made it difficult to understand what Nabokov really meant. I still tried to remain as close as possible to the original while writing a fluid translation. I always use a variety of dictionaries, French and English, as well as glossaries with synonyms, most of them on my hard disk, others online.

ANNA RAFFETTO: At first I read all the cards to get a clear idea of the text; then I concentrated on the first chapter and typed the Italian version directly, consulting both monolingual and bilingual dictionaries. I did the same for the following chapters and sections of the book.

YURI LEVING: *Did you attempt to rearrange the text that you received from the editor/agent/publisher?*

TADASHI WAKASHIMA: Yes. When you try to rearrange the text of *Laura*, two cards that stand out as "odd pieces" are those that describe the reunion between Ivan and Flora at a central European resort. The trouble is that they should come *after* the provisional ending in which Flora waits for "someone" on a station platform. Besides, Ivan refers to himself as "I" in the usual first-person narration, which he almost never does in previous chapters. I am at a loss as to where to fit them in the whole scheme of the book, but there must surely be some unfathomable reason why Nabokov wrote them.

GENNADY BARABTARLO: The lines preserved on cards 120–1 (distant war, reunion, St Esmeralda) are indeed the most enigmatic in the series; they cast a strange reverse light on this ghostly novel. Placing them anywhere in the batch with certainty is impossible. Nevertheless, I am more or less sure that they cannot be placed after cards 112–14, as Tadashi Wakashima suggests, one of the two chief reasons being that the "she" of the "rotunda reunion" can scarcely be Flora, because assuming that Flora can be "brimming with religious fervor" would capitally change her character's complex. (The other reason has to do with my notion of the book's provisional ending). I think that the cards are from *My Laura*, and that Laura is very different from her original (who is reading the book at the railway station). If anything, these cards prove that we can know very little of the general design which, if realized, might have shocked us all.
RIEN VERHOEF: No, I received my first version quite early (autumn 2008), followed by several other versions, sometimes partly reshuffled by Dmitri Nabokov (I assume). Each time I kept to the order I received as a translator.
GENNADY BARABTARLO: During an early round of consultations I proposed that in the last third of the batch there might be the novel's provisional ending – cards 112–14 (waiting for the train). In the essay appended to the Russian edition I explain my reasons at some length. This cautious proposition was guardedly or silently accepted by the few participants at that initial round table. So the second transcription sent to me, which I used for translation (with the cards *en regard*), already had this alternative ending, and that is how the Russian edition has it. Besides, the seven working cards (culled quotations, etc.) were collected in an appendix.
ANNA RAFFETTO: I did not make any attempts to rearrange the text, but I faithfully followed the transcription of the cards, made first by Dmitri Nabokov. Later, through Andrew Wylie, I received a new transcription, made by Knopf editorial staff, which showed some variant readings.

At an advanced stage of my work, just because I wanted to dispel any doubts, I checked both the original text of *Laura* (i.e., the cards) and my translation with Dmitri Nabokov, who was very helpful in stating the correct interpretation of some words, signs, or sentences, and eventually approved of my work.

MAURICE COUTURIER: No, not at all. I was not even tempted to try it. I have just written an article for *La Revue des Deux Mondes* in which I explain what Nabokov's manuscript means to me without attempting to figure out what the finished novel could have been like. I have my doubts, by the way, about the reports that the cards have been preserved in their original order.

YURI LEVING: *It is almost a norm, as we know, for canonical texts to be retranslated over time in order to accommodate the language and culture of contemporary readers (Tolstoy and Dostoevsky being regulars in such backlists). Did you have to find or invent any special stylistic registers and tonality for the most adequate rendering of* Laura *into your target language, considering the unusual time leap: the work was written over thirty years ago but revealed for the first time only in a modern context?*

GENNADY BARABTARLO: We know, too, that what is now taken for the norm as often as not is an abnormality. To adjust the language of the translation of an old piece of prose to modern taste is to betray the author, to do disservice to the reader, and thus deeply wrong, in my opinion. It is natural and right for a new translation of an old work to be felt anachronistic. I hold with those who think that language, and therefore culture, generally progresses down a fairly steep slope. While the English language is a sad case in point, the Russian, after suffering what Mandelstam called a crushing severing of the spinal cord, is in a state of utter deformation and destitution, infixed as it is with criminal cant, large fragments of Soviet political jargon, bits of stiff profanity, and undigested pieces of pidgin English and bloganeering. Translating Nabokov, whose Russian was as different from today's usage as H.W. Fowler's English is from Ebonic, into *his native tongue* is an unexampled challenge; it is unlikely that there is anybody left who would be up to the task nowadays. Myself included, of course, for in spite of the painstaking care I took to reproduce Nabokov's Russian in diction and style, my version, too, inevitably suffers from inbred flaws of usage, some of which I cannot correct because I simply do not see them, blinded by the prevailing linguistic conditions.

RIEN VERHOEF: To me, it did not feel that way. This might have to do with the fact that I started as a translator around the time Nabokov died. So, in a way, my register and tonality neatly cover the time gap.

MAURICE COUTURIER: The geographical and historical context of Nabokov's text is so vague that the problem hardly arises. It is its fragmentary nature that is a problem.

ANNA RAFFETTO: No, it was not necessary for me to seek out any special stylistic registers. *Laura*'s language is still living and actual, so it can be easily transposed into my target Italian.

TADASHI WAKASHIMA: Nabokov's best works are eternally modern, and never become mere museum pieces. My guess is that Nabokov himself wanted to believe this. His recurrent theme of "future recollection" can be regarded as the manifestation of this belief (e.g. "A Guide to Berlin"). The particular case in point is *Lolita*. Humbert's assumption that "this book is being read ... in the first years of 2000 A.D. (1935 plus eighty or ninety, live long, my love)" must also surely be Nabokov's.[7] That is why Lolita speaks like a Japanese teenage girl circa 2000 in my new translation of *Lolita*. In the same vein, in my translation of *Laura*, I wanted Flora to be more liberated than Lolita. After all, she dies only in *My Laura*, not in *Laura*.

YURI LEVING: *Umberto Eco states that "a translation is an actualized and manifested interpretation."*[8] *Eco's semiotic concept of "an open text" (text as an internally dynamic and psychologically engaged field that allows multiple interpretation by the readers actively mediating between mind and society and life) also seems apt in grappling with the incompleteness of Nabokov's last novel. What relevance does this critical discourse have to your own approaches in translating the cryptic Laura?*

GENNADY BARABTARLO: None. However, my inverted commas around "exact" in the answer above may have something to do with one possible extension of these words. No translation can be really exact in principle, if one understands the notion of "idiomatic" as peculiar to a national language or its part. The best translation is a hyperbolic curve ever tending toward the ordinate axis of the original but never touching it.

ANNA RAFFETTO: I think that Umberto Eco's concept of "an open text" fits perfectly with *Laura*, but I did not recall it while I was working on *Laura*.

RIEN VERHOEF: Translating cryptic parts differs from just reading them. A translator simply has to fill in more gaps than a reader, forced by the laws of his own language. For mostly grammatical reasons, unfinished sentences cannot be left unfinished *in exactly the same way* in another language.

TADASHI WAKASHIMA: In Eco's concept of "the open work," the author offers the reader a work to be completed.[9] We must bear in mind that Nabokov never allowed such openness. But the case of an incomplete novel is entirely a different matter. The book, not the author, invites active participation from the reader to complete the picture.

MAURICE COUTURIER: In the present case, because of the incompleteness of the text, I don't have the feeling that my translation is an "actualized and manifested interpretation," simply a faithful rendition. Nabokov didn't deliberately write an open text; he didn't have time to complete it, which is a different matter altogether.

GENNADY BARABTARLO: *Laura*'s text can be called cryptic only inasmuch as it is a very incomplete assemblage of parts of a complex machine whose blueprint is gone with the designer. To echo Humbert, any translator is an interpreter *par excellence*, yet when one translates fragments, many of which are disjoined and separated perhaps by whole chapters, one should stick to the task at hand. An honest translator tends to be more literal in case of doubt, and *Laura*'s case is just that.

YURI LEVING: *Does the unfinished text with its numerous gaps make any better sense and seem more coherent to you now – whether during the process of translation or after it had been completed and edited in your target language?*

RIEN VERHOEF: Almost by definition – translating is very, very close reading. And it certainly leads to deeper understanding, though not always – sometimes it's rather the puzzlement that deepens.

GENNADY BARABTARLO: Doubtless so. But this is quite natural, since there is no surer method to know a literary work than to cultivate it by translating it. An understanding of a fragment is by necessity impaired, perhaps impossible, yet after you have spent laborious time handling the component words, some areas of the blank space appear as nebulae of recognizable shape. For example, I can now venture a reasonably stable supposition that, in *My Laura*, Flora's Russian lover makes Philidor Sauvage annihilate his wayward wife by hypnotic telethanasia, moving his eraser from toe to tête; this is why Wendy Carr insists that Flora read the passage about Laura's "wonderful death" at what I take to be the book's finale. If so, it would appear that "Ivan Vaughn" (if that is the novelist's real or pen name) had learned of Philip Wild's self-expunging experiments from Laura's original, Flora, who *had* after all gone through her husband's notes despite her tipsy denial in the first sentences of the novel. Of course, the trouble with suppositions about *Laura* is that they are cheaply incontestable, because proof or disproof lurks within the text that does not exist.

TADASHI WAKASHIMA: Yes. Generally speaking, translation pays, not in monetary terms but in that it deepens my understanding of the text.

ANNA RAFFETTO: The different plots of *Laura*, the various levels of meaning of its stories, became clearer and clearer while I was going over every passage looking for possible mistakes.

The work was like a puzzle for me: only when the right pieces found their own places (I mean, only when I understood the correct interpretation of a single card related to subsequent or previous ones) the drawing became clearly visible.

MAURICE COUTURIER: The first time I read the manuscript, I was very disappointed. It does make a little more sense to me now after translating it, though there still are many things I don't understand. The finished novel was obviously going to be highly metafictional.

YURI LEVING: *What do you draw from the fact that the real, original fragments of Laura remained unrecognized during the 1999 Nabokov prose-alike centennial competition when an excerpt was published in a specialist journal,* The Nabokovian, *concealed amid counterfeits as part of a contest to judge the best imitation of Nabokov's style? The question has a direct relation to the topic of our round table discussion because this surprising result means that even expert scholars failed to accept the stylistic idiosyncrasies of the writer's late work. Does this therefore mean, in turn, that you could feel more manoeuvrability or enjoy a greater freedom of lexical and linguistic choices in bringing out the "new" old text by the long-departed author?*

GENNADY BARABTARLO: It would be awkward for me to engage in this discussion because it was I who instigated that competition and suggested its format to Stephen Parker; I even entered two of my own imitations. The last sentence in your question rings true, by my experience.

ANNA RAFFETTO: I think that the translation of *Laura* requires the same accuracy as the other works by Nabokov. Respecting the author's stylistic and lexical choices has always been a "must" to me. In case of *Laura* the "new 'old text'" does not seem to me so *old* as to ask great freedom of lexical and linguistic choices.

TADASHI WAKASHIMA: Personally, the episode means almost nothing, although it is surprising indeed. I endorse Michael Wood's distinction between signature and style in Nabokov's writings.[10] One can imitate his signature (or "stylistic idiosyncrasies") if one is good enough, as the episode shows, but no one can do what Nabokov does in his distinctive style.

MAURICE COUTURIER: It is quite understandable, I think, the text being so fragmentary and unpolished; it bears fewer traces of Nabokov's highly elaborate poetic language than any of his other works.

RIEN VERHOEF: I would say this is rather reassuring. Hurrah for Nabokov's originality and unpredictability. I don't think it affects my own feeling of manoeuvrability or freedom, since this is governed much more by the writer's text than by the writer as a looming figure.

YURI LEVING: *Do you find this last work different, radically or subtly, from the previous writings by Nabokov that you have translated?*

ANNA RAFFETTO: *Laura*'s themes do not seem very different from those dealt with in Nabokov's other books. In the first chapters I found much of the Nabokov we know and love: a mocking view of social rites; a disenchanted diagnosis of the impossibility of true love; the fleetingness of desire; a cheerful view of inescapable death – death that eventually fades away in the spells of conjuring tricks (as it always happens in his works); man's stubborn longing for control over his life; man's loneliness; and his wandering in a hall of mirrors where there are no boundaries between reality and illusion. Obviously, we have to consider that *Laura* is only an unfinished novel and not the final result of an artistic creation.

TADASHI WAKASHIMA: For a Japanese translator, *Laura* causes the extremely difficult problem of rendering (free) indirect discourse. The same thing can be said of *Lolita* and *Transparent Things*.

Another point worth mentioning is that Flora and Lolita share some similar experiences and, other than that, *Laura* contains many glancing allusions to *Lolita*. But whereas Lolita is captured by Humbert's warped imagination, Flora is ultimately free – that is the fundamental difference between the two works.

RIEN VERHOEF: Yes, but I had a strong feeling this it was a least partly because of the unfinished state of the book (and the prose).

GENNADY BARABTARLO: It is easy to forget that this is not really his *last work*, only the last thing he was working on: pieces of a vessel of unknown shape or purpose. One therefore cannot really employ any serious comparison. With tight-lipped reservation, I can say that the design might have been of a concentric kind, not unlike that of *Pale Fire*; that the prose here moves faster, with more torque and on stiffer suspension and takes turns with even less body roll than before; and that even though none of Nabokov's novels avoids the central theme of mortality, nowhere is it treated so directly and yet so enigmatically.
YURI LEVING: *Could you cite any specific challenges of translating* Laura *(compared with either another Nabokov work or any other classical or contemporary writer) that you experienced while working on this project?*
RIEN VERHOEF: Again, mainly the unfinished state.
GENNADY BARABTARLO: Translating fragments is in a way technically easier because one is not expected to bring up totally clear sense in an orphaned or incomplete sentence or wrap up an abandoned or disconnected passage. On other hand, you ought to be on guard to resist the temptation to render not the text but your conjecture or to improve on the original: to fill a small gap, to dock a prolixity, to enliven a dull spot.

One cardinal difficulty in translating *Laura* into Russian, in addition to the one mentioned above (translating an author into his mother tongue, which is gone, along with his motherland), is that the traditional Russian literary language is very chaste, compared to the English of the second half of the 20th century. Many erotic terms accepted now in English prose, especially those related to intercourse, are not available to an honest translator into Russian: the choice is between crude anatomy and winding circumlocution. There is, for example, no good way to translate even "lovemaking" (there is a curious isogram to the Latin "coitus," but that's hardly the same), and no way at all to translate "to make love." Fortunately, Nabokov never uses Billingsgate or expletives that have become pepper and salt on the anglophone writer's table; still more fortunately, he usually resorts to tropism in describing a love scene, and metaphors are easier to transplant.

ANNA RAFFETTO: I could cite, for instance, section D [Chapter Six], or D Three, but it means nothing in comparison with the challenges of translating the poem *Pale Fire*.

MAURICE COUTURIER: The difficulty between French and English when these two languages are compared is often the question of vocabulary; the fact, for instance, that so many verbs can't be turned into adjectives or nouns as they can in English, and also the fact that our syntax is so complex and not very flexible. Remember what Nabokov said about translating from English into French. A French translation is usually about 25 per cent longer than the English original.

TADASHI WAKASHIMA: A special challenge for me was the problem of how to render "Was I game now for another round, she wanted to know" in Japanese. That is the sentence in which the absent I-narrator, wittingly or not (I opt for the former), reveals himself *only once,* in Chapter One, when translating Flora's utterance into indirect discourse.

As I explained above, indirect discourse is usually translated as direct discourse with the *to*-suffix. Then, the lexical translation of this sentence would be:

あなた、もう一回戦できる？ と彼女はたずねた。

[Anata, moo ikkaisen dekiru? to kanojo wa tazuneta.]

「あなた」(anata) is a common Japanese pronoun for the second person. But the problem is, how to slip in the first person singular 「私」[watashi (= I)] here? Adding「私に」[watashi ni (= me)] to 「彼女はたずねた」[kanojo wa tazuneta (= she asked)] is too easy, and feels like cheating. Moreover, it does not make you laugh as the original sentence does. So, I thought it impossible to translate this into Japanese. Then one day, I hit upon a crazy solution:

ぼく、もう一回戦できる？ と彼女はたずねた。

[Boku, moo ikkaisen dekiru? to kanojo wa tazuneta.]

As every Japanese learner knows, 「ぼく」[boku] is the most common personal pronoun used mostly by young men and boys. But the trick here is that it can be used as an address to a child (equivalent to "kid" in English). In this sense, 「ぼく」[boku] means both "I" and "you."

During the whole process of seduction and lovemaking, Flora always takes the upper hand. So I made Flora mockingly call Ivan "kid." I only hope that it is funny and Nabokov would approve of my solution.

GENNADY BARABTARLO: A curious psycholinguistic difference; that sentence does not strike so much as a smile in me, let alone a laugh. By the way, we probably should not assume so easily that "Ivan Vaughn," scribbled once on top of a card (59), was indeed the intended name for the belletristic lover, although it's tempting because of the Van Veen association.

MAURICE COUTURIER: As a specific challenge I can cite a sentence from page 31 in the Knopf edition: "The position of her head, its trustful poximity [sic], its gratefully shouldered weight, the tickle of her hair, endured all through the drive." The phrase is ambiguous: it could be either the driver's or the girl's sensation. I preserved the ambiguity in the French translation: "La position de sa tête, sa proximité confiante, son fardeau posé sur l'épaule avec gratitude, le chatouillement de ses cheveux, persistèrent pendant tout le trajet en voiture."

GENNADY BARABTARLO: They are riding in the back seat of a cab he called to take her home, she is resting her head on his shoulder, his ear and cheek tickled by her hair. I see no ambiguity here.

YURI LEVING: *To what extent was it necessary for you, in the process of translating, to make suppositions about the work's possible integrity or its probable general concept and author's message?*

TADASHI WAKASHIMA: I always think that the translator's task is to render the intentions of the implied author as faithfully as possible. This presupposes the work's integrity, and the case of *Laura* is no exception, however incomplete it actually is.

ANNA RAFFETTO: Several times I tried to find connections between the different sections of *Laura*, but eventually I gave up; it was impossible for me to find any overall meaning. As to the second part of your question, I think I have already explained my point of view some lines above.

MAURICE COUTURIER: It is not always easy to decide what Nabokov meant. While translating *Lolita* I also found out that there was a certain vagueness at times in his prose. I believe that if *Lolita* had been published in America or England, the publisher would have suggested a number of corrections, as the editor Katharine White did, for instance, for the *New Yorker* articles.

GENNADY BARABTARLO: Since one knows in advance that the text at hand has neither integrity nor explicit design, one can be quite carefree about it and go about the business of rendering coherent pieces coherently and incoherent, incoherently.

As for the message, we all know that the only kind our author admitted was transnatural – enormously hard to detect even in his finished novels, to say nothing of *Laura*'s sunderances.

RIEN VERHOEF: To me, as a translator, this aspect did not really play a role.

YURI LEVING: *The Knopf and Penguin hardback editions of the original text have been praised as beautiful and inspirational (or, as Eric Naiman puts it in the* San Francisco Chronicle, *a "gorgeous book, which eventually will be seen, when it is packaged less distractingly, as one of the most interesting short stories Nabokov never wrote").*[11] *Are you satisfied with the way your translation has been published from an aesthetic point of view (the cover design choices, the peculiarities of reproduction – i.e., cards scanned and/or perforated, detached in a box, or simply as a text printed* en regard *to a facsimile of the original cards, etc.)? Were you consulted in the process? If not, what would you do differently?*

RIEN VERHOEF: The Dutch edition followed the original, with the cards scanned (front and back), though under the cards it has the translation instead of the English transcription. At my express request, the perforation was copied. This was a very expensive process, of course, but in the end the publisher accepted my argument that *not* perforating the cards would be like travelling to Venice and not taking a gondola, because they're so expensive. I'm very grateful the publisher found this convincing. The reward in publicity was almost instantaneous: on the day it came out, *Laura* was discussed extensively on a popular Dutch TV show and, amid Ohs and Ahs, one of the cards was pressed out.

GENNADY BARABTARLO: Chip Kidd's dust jacket is indeed excellent, and so is the book's design, although I should think that the half-cocked perforation around each card looks like a coy typographical tease. Nobody in his right mind is going to take the publisher's invitation to detach and shuffle the cards. The German *de luxe* solution (a separate stack of superbly reproduced cards lurking beneath a toothy book in a slipcase) is more elegant.

The Russian edition came out in two hardbound versions: a relatively slim sextodecimo for the masses (a 50,000 initial run, followed by 80,000), with Dmitri Nabokov's preface (25 pp.), the text (95 pp., with cards numbered throughout in the margins), and my afterword essay

(57 pp.); and an expensive limited edition (10,000 copies in November, plus another 10,000 in December, with some corrections): an octavo that imitates the Knopf design, down to the lettering fading to naught on the dust jacket, minus the "tear here" stitching along the cards' perimeter, plus everything contained in the mass edition. I should like to add that in January 2010 Azbooka Publishers issued a revised second edition of both versions, with a score of important corrections inserted, which however looks identical to the first and is silent about the revision. One way to tell is to see whether Daisy is translated as Dalia (1st) or *Deizi* (revised).

As for the cover design, I had had little luck with the publisher previously, protesting Pnin's Garibaldi beard and pipe (a picture by André Derain; they subsequently erased the beard and replaced the pipe with a fountain pen) and giving up on the moon-faced dandy in a top hat posing for the cover of *The Real Life of Sebastian Knight.* In the case of *Laura,* I suggested that they integrate Botticelli's Flora, because of a certain facial and sensual affinity (as described on card 43) and because in Nabokov's preceding novel, N. proposes to Anna Blagovo by urging her attention to the "fifth girl from left" in the *Primavera.* Much to my astonishment they ran away with the idea and plastered "the fifth girl" full face on the cover and spine towering over a book open flat at her breast level, with an inch-tall contrastive "*Laura*" blazing at you from a ten-foot distance and the barely visible "*and her original*" in minuscule. That, combined with a tremendous pre- and post-publication advertising effort, helped to sell the first run in two days, and the second, in the next three weeks; then followed the launch of a third (revised) edition and a paperback version. The title was propelled to the top of the bestseller list, from which it has been slowly sliding down, perfectly in step with *My Laura*'s dignified descent as described on cards 59 and 60. It suddenly jumped back to number two in late February, below a "Dan Brown" title and above a Russian grammar textbook.

ANNA RAFFETTO: I very much like the Italian edition, which perfectly matches the plain and elegant style of the previous Nabokovian editions printed by Adelphi since 1991.

The cover reproduces the last card ("efface, expunge") with the same squared paper. The cards were scanned in black and white and printed on the upper side of each page; the relative translation is printed beneath, on the same page. At the beginning of the book, four cards have been reproduced as plates (in three-colour print) as samples of the original recto and verso.

The publishing house asked for my view about the layout of the book and showed me all the proofs.

MAURICE COUTURIER: The French translation also preserves the page setting adopted in the American edition. I was consulted by the publisher from the beginning.

TADASHI WAKASHIMA: Japanese books are usually written top-to-bottom, right-to-left, and bound on the right. This way of Japanese bookbinding obviously causes a problem when you try to incorporate Nabokov's cards with the Japanese text. To solve this problem, my publisher came up with a brilliant idea: the cards and the text run in opposite directions, and their ends meet in the middle of the book! It is a pity that this idea was not realized after all because it was too unconventional. Anyway, my publisher asked my opinion about every aspect of book-making, and the final product is quite satisfactory to me.

YURI LEVING: *Was the fact that Nabokov did not wish this work to be published of any importance to you while you were translating* Laura*?*

TADASHI WAKASHIMA: None at all.

ANNA RAFFETTO: According to Bulgakov's sulphurous Woland, I believe that "the manuscripts don't burn": they cannot burn when only one person knows about their existence. *Laura* is a door to Nabokov's workroom, and Dmitri Nabokov could not give up on opening it for all of us. That was my mind while I was translating *Laura*.

RIEN VERHOEF: It was all the more reason to do my very best in order not to embarrass "the long-departed author."

GENNADY BARABTARLO: Before I began translating, during the debates in which I took part – yes (I advised against publication). Then, in the course of work, one gets used to the thought that a house-painter who was handed the keys to the house by its owner is not an intruder, no matter what the neighbours may think.

MAURICE COUTURIER: I never paid much attention to the debate about Dmitri's decision to publish the book. I am grateful to him, in fact, for allowing us to overhear the last breath of a genius I have always admired.

Afterword

The Last Word – Or Not? On Some Cards Named *Laura*[1]

BRIAN BOYD

On occasion, Nabokov's novels took a long time to finish and publish: nineteen years, for example, from first composition to complete publication of *The Gift*. *The Original of Laura* will never be finished and had to wait over thirty years to be published. But the longer that particular dam filled, the greater the flood when it broke. *The Gift*'s publication in 1952 barely made a splash. Even *Lolita* had to wait fifteen years from first publication for the first two books about it to trickle out.[2] Within two years *The Original of Laura*, less than a tenth as long, has already set afloat two books, two special issues of journals, and reviews and opinions by writers ranging from Martin Amis and John Banville to Tom Stoppard and Michael Wood.[3] What a pleasure to see so much of that flood of first responses stored in *this* rich reservoir, along with later reflections on the uniqueness of the text and of the manner of its publication, translation, and reception.

On 16 November 2009, on the eve of publication, the Poetry Center at the 92nd Street YMHA, America's premier literary venue – where Nabokov read in public for the second-to-last time on 2 April 1964 – novelist Martin Amis, the book's designer Chip Kidd and I helped launch *The Original of Laura*, in "A Celebration of Vladimir Nabokov." The event was apparently broadcast live across US campuses.[4] Nabokov began the show, in splendid voice, by means of a recording from his 1964 performance, with a recitation of "The Ballad of Longwood Glen." What follows is an expanded version of my talk, amplified here and there by later reflections and reactions to what others have written, including *The Shades of Laura*.[5]

In 1973, four years before his death, Nabokov had the initial inkling of what became *The Original of Laura*, but first he had to finish *Look at the Harlequins!* and then, driven by a sense of personal honour, to revise and virtually rewrite the translation of *Ada* for the French publisher, after the first translator's breakdown. At the age of seventy-six, his intense work on the translation, beginning at five a.m. each morning, drained him, as did severe falls, operations, and infections over the next two years, and he could not finish *The Original of Laura* before his death in 1977.[6] Sometime earlier, he asked his wife to promise to destroy the manuscript should it be left uncompleted. She could not bring herself to do so.

Two years after his death, I finished my PhD at the University of Toronto. After reading my dissertation, Véra invited me to visit her in Montreux; after the visit, she asked me to sort out Nabokov's archive for her. Although from late 1979 I had free access to the archive, I could not see other materials that Véra guarded in her bedroom: Nabokov's letters to his parents and to her, his diaries, and *The Original of Laura*. By mid-1981 she agreed even to condone my working on a biography and, in principle, to allow me access to all I wished to see. She gradually allowed me access first to Nabokov's letters to his parents, then to what she chose to read into my tape recorder of his letters to her. Not until February 1987, as I was already working on Nabokov's American years, did she at last agree to my entreaties to read Nabokov's final but unfinished fiction. She placed the little box of index cards on the maroon-and-silver striped period sofa on the west side of her narrow living room and monitored me from the matching sofa two metres away on the east side. I could read the manuscript once only and could not take any notes. I also had to agree to delete anything she wished of what I might write about the novel as a result of this reading. The conditions could hardly have been worse.

Not long afterward, on Dmitri Nabokov's next visit to Montreux, he and his mother asked me what I thought they should do with the manuscript of *The Original of Laura*. I said, to my own surprise, "Destroy it." How glad I am now that they ignored my advice and that their attachment to Nabokov's work overrode even their respect for his last wish.

In 1950, Nabokov would have burned another manuscript of another still incomplete book, entitled *Lolita*, if Véra had not stopped him on his way to the incinerator. Of course, Nabokov, Véra, Dmitri, and the whole world have good reason to be thankful that *that* burning never took place. But he finished *Lolita*, and he came nowhere near finishing *The Original of Laura*. So why am *I* now thankful about *this* publication?

The Original of Laura could have been published poorly, as if it were a new *Lolita* or at least a new *Pnin*. Instead, it was better published than I could have imagined.[7] Subtitled "A Novel in Fragments" on the cover and "(Dying Is Fun)" on the title page, the index cards now bound into book form suitably flaunt their unfinishedness. Readers should not expect a new story to rival *Lolita*'s intensity or a new character to match Pnin's pathos but, rather, glimpses of a famously demanding writer still challenging his readers and himself, in his late seventies, with death closing in.

What troubled me so much when I first read *The Original of Laura* and recommended that VN's wishes should be followed and the text destroyed? And what has changed so much in my sense of the novel that I welcomed its publication?

All of my initial dissatisfactions have been echoed in the responses of such gifted reviewers as Martin Amis, John Banville, Jonathan Bate, Alexander Theroux, and Aleksandar Hemon.

My first disappointment was that the fragments remain just that. I knew that Nabokov had had the first idea for the novel almost four years before his death, and that when he still had more than fourteen months to live Véra reported that he was "about half way" to completion.[8] I expected much more than I found. Reading and understanding require trust. The embryonic nature of the text sapped my trust, especially when I could read it only once under Véra's wary eye. For reviewers, their reluctance to trust an inchoate Nabokov text, too, was compounded by their suspicions about the rationale for its publication.

My second regret was that there were no sympathetic characters and no one who looms large in the imagination like Luzhin, Humbert, Pnin, Kinbote, or Van Veen.

The third was that the narrative's driveshaft seemed broken. In *Lolita*, *Pale Fire*, and *Ada*, Nabokov reinvents fiction without forfeiting the pleasures of plot. *The Original of Laura* has a beginning, middle, and end, but it's hard to see how readers would have been impelled from one to the next even if the novel was completed.

The fourth was the recurrence of unpleasantly heartless sex, as in *Transparent Things*, and the fifth, the recurrence of a *Lolita* theme. Nabokov recycled Lolita's name, and much more, in *Pale Fire*, *Ada*, and *Look at the Harlequins!* In *The Original of Laura* he introduces a character called Hubert H. Hubert, the partner of Flora's mother. When his hand touches twelve-year-old Flora's legs under the bedclothes, she kicks him in the groin. Do we really need a *fourth* reprise of *Lolita*, even with this twist?

The sixth disappointment was that the hero has a problem too strange to engage the imagination. Luzhin's love of chess haunts even readers who cannot play the game. Humbert's desire for Lolita compels readers despite their feelings about child rape. But in Nabokov's last completed novel, *Look at the Harlequins!*, Vadim Vadimych's maddening problem is merely that he can't imagine turning around to walk the other way along a street, an act that he can readily perform in real life but that sends his imagination spinning – and a problem that has always failed to turn *my* imagination. In *The Original of Laura*, Philip Wild wants to find out how to *will* his own body dead, inch by inch, from his feet upward, so that dying becomes fun and a reversible relief from the itch of being. Most of us surely think about death, and most of us have times when we wouldn't mind redrawing our figures. But Philip Wild's obsessive quest to erase his body seems remote from ordinary human preoccupations.

My seventh concern was the novel's style. In a 1974 review, a stern young Martin Amis had greeted *Look at the Harlequins!*: "[Its] unnerving deficiency ... is the crudity of its prose. ... In the book's 250-odd pages I found only four passages that were genuinely haunting and beautiful; in an earlier Nabokov it would be hard to find as many that were not."[9] I, too, was sadly disappointed by *Look at the Harlequins!* and wondered if it marked an irreversible decline in Nabokov's powers. Yet he still sparkled in interviews and introductions. As his biographer, I sweated in 1987 as I picked up the first of the *Laura* index cards: would I be able to describe Nabokov's invention as undimmed, or would the manuscript confirm a decline? My fraught first reading, alas, bore out my fears. Above all, I felt that whatever *might* have become of the novel, the cards that survived fell far short of Nabokov's standards and should be destroyed as he wished.

If you have not yet read *The Original of Laura* you will now be thinking that you need not bother. Pay attention: I want to change your mind. And rest assured that I'm not someone who approves of everything

Nabokov wrote: I have sometimes been harsher than anyone on those of his works I think not up to his high standards.

My estimation of *The Original of Laura* has changed dramatically. It's not another *Lolita* or *Pale Fire*, but it could have been – it already is – both another ground-breaking Nabokov novel and a priceless and unique glimpse into his workshop. (I'm fascinated, now, to see in the round table discussion in this volume that Leland de la Durantaye thinks the decision to publish was wrong *but also* that the novel, if completed "could have developed into as fine a work as, say, *Ada*.") What's changed my mind? Not reading under impossible conditions. Not reading with fixed expectations. Reading for what's there and not for what's missing. Rereading. Trusting more. *Re*-rereading, and trusting still more.

My first disappointment was that the novel was so fragmentary, so unfinished. It still is, but there's a strong beginning, a vivid middle, a wry end, and an already intricate design. The more I reread the more I think that Nabokov may indeed have been nearly halfway to another short novel like *The Eye* or *Transparent Things*. Gennady Barbatarlo in his essay in this volume disagrees, but what he adduces as new lines to be developed often seem like indecisiveness about character names, not whole new developments.

My second disappointment was with the characters. True, none is sympathetic. But the heroine, Flora, is deliciously unlikable, and her husband, the neurologist Philip Wild, is an unforgettable presence from his tartan booties and ingrown toenails to his Buddha-like bulk and brilliant brain trying to erase his feet.

My third lay with the plot. But if there is little plot tension there is also headlong action from reckless Flora and comic inertia from Wild's repeated self-erasures. Perhaps one or two of Nabokov's novels lacks a powerful plot impetus. Unless I'm mistaken, as you know by now I can be, *The Original of Laura* would have offered different pleasures from those of suspense: the contrasts of helter-skelter narration and meditative stasis,[10] along with puzzles about who has created and who has obliterated whom.

Three problems down, four to go. You'll still be far from persuaded.

My fourth and fifth: the frequent focus on sex and the replay of the *Lolita* theme. Why I thought the former disappointing on first encounter I now can't imagine. I now find Nabokov's descriptions of sex here hilariously unappetizing, prodigiously unsatisfying emotionally, and often physically comic in their painful shortcomings. Just forget the tension of *Lolita* or the ecstatic, "passionate pump-joy" release of *Ada*;[11] forget, above all, the romance of first love in *Speak, Memory* or in *Mary*. Here's the different world of *The Original of Laura*:

> Flora was barely fourteen when she lost her virginity to a coeval, a handsome ballboy at the Carlton Courts in Cannes. Three or four broken porch steps – which was all that remained of an ornate public toilet or some ancient templet – smothered in mints and campanulas and surrounded by junipers, formed the site of a duty she had resolved to perform rather than a casual pleasure she was now learning to taste. She observed with quiet interest the difficulty Jules had of drawing a junior-size sheath over an organ that looked abnormally stout and at full erection had a head turned somewhat askew as if wary of receiving a backhand slap at the ~~decisive moment~~. Flora let Jules do everything he desired except kiss her on the mouth, and the only words said referred to the next assignation. (77–9)

Nabokov has focused on sex before, but never has he shown it so divorced from feeling. But he surely amuses and appalls us in a new way with the sexual activity he depicts here.

Indeed, I think he uses the starkness of sex in this novel – so "far from the poetic euphemisms in which Humbert draped his prose," as Yannicke Chupin observes in her fine discussion of the uniqueness of Nabokov's treatment of sex in this passage[12] – to veil design, to conceal his art under the appearance of brutalism. Half of the novel focuses on Flora's husband's attempt to obliterate himself, and to do it again and again. Here, in the first decisive action reported from her life, apart from her kicking Hubert H. Hubert in the groin, Flora stages her own de*flora*tion – in a physical process she too will want to repeat compulsively. Nabokov makes this stark defloration, so different in its details, somehow analogous to Philip Wild's self-erasure. I do not know where this would have led, but I appreciate the glimpses of design emerging behind this new mode of Nabokovian concealment – by concealing, perversely, nothing of the sexual organs.

A little later in the same chapter, Nabokov writes: "This is Flora of the close-set dark-blue eyes and cruel mouth recollecting in her midtwenties fragments of her past, with details lost or put back in the wrong order, TAIL betwe[e]n DELTA and SLIT, on dusty dim shelves, this is she" (85). These in fact are the very words that provoke Chupin's comment on the contrast between this novel's bluntness and Humbert's imagistic obliqueness. But again, the in-your-face starkness of those capitals, and the anatomical parts they stand for, and their indecorousness, make them seem coarsely unmotivated, so that we don't at first notice that these capitalized words are anagrams of the word "details" in the preceding phrase. Responding to new degrees of sexual frankness possible in the mid-1970s, and the inartistic ways they are deployed,[13] Nabokov finds his own new possibilities even in naked fact.

My fifth concern yielded even greater surprises. Nabokov evokes Humbert Humbert not to replay *Lolita* but to mislead our expectations. Mr Hubert H. Hubert lost a twelve-year-old daughter when she was run over by a truck. He sees her in a sense resurrected in Flora, who is Daisy's age when she died, and wants to be nearer Flora than she wants him to be – wants, even, to brush her hair with his lips. But as far as I can see – and Ellen Pifer's fine analysis of Hubert's role (in this volume) confirms this with great sensitivity – he feels toward her only as the father of the lost daughter of whom Flora keeps reminding him. Flora, who knows about sex but not about love, misreads his intentions, as do readers, including this first-time reader, misled by Nabokov's expert deception. The real link to *Lolita* we should make from Hubert H. Hubert is not to Humbert crushing Lolita under his memory of "Annabel Leigh," but to the Kasbeam barber, whom Nabokov identifies in his essay "On a Book Entitled *Lolita*" as one of "the nerves of the novel ... the secret points, the subliminal co-ordinates by means of which the book is plotted."[14] The barber appears in a sentence that, Nabokov reports, cost him a month of work: "In Kasbeam a very old barber gave me a very mediocre haircut: he babbled of a baseball-playing son of his, and, at every explodent, spat into my neck, and every now and then wiped his glasses on my sheet-wrap, or interrupted his tremulous scissor work to produce faded newspaper clippings, and so inattentive was I that it came as a shock to realize as he pointed to an easeled photograph among the ancient gray lotions, that the mustached young ball player had been dead for the last thirty years."[15]

Hubert H. Hubert feels a tender love for his dead Daisy, and would like to offer the same to Flora, but Flora understands only sex, not love, not tenderness, and repays his attentions with a kick in the crotch. Through the Hubert name and other *Lolita* echoes, Nabokov dupes us at first into misreading the scene just as hard-bitten Flora does. But in this novel of human erasures, Daisy's death has *not* been erased for her father, who remembers his lost child so painfully, so hopelessly. Nabokov has hidden under our noses the beating core of tenderness in this apparently heartlessly hard novel: Flora as a potential Daisy, not as Lolita, is one of *this* novel's "secret points."

And, to offer an incidental extra concerning echoes of *Lolita:* Philip Wild's first love, Aurora Lee, echoes of course Annabel Leigh in *Lolita*, in name as in role, but just as Annabel's surname respells that of a famous nineteenth-century poem, Poe's "Annabel Lee" (1849), so Aurora's, in return, respells, in neat reverse fashion, that of another, Elizabeth Barrett Browning's *Aurora Leigh* (1856).

My sixth problem was that Philip Wild's obsession with willing his own death, erasing himself by inches so that he can restore himself by inches – so that death can dance to his tune – seems so remote from our experience and our desires. Wild's quest is certainly singular. But many of us have wished to shed intense pain or discard excess weight. Wild wants both. Many have sought to train the mind to control and transcend self, through meditation, and Wild has not only the shape of the fattest Buddha but the same urge to reach nirvana (the text makes reference to both) and to eliminate the self. Life has pained him, with his vast bulk, abscessed toes, writhing gut, and the "anthology of humiliation" (219) his life has been since he married Flora. The word *anthology* derives from the Greek for "collecting flowers" but, in Wild's case, his Flora casually plucks and casually or viciously jettisons other men.

Nabokov has some sympathy with Wild in his humiliation, and so should we, but he is no Pnin. All of us might wish at times that we could control our own death or restoration, but Nabokov surely presents Wild's as exactly the wrong way to transcend death. Eliminating the self promises no worthwhile passage beyond life. The only transcendence of death Nabokov could imagine wanting would take the self *through* death to a freer realm of being, but without denying its accumulated experience: "I am ready to become a floweret / Or a fat fly," John Shade writes in *Pale Fire*, "but never, to forget."[16] In *Ada*, Van Veen explains "the worst part of dying": "the wrench of relinquishing forever all one's memories – that's a commonplace, but what courage man must have had to go through that commonplace again and again and not give up the rigmarole of accumulating again and again the riches of consciousness that will be snatched away!"[17]

Wild obsessively tries to will his own elimination, but for Nabokov self-elimination can only be the falsest kind of self-transcendence. Wild's ingrown toenails cause him agony. On one occasion, as he lies on a mattress in his bath, again willing away what he can, he not only seems to erase his toes but decides not to restore them when he emerges from his hypnotic trance. As he opens his eyes, his heart sinks when he sees that his toes are intact, but when he scrambles out of the tub, he falls flat on the tiled floor. To his "intense joy," his toes are "in a state of indescribable numbness. They looked all right, though ... all was rubber and rot. The immediate setting in of decay was especially sensationally [sic]" (165–7).

For many over many millennia, but never more than for Nabokov, transcending death has seemed somehow akin to escaping earth's gravity. Fat Philip Wild flopping over on erased toes succumbs to gravity more grotesquely than ever. His obsessive quest seems an apotheosis of self and of stasis, a self-fixated and self-enclosed attempt to circumvent the limits to the self that death imposes. To the extent that Nabokov imagines possibly passing through death – and that's to a very considerable extent – he sees it as a transition that hurtles the self into a state retaining accumulated selfhood but no longer subjected to "the solitary confinement of [the] soul."[18] Wild conjures up an image of an "I," "our favorite pronoun" (137), on his mental blackboard, its three bars representing his legs, torso, and head, and he sees his auto-hypnosis as akin to successively rubbing out each bar.

Images of erasure or self-deletion pervade the whole novel in ways that reveal Nabokov's customary care in constructing and concealing his patterns. To take one example: Wild feels delight and relief at erasing his ingrown toenails. Flora, by contrast, wipes not a mental blackboard but her own flesh: she requires her partner to withdraw before ejaculation and promptly wipes the semen off her groin or, as the novel once phrases it, her "inguen" (121). How many know this word means "groin"? *Ingrown–inguen*: Nabokov covertly links Wild erasing his own life, rubbing out his toes, with Flora briskly wiping off the possibility of new life. The Roman Flora was a fertility goddess; Nabokov's Flora, a sterility goddess.

Art can offer a kind of immortality, a different promise of transcending death. But not here, not in this novel. Flora's grandfather, a painter of once-admired sentimental landscapes, falls forever out of favour: "What can be sadder than a discouraged artist dying not from his own commonplace maladies, but from the cancer of oblivion invading his once famous pictures such as 'April in Yalta' or 'The Old Bridge'?" (43–5). His son, a photographer, films his own suicide, *his* being rubbed out. The photographer's wife, Flora's mother, a ballerina known only as Lanskaya, finds her art fading as her body ages. Flora becomes the subject of a kiss-and-tell novel, *My Laura*, which aims not to immortalize but to expunge her: "The 'I' of the book is a neurotic and hesitant man of letters, who destroys his mistress in the act of portraying her" (121). The laurel was associated with literary immortality because its leaves last so long after they detach. Flora, so eager to be deflowered, remains alive at the end of the novel; unlike her husband, obsessed with his own death, she ends *The Original of Laura* refusing to look at the novel *My Laura* lying on her lap and at what a friend recommends as "your wonderful death ... the craziest death in the world" (227).

We come to my seventh concern, the novel's style. For an older and still sterner Martin Amis, this by itself would be decisive. In 1999, for the centenary of Nabokov's birth, the oldest of the five journals devoted to him, the *Nabokovian*, decided to stage a Nabokov write-alike contest. A panel of judges selected three submissions, which appeared alongside what were announced as two "never before published pieces of Nabokov's prose"[19] – both, in fact, from *The Original of Laura* – that, readers were informed, Dmitri had supplied. Subscribers were invited to pick the original of Vladimir. Delightfully, most picked as Nabokov's a passage by Charles Nicol, an academic and writer who has been publishing superb work on Nabokov for more than thirty years, and *no one* picked the passages from *The Original of Laura*. Nobody picked Nabokov as the one who wrote most like Nabokov.

What does that tell us? I think it indicates that even Nabokovians either misconstrue Nabokov's style or underestimate how new it can be from work to work. We can recognize on sight many hallmarks of his style when we see them "on site," and we can find many of them already on his construction site for *The Original of Laura*. But we have not sufficiently recognized how much Nabokov also modifies his style and reweights particular features in each work. To take his best English works: the high, controlled elegance of *Speak, Memory* differs radically from *Lolita*'s neurotic twitchiness, and both from *Pale Fire*'s would-be cloudless craziness, and all three from *Ada*'s rococo supersaturation – and all four from *The Original of Laura*.

That no one picked the *Laura* passages in the write-alike contest suggests to me not that Nabokov isn't writing up to par here but, on the contrary, that he's playing his usual game of *changing* or reinventing his game subtly to suit the special world of the work.

Nabokov has a reputation as a great prose stylist, perhaps even the greatest. *The Original of Laura* makes me want to rethink what constitutes the distinctively Nabokovian: not just elevated prose, a recondite lexicon, elegant quicksilver sentences, minute precision of visual detail, pointed allusion, foregrounded verbal combinatory play, cryptic crossword-type challenges, and lucid elusiveness. His style may be most extraordinary not so much as *prose* but as *story*. Unlike "Lolita, light of my life, fire of my loins," the thirteen words of the opening sentence of *The Original of Laura* would win no place in dictionaries of quotations and no prizes as prose, but they offer anything but an insipid incipit. I won't quote them yet but, taken out of context, the first sentence offers plain words that muffle even their plain declarative force with a doubled concession – but as storytelling, the sentence astounds. It does more as *story* than we had any right to expect of a first sentence, until now.

Nabokov stressed transition among character, description, report, speech, and reflection as the most demanding skill in storytelling. He sought new ways to shift from one to another, new ways to speed up the shifts or slow them down or highlight or veil them. He wanted to both extend the possibilities in narrative at every moment and to show readers how nimbly their minds can move from present to past or possible future, from outside a character to inside, from here to there, from actual to possible or impossible, counterfactual or suppositional. In *On the Origin of Stories*,[20] I marshal the evidence that we have evolved into a storytelling species and that the key reason we have done so is because stories improve still further the social cognition and hence the perspectival shifts that had already reached such a high level in our species. From childhood pretend play to adult fiction, we speed up the capacity of our minds to leap beyond our here and now by taking on new roles, sidling and sliding this way and that through time, space, minds, and modalities, thanks to the intense doses of social information we deal with in fiction. No one has taken this further than Nabokov does in his last novel. Narratologists and novelists alike will focus for a long time on the opening chapter of *The Original of Laura* as proof of the new finds still to be made in fiction.

The Original of Laura starts with an answer, but we never learn the question, and we never quite keep up with the pace of the story. It reminds me of the myth of Atalanta and the golden apples. At top speed it picks up a stray fact, darts aside, nonchalantly drops one subject, gathers up another, and still races ahead – unless it slows down and all but stops, with Philip Wild, as he tries again and again to erase himself.

Nabokov not only rewrites narrative texture but from novel to novel reshapes narrative structure. In *The Original of Laura* he plays with the erasure of human selves. Philip Wild tries to dispense with his body by degrees. The author of *My Laura* aims to eliminate Flora. As you read the novel's first chapter, look for the unprecedented way Nabokov makes the narrator imply himself and conceal or erase himself throughout – while Laura disregards her new lover, dumps an old one, and ignores her husband.

Do not expect in *The Original of Laura* the high lyricism of sentiment and sentence found in *Lolita*, *Pale Fire*, and *Ada*. Instead, look for how much Nabokov does once again by inverting what he values most but, as always, in a new way. He inverts love as a path to self-transcendence (through procreation, through the tender attunement of lovemaking, through sharing a life with another) in Flora – as sterility goddess wiping the semen off her groin, in her heartless promiscuity, in the "anthology of humiliation" she offers her husband. Art becomes not a way to self-transcendence here but, rather, the vengeful obliteration of others or the narrator's skulking effacement of the tattle-tale self. Nabokov sees death as a possible release from the confines of the self, not an erasing of the self like Philip Wild's or an evasion of its limits like Flora's.

Nabokov offers us, in the suppleness and speed of our imaginations as he sends us hurtling along the black trails of his story, a route beyond the rapacity of the sexual self in Flora or the stagnation of the cerebral self in Philip – and, if we invert his inversions, what he famously called "a sense of being somehow, somewhere, connected with other states of being where art (curiosity, tenderness, kindness, ecstasy) is the norm."[21]

In some of the many interviews *The Original of Laura* has provoked I have sometimes illustrated the reasons for my reversal of judgment in terms of the excitement I now feel at the opening of the novel and its narrative novelty.

David Gates, in the *New York Times Book Review*, quotes me and asks: "Does Boyd mean the device of beginning a novel *in medias res*, with a character answering a question we don't get to hear? Virginia Woolf did the same thing in the first sentence of *To the Lighthouse*." True, Woolf's landmark novel does begin "'Yes, of course, if it's fine tomorrow,' said Mrs. Ramsay. 'But you'll have to be up with the lark,' she added." The suddenness of that opening, and its clear announcement of a planned excursion, magnificently sets up the thwarted expedition to the lighthouse.

But Nabokov's openings are still more extraordinary, from, "In the second place, because he was possessed by a mad hankering after Russia"[22] to "Lolita, light of my life, fire of my loins," to the parodic mistranslation and reversal of Tolstoy's famous first sentence of *Anna Karenina* in the first sentence of *Ada*, to the bizarre address from a dead narrator to a living character at the start of *Transparent Things*: "Here's the person I want. Hullo, person. Doesn't hear me."[23]

And here's the opening sentence of *The Original of Laura*: "Her husband, she answered, was a writer, too – at least, after a fashion" (1). After those other famous first lines, what is it that strikes me as just as remarkable about this succession of individually unremarkable words?

Let me unpack my pleasure. The first word, "Her," a third-person possessive pronoun, already implies a female possessor we do not know and cannot identify as the narrator. "She" comes along at the third word, but she remains unidentified.

Over the last couple of centuries, fiction has tended to shorten exposition and even to begin more and more often *in medias res*. For this reason, direct speech as a more immediate and dramatic entry has become increasingly common in twentieth-century fiction. But indirect speech implies a narrator doing the reporting, and usually follows the narrator's establishment of the character's identity. Here we have neither the identity of the character nor the confident establishment of the narrator. Over the next few sentences the volubility of the still-unnamed woman continues to hold the narrator at bay.

As Tadashi Wakashima has also explained, we can infer what provokes "her" response: a preceding "I am a writer."[24] "She" then answers: "My husband is a writer, too – at least, after a fashion." Later in the long first paragraph we discover that "she" is Flora, that she is at a party, that she is drunk, that she "wished to be taken home or preferably to some cool quiet place with a clean bed and room service" (3). In another paragraph she has been offered and has eagerly accepted the apartment of friends and has begun to undress there to make love with someone whom she has picked up at the party, someone whom we cannot see clearly. As the lovemaking scene enfolds us and unfolds itself, we recognize Flora's sexual partner as the narrator, yet we also see that he avoids identifying or describing himself or reporting his actions as his, by dint of referring to them only through nonfinite verbs. The narrator, we infer, is the writer whom Flora has just met at the party, when she is already drunk, when she has asked what he does, when he has replied, and when she in turn answers, in the opening line of the novel. There she refers disparagingly to her husband – the very husband this new lover will return her to late in the chapter, after dawn, to add another rank flower to his "anthology of humiliation." She refers to her husband's being a writer, a profession she casually insults four short sentences later, despite being already in the process of picking up this other self-effacing writer – who in writing this very scene, in these very words, in his roman à clef *My Laura*, has his revenge on her heartlessness.

No one has ever packed so much story into the choice of the opening word ("Her"), the opening mode (indirect speech), and the opening declaration and its antecedents and consequences in terms of narrative action, narrative voice, and narrative aim. At the same time as he manages all this, Nabokov also shows the narrator *effacing* himself and *deleting* Flora as he portrays her (before killing her off fictively later in *My Laura*) mentioning her husband as "a writer of sorts," whose "mysterious manuscript" itself recounts how he *erases* himself, in another doomed attempt at transcending, or expunging, the self.

After reading Martin Amis's negative review of *The Original of Laura* on the day we were to appear in New York on the eve of the novel's publication, I gave him to read the printout of a review I had written for publication later that week.[25] Handing it back, he had to say he disagreed with my claim that the opening shows Nabokov "at the peak of his powers." I stand by, and I can now explain, my claim.

A postscript. William Deresiewicz, in his *New Republic* review of *The Original of Laura,* wonders if the volume really contains all that survives, given that Nabokov in April 1976 implied a larger novel, already well advanced in composition.[26] In February 2011, I stayed with Dmitri Nabokov in Montreux, and in search of other material for a different project, came upon another twenty cards that clearly belong to *The Original of Laura* and contain about another 1,200 words. Presumably this material, located by Dmitri's archivist, Antonio Epicoco, was not kept by Nabokov in the index-card box where the bulk of the novel was found. The name *A Passing Fashion* at the start of the longest sequence (dated 7 September 1975), a name Nabokov discarded by 16 February 1976, for *The Original of Laura*, may indicate that some of this rediscovered material reflects an older conception of the novel. The first long sequence, of nearly 700 words, has no obvious relation with anything in the published volume, apart from the name A.N.D. (also spelled out here as "Anthony N. Day") of *Laura*'s "Medical Intermezzo" (175–7), and has a careening scenic verve unlike anything in the published novel. One card is headed "TOOL"; another suggestively links the novel about Laura, who in that novel-within-the-novel is married to the author of a book on suicide, in a way probably anterior to what we have in the current *The Original of Laura.* Dmitri and his agent and publishers now know about the new material. The original *Original of Laura* will not be the last word.

Notes

YURI LEVING: NABOKOV'S "SWAN SONG"

1 Vladimir Nabokov, *The Original of Laura (Dying is Fun)*, ed. Dmitri Nabokov (New York: Knopf / London: Penguin, 2009). All page references follow this edition.

2 Michael Antman, "Genius Erased," *PopMatters Magazine*, 20 November 2009. See pp. 194–7 in this volume.

3 John Banville, "Trump Cards: Controversy Surrounds the Publication of Nabokov's Last, Unfinished Work," *Bookforum*, December/January 2010. See pp. 169–73 in this volume.

4 The original title, *La Misteriosa Fiamma della Regina Loana*, was first published in Italian in 2004. An English translation by Geoffrey Brock appeared a year later (Boston: Houghton Mifflin Harcourt, 2005).

5 English edition: Gabriel García Márquez, *Memories of My Melancholy Whores*, trans.Edith Grossman (New York: Knopf, 2005).

6 Certain similarities between Nabokov's and Márquez's fiction have been noted earlier. On *Memories of My Melancholy Whores* and Nabokov's *Lolita*, see Gene H. Bell-Villada, *Garcia Marquez: The Man and His Work* (Chapel Hill: The University of North Carolina Press, 2010), 261.

7 A few more representative quotes: "True to form, his latest novella is a trick of a book ... But the novel turns out to be a decoy in more ways than one: throughout the apparently simple story, you anticipate a mode that does not come – magical-realism, erotica, memoir, children's fiction" (Gaby Wood, *The Guardian*); "[T]he resulting memories are not melancholy, not even sad, but merely pitiful and disappointing" (Alberto Manguel, *The Guardian*); "The

scenes and descriptions when the writing ignites are fewer and further between than in any earlier [writings]" (Amanda Hopkinson, *The Independent*); "Measured by the highest standards, [the book] is not a major achievement. Nor is its slightness just a consequence of its brevity ... Yet the goal of [the book] is a brave one: to speak on behalf of the desire of older men for underage girls, that is, to speak on behalf of pedophilia, or at least show that pedophilia need not be a dead end for either lover or beloved" (J.M. Coetzee, *The New York Review of Books*); "That [the author] expects the reader to salute an ancient man's victory over a child, rather than see it as pathetic or monstrous, is the latest measure of his fiction's heroic contempt for reality" (Adam Kirsch, *The New York Sun*); "The cunning of [the book] lies in the utter – and utterly unexpected – reliability of its narrator ... because his story is, like the saint's, a conversion narrative" (Terrence Rafferty, *The New York Times Book Review*); "There are careless touches, as though [the author] were weary of his creations" (Caroline Moore, *Sunday Telegraph*); "In size, style and subject matter, this is a work suffused with a sense of exhaustion" (Andrew Holgate, *Sunday Times*); "Magic and cynicism, love and power, corruption and redemption ... There is not in this slender book one stale sentence" (Ruth Scurr, *The Times*); "As publishing sensations go, this was spectacular. The trouble is that the 109-page [book] – for all its warmth, humour and magnificent linguistic invention – ultimately emerges as a slight piece of work ... This novel is an imperfectly formed little jewel – sadly, not one destined to sparkle in the memory alongside the finest works of [the writer]" (Adam Feinstein, *Times Literary Supplement*). See the complete list with bibliographic references at www.complete-review.com/reviews/garciamg/mmwhores.htm (accessed 1 June 2011).

8 For more on the socio-cultural implications of the publication of *Laura*, see my article "Interpreting Voids: Vladimir Nabokov's Last Incomplete Novel *The Original of Laura*," *The Russian Review* 70, no. 2 (April 2011): 198–214.

9 Ibid.

10 Pierre Bourdieu, *The Rules of Art: Genesis and Structure of the Literary Field*, trans. Susan Emanuel (Stanford: Stanford University Press, 1996), 169.

11 Michael Dirda, "Vladimir Nabokov, Reduced to Notes," *The Washington Post*, 19 November 2009. See p. 184 in this volume.

12 Ibid.

13 The round table participants received the first set of questions simultaneously; the responses were compiled in logical order, and the text was circulated a second time with a request to participants to expand on their answers and

engage directly with the other participants' opinions; the resulting text, after editing, was distributed to the group for final remarks. The three rounds occurred at one-month intervals.

14 Umberto Eco, *The Role of The Reader: Explorations in the Semiotics of Texts* (Indiana: Indiana University Press, 1984), 35.

15 Leving, "Interpreting Voids," 207–14.

BRIAN BOYD AND YURI LEVING: CHRONOLOGY OF THE NOVEL

1 All quotations from the Nabokov archives were transcribed by Brian Boyd at Montreux, 1980–1982. The original manucripts are now housed in the Henry W. and Albert A. Berg Collection, New York Public Library. Quoted by permission of the Nabokov estate.

2 Craig Offman, "Dmitri Nabokov on his Father's Unfinished Novel," *Salon,* 19 April 1999, www.salon.com/books/log/1999/04/19/nabokov.

3 John Banville, "Trump Cards: Controversy Surrounds the Publication of Nabokov's Last, Unfinished Work," *Bookforum* December/January 2010. See pages 169–73 in this volume.

GALYA DIMENT ET AL.: PUBLISHING *LAURA*

1 *Editor's note:* "Vladimir Nabokov: Letters to Vera," *Snob* 11, no. 26 (November 2010).

2 Vladimir Nabokov, *The Annotated Lolita,* ed. Alfred Appel Jr. (New York: Vintage, 1991).

3 Angus Phillips, "How Books Are Positioned in the Market: Reading the Cover," in *Judging a Book By Its Cover: Fans, Publishers, Designers, and the Marketing of Fiction,* ed. Nicole Matthews and Nickianne Moody (Aldershot, Hants: Ashgate, 2007), 19.

4 See John Gall, "The Nabokov Collection," *Design Observer,* 20 October 2009, http://observatory.designobserver.com/entry.html?entry=11597

5 *Editor's note:* Olympia Press, a Paris-based publishing house launched in 1953 by Maurice Girodias, was the original publisher of *Lolita.*

6 See Carolyn Kellogg, "Nathalie Portman's 'Lolita' clutch, *Los Angeles Times,* 4 December 2010, http://latimesblogs.latimes.com/jacketcopy/2010/12/natalie-portmans-lolita-clutch.html

7 *Editor's note:* The library edition of the book has non-removable cards.

8 Jason Epstein, *Book Business: Publishing past, present, and future* (New York: Norton, 2001), 173.

9 Patrick Forsyth and Robin Birn, *Marketing for Publishing* (New York: Routledge, 1997), 1.

10 Vladimir Nabokov, *Speak, Memory* (New York: Vintage International, 1989), 268.

11 *Playboy*, December 2009, 44–8.

12 Dmitri Nabokov, "Regarding *The Original of Laura*," *The Nabokovian* 63 (2009): 6.

13 See reviews in this volume.

14 See D.T. Max's article by the same title in *The New Yorker*, 19 June 2006, www.newyorker.com/archive/2006/06/19/060619fa_fact

15 David Lodge, "Shored against his Ruins," *Literary Review*, December 2009 / January 2010, www.literaryreview.co.uk/lodge_12_09.html

16 Aleksandar Hemon, "Hands Off Nabokov: Why *The Original of Laura* Should Never have Become a Book," 10 November 2009, www.slate.com/id/2235023/

17 Mary Benjamin, "Autographs; A Key to Collecting," *The Collector*, September 1948.

18 See Carolyn H. Sung, "Your Manuscripts and the Scholarly World," in *Autographs and Manuscripts: A Collector's Manual*, ed. Edmund Berkeley, Jr. (New York: Charles Scribner's Sons, 1978), 160.

19 Addendum: It did sell, finally, at Christie's London on 23 November 2010 for £64,000 plus the buyer's premium of £14,050. Altogether, that's about $124,000. Compare that to the $280,000 (without the premium) it didn't get knocked down for in December 2009 because it didn't reach the reserve price. *Editor's note:* This round-table discussion was held before Nabokov's manuscript was sold.

20 Thomas Leveritt, "*The Original of Laura*, By Vladimir Nabokov: if only this had been burnt, as the author had ordered," *The Independent*, 3 January 2010, www.independent.co.uk/arts-entertainment/books/reviews/the-original-of-laura-by-vladimir-nabokov-1850030.html

21 *Editor's note:* See note 19, above.

22 See Nicholson Baker, *Double Fold: Libraries and the Assault on Paper* (New York: Vintage Books/Random House, 2001).

23 Brian Boyd, "Nabokov Lives On," *The American Scholar* 79, no. 2 (Spring 2010): 45–58.

24 Michael Dirda, "Vladimir Nabokov, Reduced to Notes," *The Washington Post,* 19 November 2009. See pages 184–6 in this volume.

25 David Gates, "Nabokov's Last Puzzle," *The New York Times' Sunday Book Review* 11 November 2009, www.nytimes.com/2009/11/15/books/review/Gates-t.html?pagewanted=all&_r=0

26 Sam Anderson, "A Glorious Mess," *The New York Magazine* 15 November 2009, http://nymag.com/arts/books/reviews/62036/

27 Alexander Theroux, "In the Cards, A Last Hand," *The Wall Street Journal* (20 November 2009): W15. See pages 174–7 in this volume.

28 *Editor's note: The Tale of Igor's Campaign* is an anonymous medieval epic poem written in the Old East Slavic language that Nabokov translated into English.

29 Nabokov, *The Gift* (New York: Vintage International, 1991), 334.

30 See "Institutionalizing Nabokov: Museum, Archive, Exhibition," *Nabokov Online Journal* 3 (2009).

MICHAEL WOOD: VANISHING FRAGMENTS

1 This review article first appeared under the title "What Happened To Flora?" in *London Review of Books* 32, no. 1 (7 January 2010): 13–14, and was adapted by the author for this volume.

2 Vladimir Nabokov, *Lolita* (New York: Vintage, 1997), 314.

3 Vladimir Nabokov, *Selected Letters 1940–1977,* ed. Dmitri Nabokov and Matthew J. Bruccoli (London: Weidenfeld and Nicolson, 1990), 562.

4 Ibid.

5 Vladimir Nabokov, *Pnin* (London: Penguin, 1997), 23–4.

6 Nabokov, *Selected Letters*, 562.

7 Brian Boyd, *Vladimir Nabokov: the American Years* (Princeton: Princeton University Press, 1991), 653.

8 Ibid., 654.

9 Vladimir Nabokov, *The Original of Laura (Dying is Fun),* ed. Dmitri Nabokov (New York: Knopf / London: Penguin, 2009). All page references follow this edition.

10 Vladimir Nabokov, *Ada* (New York: Vintage, 1990), 8.

11 Quotations from *The Original of Laura* include interpolations made in square brackets in the Knopf edition; for clarity, further minor interpolations and the notation "sic" also occur in some quotations that appear in the present volume.

12 Vladimir Nabokov, *Strong Opinions* (New York: Vintage, 1990), 154–5.

13 Nabokov, *Ada,* iv.

14 Ibid., 587.

GENNADY BARABTARLO: TERMINATING THE PHRASE

1 See Gennady Barabtarlo, *Aerial View* (New York: Peter Lang, 1993), 193–7.

2 "Let's suppose that I so shuffle, twist, mix, rechew and rebelch everything, add such spices of my own and impregnate things so much with myself that nothing remains of the autobiography but dust – the kind of dust, of course, which makes the most orange of skies." Vladimir Nabokov, *The Gift* (New York: Vintage, 1991), 376.

3 Ibid., 193. "Now I'll ask them [Fyodor's publishers] to make little holes around them [his poems] with a perforator – you know, like coupons, so that you can tear them out more easily."

4 Brian Boyd, *Vladimir Nabokov: The American Years* (Princeton: Princeton University Press, 1991), 644.

5 Ibid., 653.

6 At the January, 2012, Nabokov conference in Auckland, Brian Boyd reported having recently come upon a dozen or so more *Laura* cards in the Montreux apartment of Dmitri Nabokov, so perhaps indeed more "capitularies" were drafted than have been published. See also Boyd's afterword to this volume.

7 Boyd, *The American Years,* 654. Card 7 has a note in the upper corner: "rewrite once more," which seems to allow that some (perhaps many) cards are a second or even a third draft.

8 Morris Bishop, in *The Italian Renaissance,* ed. J. Plumb (Boston: Houghton Mifflin Co., 1987), 166. Petrarch visited Montreux at least twice, in 1347 and 1353, one of those gratuitous yet fetching concinnities.

9 Of his Russian books, *The Eye* stands out as the shortest by far, yet even that short novel, as Nabokov called it, was fatter (100 pages), and his other short fiction "The Enchanter," of 80 pages, he called a short story.

10 *Editor's note:* Transcribed in the Knopf edition as D[a]lling. See Lara Delage-Toriel's essay in this volume, p. 271, n. 12.

11 Stanislav Shvabrin has suggested that Nabokov meant *Dalling* here, a young British football star whose fame peaked in 1975; but it is unlikely that Wild, in his New Jersey abode, should care to know the name of a British soccer player.

12 The Wilds, like almost every other of Nabokov's couples, may reliably be presumed to remain childless. Giving birth in his fiction is a lethal enterprise, and

so his married women either avoid it, or produce a child (usually just one) in the pre-narrative past: there are no toddlers in Nabokov's novels.

13 Ending his 1966 letter to Carl Proffer, about the latter's *Keys to Lolita*, Nabokov makes a remarkably clear, if playful, statement that his students should make a floating screen-saver out of: "A considerable part of what Mr Nabokov thinks has been thought up by his critics and commentators ... for whose thinking he is not responsible. Many of the delightful combinations and clues, though quite acceptable, never entered my head or are the result of an author's intuition and inspiration, not calculation and craft. Otherwise, why bother at all – in your case as well as mine." Vladimir Nabokov, *Selected Letters 1940–1977*, ed. Dmitri Nabokov and Matthew J. Bruccoli (New York: Harcourt Brace Jovanovich, 1989), 391.

14 On the other hand, Nabokov's numeration *within a given series* of cards containing an episode or a thematic string usually sets the correct order for that group.

15 Vladimir Nabokov, *The Defence* (New York: Vintage Books, 1990), 38.

16 In Sebastian Knight's last novel, *The Doubtful Asphodel*, the first-person narrator *is reported* to die in the book, taking with him a simple solution to the ultimate riddle of life and death just as he was about to whisper it in the eager ear of the other, reporting narrator, his half-brother V. – a design that Nabokov tried again the following year in his last Russian novel, unfinished and reduced to two published chapters with Latin titles. For more on this see my "*Taina Naita*. Narrative Stance in Nabokov's *The Real Life of Sebastian Knight*," *Partial Answers,* January 2008, 57–80.

17 As noted by Ryan Van Huijstee in his communication with Yuri Leving, there might be yet another missing layer via a reference to Elizabeth Barrett Browning, who published her novel in verse *Aurora Leigh* (1856) less than a decade after Poe's *Annabel* (editorial note, 18 September 2012).

18 I am grateful to Dr. Shvabrin of Princeton University, whose lecture on Heine and Nabokov at the University of Missouri in October 2012 brought this link to my attention.

19 *The Defence*, 37.

20 But note that it recycles, perhaps with hidden significance, a formula found in Nabokov's preceding novel: there, *Esmeralda and Her Parandrus* is the title of one of the books by the narrator, V.V.N.

21 Had Flora's lover, the author of a romance about her, known Pushkin, he might have addressed his verse to a lucky rival: "Forsooth, your mistress is no

moron. / I bear no grudge, though see it all. / She is a most enchanting *Laura*, / But I am not her Petrarch, pal." Pushkin's Don Juan, in his *Guest of Stone*, calls her "my Laura" twice, and *her* guests are decidedly not of stone.

22 There were no apostrophes in his time, and thus the visual effect matched the aural one.

23 In the eye of one expert beholder these eyes are still blue: Ronald Lightbown, *Sandro Botticelli: Life and Work* (New York: Abbeville Press Publishers, 1989), 138. A radically original recent interpretation of the possible meaning of the *Primavera* is given in Jonathan Kline's "Botticelli's *Return of Persephone:* On the Source and Subject of the *Primavera,*" (*Sixteenth Century Journal* 42, no. 3 (2011): 665–89), in which Kline argues with Panofsky, Gombrich, and even Vasari. For a different but no less surprising conjecture, see Gavriel Shapiro, *The Sublime Artist's Studio: Nabokov and Painting* (Evanston: Northwestern Univeristy Press, 2009), 46–50.

24 Vladimir Nabokov, *Look at the Harlequins!* (New York: McGraw-Hill, 1974), 107.

25 *Fasti* 5:193–212. Ovid has Flora explain that her name is a Latin corruption of her original Greek name, Chloris.

26 Геометрію ихъ, Венецію ихъ / назовутъ шутовствомъ и обманомъ ["Their geometry, their Venice / they will call buffoonery and deception"]: Nabokov on his books, in his last poem.

27 One can find a curious application of the (traditional) Pygmalion *sujet* in *The Gift* in Stephen Blackwell's *Zina's Paradox* (Peter Lang: New York, 2000), 139–40.

28 Including Albert Zugsmith's 1962 screen version of De Quincey's opiatic opus (*Confessions of an Opium Eater*).

29 In a do-it-yourself interview, Nabokov pointed to the presence of this theme; his widow described it in an important preface to his posthumous collection of Russian verse (1979); Brian Boyd did the earliest study of it in his 1978 doctoral dissertation on *Ada*.

30 Nabokov, *Selected Letters*, 117.

31 Tegel, in Berlin, where his father, murdered a year earlier, was buried.

32 Letter of July 13 1923, sent from Prague to Berlin (to be published in the forthcoming collection by Knopf).

33 He also had a remarkable foreglimpse of this fall in a simultaneous prose: "Imagine me, an old gentleman, a distinguished author, gliding rapidly on my back, in the wake of my outstretched dead feet, first through that gap in the

granite, then over a pinewood, then along misty water meadows, and then simply between marges of mist, on and on, imagine that sight!" (Nabokov, *Look at the Harlequins!*, 240).

34 The last words of Pushkin's novel in Nabokov's translation are "... as I [now part] with my Onegin."

ELLEN PIFER: WORLDS APART: LOLITA, LAURA, AND THE SHADOWS OF DIFFERENCE

1 Alexander Theroux, "In the Cards, A Last Hand," *The Wall Street Journal*, 20 November 2009, W15. See pages 174–7 in this volume.

2 Most critics find that Flora, "like the heroine of *Lolita*," is "a nymphet" (Michiko Kakutani, "In a Sketchy Hall of Mirrors, Nabokov Jousts With Death and Reality," *New York Times*, 9 November 2009, www.nytimes.com/2009/11/10/books/10book.html?_r=1&pagewanted=all) and Lolita's "direct descendant" or "successor" (Michael Maar, "Speak, Nabokov," trans. Ross Benjamin, "*n + 1*," 13 November 2009, www.nplusonemag.com/speak-nabokov; Nina Krushcheva, "Nabokov's Manuscripts Don't Burn," *Moscow Times*, 4 December 2009, www.themoscowtimes.com/opinion/article/nabokovs-manuscripts-dont-burn/390855.html). She shares "the same lineage" with Lolita (David Lodge, "Shored Against His Ruins," *Literary Review,* December 2009/January 2010, www.literaryreview.co.uk/lodge_12_09.html) and suffers the same "early forced sexual experience" at the hands of a "lecher" (Christian Bourge, "Neither form nor function," *Washington Times,* 17 November 2009, www.washingtontimes.com/news/2009/nov/17/neither-form-nor-function; Theroux, "In the Cards"). Like his near-namesake, Hubert H. Hubert is an "aspiring pedophile" (David Gates, "Nabokov's Last Puzzle," *New York Times*, 11 November 2009, www.nytimes.com/2009/11/15/books/review/Gates-t.html?_r=1&pagewanted=all) or, worse yet, "a fat pedophile" (John Simon, "Gratuitous excogitations," *The New Criterion* 28, no. 6, February 2010, www.newcriterion.com/articleprint.cfm/Gratuitous-excogitations-4395) who "slobbers over a pre-teen's bed" (Amis) and belongs to a slightly "different" but equally reprehensible "species of creep" (John Lanchester, "Flashes of Flora," *New York Review of Books* 56, no. 20, 17 December 2009, www.nybooks.com/articles/archives/2009/dec/17/flashes-of-flora/). The alleged resemblance between Hubert and Humbert even leads some commentators to identify Hubert, incorrectly, as Flora's "stepfather" (Michael Dirda, "Vladimir

Nabokov, reduced to notes," *Washington Post,* 18 November, Book World; see pp. 184–6 in this volume; Aleksandar Hemon, "Hands Off Nabokov: Why *The Original of Laura* should never have become a book," *Slate* 10 November 2009, www.slate.com/id/2235023/; James Marcus, "The Original of Laura, by Vladimir Nabokov, edited by Dmitri Nabokov," *Los Angeles Times,* 15 November 2009 (see pp. 198–200 in this volume) – even though *Laura*'s text clearly indicates that Hubert, in contrast to Humbert, does not marry Flora's mother before dying of a stroke. Going still further afield, one Nabokov scholar believes that Hubert "wants to marry young Flora and is prevented from doing so a year later [after, that is, he "tries to molest" the twelve-year-old] when he "dies of a stroke in a hotel lift" (Leland De la Durantaye, "Last Wishes," *Boston Review,* January/February 2010, http://bostonreview.net/BR35.1/deladurantaye.php).

3 Martin Amis, "The Problem with Nabokov," *The Guardian* 14 November 2009. See pages 157–68 in this volume.

4 Vladimir Nabokov, *Nikolai Gogol* (New York: New Directions, 1961), 142.

5 Vladimir Nabokov, *Lolita* (New York: Vintage, 1989), 150.

6 In his chapter on *Pale Fire,* Robert Alter notes that in Zembla, "the land of semblances," the "names of its villains are anagrammatic mirror-reversals of the names of its heroes; most significantly, Jakob (or Yakob) Gradus, the Zemblan assassin chosen to track down King Charles, is an ex-glazier, and the anagrammatic mirror-reversal of Sudarg of Bokay, "a mirror maker of genius." Robert Alter, *Partial Magic: The Novel as a Self-Conscious Genre* (Berkeley: University of California Press, 1975), 188.

7 Ivan Vaughan, author of *My Laura,* the novel within Nabokov's novel, underscores the static nature of semblance when he characterizes the depiction of his novel's heroine, Laura, as a static copy of his ex-mistress Flora: "Statically – if one can put it that way – the portrait is a faithful one," comprising "fixed details" that "are absolutely true to the original" (121). The accuracy of Vaughan's account may be noted in his description of fictional Laura's "trick of opening her mouth when toweling" after sex, which corresponds rather precisely to "the mouth" Flora makes, in Chapter One, while toweling her thighs after having sex with him (25, 121).

8 Vladimir Nabokov, *Pale Fire* (New York: Putnam, 1962), 265.

9 Vladimir Nabokov, *Despair,* trans. Vladimir Nabokov (New York: Putnam, 1965), 51, Nabokov's italics.

10 Vladimir Nabokov, "On a Book Entitled *Lolita*." Afterword to *Lolita*, by Vladimir Nabokov (New York: Vintage, 1989), 314–15.

11 Nabokov, *Lolita*, 308.

12 Vladimir Nabokov, *Strong Opinions* (New York: McGraw-Hill, 1973), 11. "Deception in chess, as in art," says Nabokov, is "only part of the game; it's part of the combination, part of the delightful possibilities, illusions, vistas of thought … I think a good combination should always contain a certain element of deception" (11–12).

13 Nabokov, *Strong Opinions*, 16.

14 A different chapter, originally numbered Chapter Five, appears in a later section of the published text; as the editor observes, markings on the file card suggest that Nabokov "intended to change its number" (117).

15 Here, Wild's future wife is referred to as "Laura"; then, just before the reference to her "three years of marriage" to Wild, she is called "FLaura" (107, 111). In context, it is clear that the woman referred to in both cases is Flora. Whether the initial reference to Flora as "Laura" is deliberate on Nabokov's part is unclear, although the latter reference to "FLaura" suggests that he may have intended to merge in some way the identity of Flora with Laura, the heroine of *My Laura* – and perhaps with Aurora Lee. In the later section identified as "Wild's notes," the narrator recalls "Aurora Lee," the girl he had "pursued with hopeless desire at high-school balls" fifty years ago: "Your painted pout and cold gaze were, come to think of it, very like the official lips and eyes of Flora, my wayward wife, and your flimsy frock of black silk might have come from her recent wardrobe" (201). Just as Flora is identified as the "original" of Laura, so Aurora is evoked as the original of Flora. Introducing a potentially infinite series of "originals," their interlinking names beg the question introduced in the title, *The Original of Laura.*

16 Simon, "Gratuitous excogitations."

17 One of the few critics to question Hubert's seeming resemblance to Humbert, Brian Boyd locates Hubert's "real link to *Lolita*" in "the Kasbeam barber" ("Nabokov Lives On," *The American Scholar,* Spring 2010). In a scene that Nabokov identifies, in his afterword, as one of "the secret points" or "nerves of the novel," likely to "be skimmed over or not noticed" by most readers, Humbert receives "a very mediocre haircut" by "a very old barber" who "babbled of a baseball-playing son of his." So "inattentive was I," Humbert comments, "that it came as a shock to realize as he pointed to an easeled

photograph among the ancient gray lotions, that the mustached young ball player had been dead for the last thirty years" (Nabokov, "On a Book Entitled *Lolita*," 316; Nabokov, *Lolita*, 213).

18 In a notable departure from an otherwise negative review of *Laura* – peppered with personal slurs against Nabokov, "the ultimate control freak, not to mention one of the all-time snobs" – one critic observes what most have failed to notice: "Hubert, despite what we are seduced to believe, is no pedophile, just a sad old man – far more Pnin than Humbert – who's lost his family. He really is in love with his landlady, who reminds him of his wife, rather than with her daughter, a copy of his own, and he really does treat Flora "with a father's sudden concern" (William Deresiewicz, "Carded," *The New Republic,* 3 February 2010). Aside from his mischaracterization of Hubert as "old" rather than middle-aged, Deresiewicz accurately reads the situation. Nabokov, he goes on to point out, "asks us to search for emotional complexities beneath the conventional moral surface, even when the conventions are drawn from his own fiction." This and other insightful observations appear rather late in Deresiewicz's review – too late, in my opinion, to make up for the snide tone and cheap shots that dominate its early pages.

19 Nabokov, *Strong Opinions*, 107.

20 In *Laura,* as one of Nabokov's more astute critics observes, the author "goes out of his way to set up analogies between Laura and Lolita, and then equally far out of his way to signal differences between the two books. This is perhaps a rebuke to biographically minded critics, so keen to interrogate the 'real' origins of fictional texts." Although "we can't on the evidence tell what Nabokov was going to do with this," it seems that "he was sketching out a fictional structure that was playing with prurient responses to *Lolita* and with the general belief that fictions are always critically dependent on biographical facts" (Lanchester, "Flashes of Flora").

21 Plato, *The Republic*, in *The Dialogues of Plato*, vol. 1, trans. B. Jowett (New York: Random House, 1937) 7: 774–6.

LARA DELAGE-TORIEL: NABOKOV'S LAST SMILE

1 Dmitri Nabokov, "On Revisiting Father's Room," in *Vladimir Nabokov: A Tribute,* ed. Peter Quennell (New York: William Morrow, 1980), 136.

2 Brian Boyd, *Vladimir Nabokov: The American Years* (Princeton, New Jersey: Princeton University Press, 1991), 564.

3 John Banville, "Trump Cards," *Bookforum.com,* December/January 2010. See pages 169–73 in this volume.

4 Vladimir Nabokov, *Pnin* (New York: Doubleday, 1957), 20.

5 Lewis Carroll, *Alice's Adventures in Wonderland* (1865). Full text available on the Gutenberg Project site: www.cs.cmu.edu/~rgs/alice-table.html

6 This situation echoes Nabokov's desire to write "[a] novel without an I, without a he, but with the narrator, the gliding eye, being implied throughout" (Boyd, *American Years,* 644).

7 William Gass, *On Being Blue: A Philosophical Inquiry* (Boston: Godine, 1976), 84.

8 Ibid., 86.

9 "*Interprète*" is a French word that can signify "interpreter" in the sense of an exegete of texts, signs, or dreams, a translator, and a singer or performer.

10 Vladimir Nabokov, *The Real Life of Sebastian Knight* (London: Penguin, 1995 [1941]), 30.

11 Vladimir Nabokov, Commentary to Aleksandr Pushkin's *Eugene Onegin: A Novel in Verse,* vol. 1 (Princeton: Bollingen, 1964), 15.

12 The printed text tentatively gives "D[a]lling" (135), yet Nabokov's handwriting would suggest "Delling."

13 Vladimir Nabokov, *Lectures on Literature,* ed. Fredson Bowers (New York: Harcourt Brace Jovanovich / Bruccoli Clark, 1980), 270.

14 Vladimir Nabokov, *Strong Opinions* (New York: Vintage International, 1990 [1973]), 27.

15 Vladimir Nabokov, *Dear Bunny, Dear Volodya: The Nabokov–Wilson Letters, 1940–1971,* ed. Simon Karlinsky (Berkeley: University of California Press, 2001), 123.

16 Vladimir Nabokov, *The Annotated Lolita* (London: Penguin, 1995 [1970]), 63.

17 Ibid., 58, 59.

18 I offer a more detailed analysis of this scene in *"Lolita" de Vladimir Nabokov et de Stanley Kubrick* (Paris: Editions du Temps, 2009), 87–90.

19 Vladimir Nabokov, *Pnin* (London: Heinemann, 1959), 38.

20 Ibid., 38, 12.

21 Ibid., 38.

22 The tongue is also compared to a "punchinello" (*Pnin,* 66). For more on this aspect, see Savelii Senderovich and Yelena Shvarts, "The Tongue, That Punchinello: A Commentary on Nabokov's *Pnin,*" *Nabokov Studies* 8 (2004): 23–41. For the question of pain in *Pnin,* see Stephen Casmier, "A Speck of Coal Dust:

Vladimir Nabokov's *Pnin* and the Possibility of Translation," *Nabokov Studies* 8 (2004): 71–86.

23 Nabokov, *Pnin*, 126. In February 1952, a routine X-ray revealed that Nabokov had a "'Shadow behind the Heart' – something that has been haunting me for more than ten years and that no doctor has been able to explain – but what a wonderful title for an old-fashioned novel!" (Boyd, *American Years*, 216). I trace the significance of this shadow in *Pnin* using two different perspectives, in "'A Shadow behind the Heart': l'Étranger au cœur de l'intime dans *Pnin* de Nabokov," *LISA* 8, no. 2 (2009): 130–4, http://lisa.revues.org/index324.html; and in "Disclosures under Seal: Nabokov, Secrecy and the Reader," *Cycnos* 24, no. 1 (2007): 69–79, http://revel.unice.fr/cycnos/index.html?id=1048.

24 Nabokov, *The Annotated Lolita*, 14–15.

25 Ecstasy is associated with self-destruction no less than five times, pages 139, 171, 183, 213, 267.

26 See J. Hughes, P. Clark, and L. Klenerman, "The importance of the toes in walking," *Journal of Bone and Joint Surgery* 72, no. 2 (1990): 245–51; Hsin-Yi Kathy Cheng et al., "The importance of the great toe in balance performance." In *BioMech '07 Proceedings of the Fifth IASTED International Conference on Biomechanics* (Anaheim, Ca.: ACTA Press 2007), 59–63.

27 Vladimir Nabokov, *Look at the Harlequins!* (New York: McGraw-Hill, 1974), 252.

28 *corps à corps*: a French expression designating a close embrace; *à fleur de peau*: a French expression designating something that brushes the skin, most often used figuratively to express great sensitivity.

MICHAEL RODGERS: *THE ORIGINAL OF LAURA* AND NIETZSCHE: A ZARATHUSTRAN TOOL?

1 Vladimir Nabokov, *The Original of Laura (Dying is Fun)*, ed. Dmitri Nabokov (New York: Knopf / London: Penguin, 2009). All page references follow this edition.

2 Vladimir Nabokov, *Pale Fire* (London: Penguin Books, 2000 [1962]), 53.

3 It is uncertain whether Nabokov's "tacite" (opposed to "tacit") is intentionally ironic.

4 Friedrich Nietzsche, *Thus Spoke Zarathustra*, trans. R.J. Hollingdale (London: Penguin Books, 1969 [1883–1885]), 97.

5 The double use of the deictic "that" adds strength to this suggestion.

6 John Simon argues, "Why is Montherlant misspelled 'Montherland'? Out of sloppiness, patronizing indifference, or the sake of a jeering parallel with Morand?" ("Gratuitous Excogitations," *The New Criterion,* February 2010).

7 Having consulted with the British Library and the *TLS* Centenary Archive (1902–1990), I can state that an issue of the *Times Literary Supplement* was indeed published on 16 January 1976, yet this issue contains no explicit mention of Nietzsche.

8 John Burt Foster, *Nabokov's Art of Memory and European Modernism* (Princeton: Princeton University Press, 1993), 39.

9 Bernice Glatzer Rosenthal, *Nietzsche and Soviet Culture: Ally and Adversary* (Cambridge: Cambridge University Press, 1994), 2.

10 Edith Clowes, *The Revolution of Moral Consciousness: Nietzsche in Russian Literature, 1890–1914* (Illinois: Northern Illinois University Press, 1988), 16.

11 Simon Karlinsky, *Dear Bunny, Dear Volodya: The Nabokov–Wilson Letters, 1940–1971* (California: California University Press, 2001), 246. For more detail, see Vladimir E. Alexandrov's essay, "Nabokov and the Silver Age of Russian Culture," in *Nabokov's Otherworld* (Princeton: Princeton University Press, 1991). In *Strong Opinions* (New York: Vintage Books, 1990 [1973]), Nabokov famously listed Andrei Bely's *Petersburg* (1913) among his favourite novels of the twentieth century (57). Rosenthal, in turn, notes that Bely thought of *Zarathustra* as his manual (431).

12 One possible reason for this particular refutation, or suppression, may be that Nabokov wanted to distance himself from the appropriation of Nietzsche by the Nazis. Astore and Showalter (*Hindenburg: Icon of German Militarism* [Virginia: Potomac Books, 2005] 99) report that the three books given to Nazi soldiers were Hitler's *Mein Kampf,* Alfred Rosenberg's *Myth of the Twentieth Century,* and Nietzsche's *Thus Spoke Zarathustra.*

13 Brian Boyd, *Vladimir Nabokov: The Russian Years* (Princeton: Princeton University Press, 1993), 76, 150; Thomas Karshan, *Nabokov and the Art of Play* (Oxford: Oxford University Press, 2011), 44.

14 Foster, *European Modernism,* 67. Here, Foster is quoting from Nietzsche's *Ecce Homo,* "Why I Write Such Good Books: *Thus Spoke Zarathustra,* in *Werke* 2: 1128, and from Nabokov's *The Defense,* trans. Michael Scammell in collaboration with the author (New York: Putnam's, 1964).

15 See Clowes, *Moral Consciousness,* 18, for more detail. The mountain motif can also be seen in Nabokov's early collection of poems, *The Empyrean Path* (Gornii Put') (1923), *Glory* (Podvig) (1932), "Spring in Fialta" (1936), and in his

essay "Good Readers and Good Writers" in *Lectures on Literature,* ed. Fredson Bowers (London: Weidenfeld and Nicolson, 1980), 2.

16 Nietzsche's idea of the "will to power" can be seen as antithetical to Arthur Schopenhauer's belief in the "will to live."

17 Laurence Lampert, *Nietzsche's Teaching: An Interpretation of Thus Spoke Zarathustra* (New Haven: Yale University Press, 1986), 19.

18 Leland de la Durantaye, "Last Wishes," *Boston Review*, January/February 2010.

19 Nietzsche, *Zarathustra*, 59.

20 Lampert, *An Interpretation*, 37.

21 Nietzsche, *Zarathustra*, 63.

22 Ibid., 61.

23 Ibid., 97, 99.

24 Michael Tanner, *Nietzsche: A Very Short Introduction* (London: Oxford University Press, 2000), 54. In the essay "Good Readers and Good Writers" in *Lectures on Literature* (1980), Nabokov states, "Propagandist, moralist, prophet – this is the rising sequence" (6).

25 Nietzsche, *Zarathustra*, 52–3; Lampert, *An Interpretation*, 29.

26 It is interesting that "surmise" is used: "to infer (something) from incomplete or uncertain evidence" (Collins English Dictionary).

27 Lampert, *An Interpretation*, 16.

28 Ibid., 24.

29 Nietzsche, *Zarathustra*, 98.

30 Lampert, *An Interpretation*, 24.

31 Ibid., 27.

32 Nietzsche, *Zarathustra*, 63; Lampert, *An Interpretation*, 39.

33 *The New Criterion,* February 2010.

34 James Liu, "The Original of Laura," *The Front Table*, 12 January 2010.

35 Barbara Wyllie, "The Original of Laura (Dying Is Fun)," *Literary Encyclopedia,* 15 January 2010.

36 The brevity of Daisy's death, and Aurora Lee's (205), recalls the death "(picnic, lightning)" of Humbert's mother in *Lolita* (London: Penguin Books, 1995 [1955]), 10.

37 *Boston Review,* January/February 2010.

38 Vladimir Nabokov, *Invitation to a Beheading* (London: Penguin Books, 2001 [1938]), 176.

39 The sentence in *Invitation to a Beheading* (23), "*That which does not have a name does not exist*" is suggestive of this affiliation.

40 There is an arguable pun where Wild is described as a "man of letters" (121). Similarly, Vaughan's claim that "Her [Flora's] exquisite bone structure immediately slipped into a novel – became in fact the secret structure of that novel, besides supporting a number of poems" (15) again equates physicality and writing.

41 Laura seems to usurp Flora in "Chapter 5" but is soon conflated with Flora as "FLaura" (111).

42 Brian Boyd, "Nabokov Lives On," *The American Scholar,* Spring 2010.

43 John Simon, "Gratuitous Excogitations," *The New Criterion,* February 2010, 62. See www.newcriterion.com/articles.cfm/Gratuitous-excogitations-4395.

44 Brian Boyd, *Pale Fire: The Magic of Artistic Discovery* (Princeton: Princeton University Press, 1999), 12.

45 Sam Anderson, "A Glorious Mess," *New York Books,* 15 November 2009.

46 *Literary Encyclopedia,* 15 January 2010.

47 Vladimir Nabokov, *Vladimir Nabokov: Selected Letters,* ed. Dmitri Nabokov and Matthew J. Brucolli (New York: Harcourt Brace Jovanovich, 1989), 562.

48 Nietzsche, *Zarathustra,* 97.

49 Durantaye, "Last Wishes," *Boston Review,* January/February 2010.

50 Nietzsche argues that "only as an aesthetic phenomenon do the world and existence appear justified." *The Birth of Tragedy and Other Writings,* ed. Raymond Geuss and Ronald Spiers (Cambridge: Cambridge University Press, 1999 [1872]), 113.

51 Arthur Symons and Richard Ellman, *The Symbolist Movement in Literature* (Montana: Kessinger Publishing, 2004 [1919]), 71.

52 Nietzsche, *Zarathustra,* 97.

BARBARA WYLLIE: LOOKING FOR FLORA

1 Vladimir Nabokov, *The Annotated Lolita,* ed. Alfred Appel Jr. (London: Penguin Books, 1991), 60.

2 Brian Boyd, *Vladimir Nabokov: The American Years* (London: Vintage, 1993), 644.

3 Except where the text of *My Laura* intrudes, briefly, at the beginning of Chapter Five (107–11).

4 Vladimir Nabokov, *The Original of Laura (Dying is Fun),* ed. Dmitri Nabokov (New York: Knopf / London: Penguin, 2009), 117. All page references follow this edition.

5 Vladimir Nabokov, *The Real Life of Sebastian Knight* (London: Penguin Books, 1964), 30.
6 Vladimir Nabokov, *Lectures on Literature* (San Diego, Ca.: Harcourt, 1980), 57.
7 Vladimir Nabokov, *Speak, Memory: An Autobiography Revisited* (London: Everyman's Library, 1999), 243.
8 Letter to Katherine White, 1951, in Vladimir Nabokov, *Selected Letters 1940–1977*, ed. Dmitri Nabokov and Matthew J. Bruccoli (New York: Harcourt Brace Jovanovich, 1989), 117.
9 Vladimir Nabokov, *Strong Opinions* (New York: McGraw-Hill, 1973), 47.
10 Vladimir Nabokov, *Ada or Ardor: A Family Chronicle* (London: Penguin Books, 1970), 461.
11 The allusion echoes the "rising perspectives" of Hugh's elevator journeys in *Transparent Things*. See W.W. Rowe, *Nabokov's Spectral Dimension* (Ann Arbor, Mich.: Ardis, 1981), 15–16.
12 Boyd, *The American Years*, 644.
13 Vladimir Nabokov, *King, Queen, Knave* (London: Penguin Books, 1993), vi.
14 Nabokov, *Strong Opinions*, 24.
15 Nabokov had an operation on a benign prostate tumour in October 1975, at the age of 76.
16 There is only one card – "Eric's notes" (235) – that can be definitely attributed to him, although he could be the ex-lover who meets Flora at her Central European resort on cards X and XX (239–41) that almost immediately follow.
17 Nabokov, *Strong Opinions*, 161; Vladimir Nabokov, "Laughter and Dreams," in *Carousel* 2 (1923): 22, quoted in Gavriel Shapiro, *Delicate Markers: Subtexts in Vladimir Nabokov's 'Invitation to a Beheading'* (New York: Peter Lang, 1998), 19.
18 Ibid., 26. Apart from "the repeated verbal and visual identification of Lucette with a bird of paradise" in *Ada*. Brian Boyd, Afternote Part One, Chapter 5, in *Ada Online*: www.ada.auckland.ac.nz. See also, Nabokov, *Ada*, 304, 332.
19 See Gerard de Vries and Don Barton Johnson, *Nabokov and the Art of Painting* (Amsterdam: Rodopi, 2006), 40–1.
20 For more on Nabokov's colour imagery, see Julian Connolly, "Black and White and Dead All Over: Color Imagery in Nabokov's Prose," *Nabokov Studies* 10 (2006). Black and white is a dominant aspect of Flora's portrayal. Her black dress is consistently contrasted with her very pale skin, distinctly echoing the look of the heroine of Nabokov's *Ada*. Connolly argues that this "impoverishing reduction" in colour is an emblem of death (see 63–4).
21 Nabokov, *Lectures on Literature*, 320.

22 Nabokov, *The Annotated Lolita*, 316.

23 Nabokov, *Selected Letters*, 209.

24 Brian Boyd, *Vladimir Nabokov: The Russian Years* (London: Vintage, 1990), 145.

25 See Nabokov, *Strong Opinions*, 189.

26 Heinrich Heine, "Lyrisches Intermezzo" no. 18, from *Buch der Lieder*, 1827, http://de.wikisource.org/wiki/Ich_grolle_nicht,_und_wenn_das_Herz_auch_bricht, trans. Barbara Wyllie. Stanislav Shvabrin contends that Nabokov had a "life-long interaction with the German poet" (correspondence with the author, February 2010). Nabokov had already alluded to another Heine poem in *Look at the Harlequins!* See Stanislav Shvabrin, "Vladimir Nabokov as Translator: The Multilingual Works of the Russian Period," unpublished PhD dissertation, UCLA, 2007, part 1.4: "'Ein Lied von der Liebsten Mein': A Study in Fullness of Sound," 68, n. 6.

27 Vladimir Nabokov, "On a Book Entitled *Lolita*," in *The Annotated Lolita*, 315.

28 Note the flower-derived names common to both Nabokov's and Flaubert's heroines, and the theme of elision that is mirrored in the shortening of Rose-Annette.

29 Gustave Flaubert, *A Sentimental Education*, trans. Douglas Parmée (Oxford and New York: Oxford University Press, 1989), 358.

30 Ibid., 359.

31 Ibid.

32 Vadim enjoys the company of Dolly, the eleven-year-old granddaughter of his landlord, Stepan Stepanov, in *Look at the Harlequins!* (London: Penguin Books, 1980), 67–8, Zina's stepfather fantasizes about a little girl in *The Gift* (London: Penguin Books, 1981), 172–3, and "A Nursery Tale" features "a somewhat decrepit but unmistakable Humbert escorting his nymphet" (*Collected Stories* (London: Penguin Books, 1997), 170, 648.

33 Nabokov, *The Annotated Lolita*, 133.

34 Ibid., 174.

35 Consider, too, the conflict that characterizes Lolita's relationship with her widowed mother, and the fact that Flora "disliked" her mother and "did not remember" (55) Adam Lind, who was only "probably" her father (47).

36 As the narrator comments, "she was still married to that hog" (239). There is no indication, in the extant text at least, that, like Rosanette, she suffers the loss of a child.

37 See nos. 1 and 3 from "Three Chess Sonnets" ("Tri shakhmatnykh soneta"), published in *Nash mir* no. 37 (30 November 1924) and reprinted in N.I.

Artemenko-Tolstoi (comp.), *Vladimir Nabokov: Sobranie sochinenii russkogo perioda v piati tomakh. 1: 1918–1925* (St Petersburg: Sympozium, 2000), 629–30. For commentary on the poems, see Thomas Karshan, *Vladimir Nabokov and the Art of Play* (Oxford: Oxford University Press, 2011), 92–4.

38 Philidor introduced two key strategies, the Philidor Defence and the Philidor Position, the latter being acknowledged as one of the most important positions in endgame theory. He also wrote a seminal book, *Analyse du jeu des Échecs*, which by 1871 had appeared across Europe in 70 editions. For more, see http://en.wikipedia.org/wiki/Fran%C3%A7ois-Andr%C3%A9_Danican_Philidor (accessed 14 March 2010).

39 This could also explain why Daisy was so distracted on her way home from school – that it was perhaps something more than the "indelible fog" and her wobbly bicycle that made her fail to notice the backing lorry (69, 59–61).

40 John Burt Foster, Jr., *Nabokov's Art of Memory and European Modernism* (Princeton, NJ: Princeton University Press, 1993), 223.

41 For commentary, see Priscilla Meyer, *Find What the Sailor Has Hidden: Vladimir Nabokov's 'Pale Fire'* (Middletown, Conn.: Wesleyan University Press, 1988), 131–2, and Brian Boyd, "'A Poem in Four Cantos': Sign and Design," in *Nabokov's 'Pale Fire': The Magic of Artistic Discovery* (Princeton, NJ: Princeton University Press, 1999), 188–206.

42 Nabokov, *The Gift*, 169.

43 Julian Connolly, *Nabokov's Early Fiction: Patterns of Self and Other* (Cambridge and New York: Cambridge University Press, 1992), 157.

44 Nabokov, *Strong Opinions*, 11.

45 Nabokov, *Lectures on Literature*, 260.

46 Nabokov, *Strong Opinions*, 11.

47 Vladimir Nabokov, *Glory* (London: Penguin Books, 1974), 11.

PAUL ARDOIN: READING THE POSTHUMOUS POSTMODERN

1 Maurice Couturier, "The Near-Tyranny of the Author: *Pale Fire*," in *Nabokov and his Fiction: New Perspectives*, ed. Julian W. Connolly (Cambridge: Cambridge University Press, 1999), 71. Couturier's reading of *Pale Fire* warns against trying to "read the text as [the author] meant it," since even the author is victim to unconscious forces that disrupt intent (66).

2 Alexandra Alter takes on the "wave of posthumous books by iconic authors [that] is stirring debate over how publishers should handle fragmentary literary

remains" in "Ghost Writers," *The Wall Street Journal,* 2 October 2009, http://online.wsj.com/article/SB10001424052970204488304574426921687042050.html. In "The Problem with Nabokov," Martin Amis reads *Laura* as another sad sign of Nabokov's decline. See pages 157–68 in this volume. Brian Boyd disagrees; he writes that the book "shows Nabokov at the peak of his powers" and that "it has been better published than I could have imagined." "*The Original of Laura,*" *Financial Times,* 23 November 2009, www.ft.com/cms/s/2/9014d314-d568-11de-81ee-00144feabdc0.html (see also pp. 243–57 in this volume). David Gates strikes a compromise in "Nabokov's Last Puzzle": the author was "an aging, ailing man," but "he was in fine form," *New York Times Sunday Book Review,* 11 November 2009, www.nytimes.com/2009/11/15/books/review/Gates-t.html. Jeanette Winterson explores *Laura* from the point of view of "someone who has burnt a novel and who burns all drafts" in "*The Original of Laura: A Novel in Fragments* by Vladimir Nabokov," *The Times Online,* 5 November 2009. Alexander Theroux suggests that the book is most useful for what its publication history says about ethics in his "In the Cards, A Last Hand," *The Wall Street Journal,* 20 November 2009, W15. See pp. 174–7 in this volume.

3 Zadie Smith, "Rereading Barthes and Nabokov," In *Changing My Mind: Occasional Essays* (New York: Penguin, 2009), 56–7.

4 Zadie Smith, *White Teeth* (New York: Vintage, 2001). Jeanette Winterson, *Sexing the Cherry* (New York: Grove Press, 1998).

5 Walter Benjamin, *Illuminations,* trans. Harry Zohn (New York: Schocken Books, 2007), 231–2.

6 Some of these motives are explored in Kate Taylor's "Nabokov's Notes for 'The Original of Laura' Go on the Auction Block," *The Wall Street Journal Speakeasy,* 12 November 2009, http://blogs.wsj.com/speakeasy/2009/page/42/.

7 Vladimir Nabokov, "Good Readers and Good Writers," in *Lectures on Literature,* 1–8 (Orlando: Harvest, 1982), 1.

8 See Anika Susan Quayle's "Lolita *Is* Dolores Haze: The 'Real' Child and the 'Real' Body in *Lolita,*" *Nabokov Online Journal* 3 (2009), for a recent rebuttal of this common way of misreading Nabokov's most famous novel.

9 Vladimir Nabokov, *Pale Fire* (New York: Vintage International, 1989). Aleksandr Pushkin, *Eugene Onegin: A Novel in Verse.* Trans. Vladimir Nabokov (Princeton, NJ: Princeton University Press, 1991).

10 Gérard Genette, *Paratexts: Thresholds of Interpretation,* trans. Jane E. Lewin (Cambridge: Cambridge University Press, 1997). Rebecca Wisor demonstrates

the continuing importance of such elements in her campaign for "Post-eclectic editions" in "Versioning Virginia Woolf: Notes toward a Post-eclectic Edition of *Three Guineas*," *Modernism/modernity* 16, no. 3 (2009): 497–535.

11 Vladimir Nabokov, *The Original of Laura (Dying is Fun)*, ed. Dmitri Nabokov (New York: Knopf / London: Penguin, 2009). The original card, as printed in the book, contains one other word or phrase that has been scribbled out with pencil.

12 See Kenneth Clay Smith, *The Book as Material Instrument: London Literary Publishing, 1885–1900*, PhD dissertation, Indiana University, 2006; Gerard de Vries and D. Barton Johnson, *Vladimir Nabokov and the Art of Painting* (Amsterdam: Amsterdam University Press, 2006); and Zoran Kuzmanovich's collaborative online reference, *Nabokov A–Z* at www.davidson.edu/academic/english/faculty/zk/vnaz/nabaz.htm.

13 Smith, *The Book as Material Instrument*, 181, 182.

14 Genette, *Paratexts*, 3.

15 Lara Delage-Toriel, "Brushing through 'Veiled Values and Translucent Undertones': Nabokov's pictorial approach to women," *Transatlantica* 1 (2006): 2–15, 6.

16 Vladimir Nabokov, *Speak, Memory* (New York: Vintage International, 1989), 77.

17 Couturier, *Near-Tyranny*, 62, 61.

18 Sarah Herbold, "'Dolorès Disparue': Reading Misogyny in *Lolita*," in *Approaches to Teaching Nabokov's* Lolita, ed. Zoran Kuzmanovich and Galya Diment (New York: MLA, 2008), 136.

19 Vladimir Nabokov, *Look at the Harlequins!* (New York: Vintage International, 1990).

20 Vladimir Nabokov, *Lolita* (New York: Vintage International, 1997), 272.

21 A book in which Cincinnatus C offers clear parallels to the experiments of *Laura*'s Dr Wild. *Invitation to a Beheading*, trans. Dmitri Nabokov (New York: Vintage International, 1989).

22 Edgar Allan Poe, "Annabel Lee," in *Complete Stories and Poems of Edgar Allan Poe* (New York: Doubleday, 1984), 738.

23 Michael Wood describes similar situations as the "moment in each book when the ontological walls give way (or could give way)" in "Nabokov's Late Fiction," in *The Cambridge Companion to Nabokov*, ed. Julian W. Connolly (Cambridge: Cambridge University Press, 2005), 201.

24 Samuel Beckett, *The Unnamable*, in *Three Novels: Molloy, Malone Dies, The Unnamable* (New York: Grove Press, 1994), 293.

25 Nabokov, "Good Readers and Good Writers," 1.

26 In "Strong Opinions and Nerve Points: Nabokov's Life and Art," Zoran Kuzmanovich stresses the importance of familiarity with Nabokov's "entire œuvre" (18) in fully understanding any small piece of it, bits that "would not divulge themselves without the reader's knowledge of all his works" (14). In *The Cambridge Companion* to Nabokov, ed. Julian W. Connolly (Cambridge: Cambridge University Press, 2005), 11–30.

27 Vladimir Nabokov, *Strong Opinions* (New York: Vintage International, 1990), 71.

28 Nabokov, *Invitation to a Beheading*, 123.

29 In "Cover to Cover: Paratextual play in Milorad Pavic's *Dictionary of the Khazars*," Ivan Callus explores contemporary novels that "make the paratext's design coextensive with the text's thematic concerns," *Electronic Book Review*, 1 January 1999, www.electronicbookreview.com/thread/internetnation/lexicographic.

30 Sarah Copland takes a pedagogical approach to the kind of book that "teaches us how to read it" (486) and its "use of its paratexts as pedagogical aids to our reading experience" (487) in her "Making It (New) as a Graduate Teaching Assistant," *Modernism/modernity* 16, no. 3 (September 2009): 485–8.

MARTIN AMIS: THE PROBLEM WITH NABOKOV

1 This review article first appeared in *The Guardian* on 14 November 2009. Reprinted by permission of the author and the Wylie agency. © 2009 Martin Amis. All rights reserved.

2 *Editor's note:* As an anonymous reader of the present volume in manuscript has pointed out, "Amis makes a major error when he states that Van and Ada are half-siblings (they are siblings on both the maternal and paternal side). If taken at face value, this misinterpretation diminishes considerably the morally scandalous nature of the book and its variety of meaningful ethical preoccupations."

JOHN BANVILLE: TRUMP CARDS

1 This review article first appeared in *Bookforum* (December/January, 2010), under the title "Trump Cards: Controversy Surrounds the Publication of Nabokov's Last, Unfinished Work." Reprinted by permission. All rights reserved.

2 Vladimir Nabokov, *The Original of Laura (Dying is Fun)*, ed. Dmitri Nabokov (New York: Knopf / London: Penguin, 2009), xvii. All page references follow this edition.
3 Ibid., xviii.

ALEXANDER THEROUX: IN THE CARDS, A LAST HAND

1 An earlier version of this review article first appeared in *The Wall Street Journal*, 20 November 2009, W15. Reprinted by permission.
2 *Editor's note:* A quotation from a landmark Cold War speech given by President John F. Kennedy in West Berlin (26 June 1963), underlining the support of the United States for West Germany after the erection of the Berlin Wall.

HELLER McALPIN: A GENEROUS GIFT TO READERS

1 This review article first appeared in *The Christian Science Monitor*, 18 November 2009. Reprinted by permission.

NATHANIEL RICH: THE NABOKOV MESS

1 This review article first appeared in *The Daily Beast* 22 November 2009. Reprinted by permission.

MICHAEL DIRDA: VLADIMIR NABOKOV, REDUCED TO NOTES

1 This review article first appeared in *The Washington Post*, 19 November 2009. Reprinted by permission.

AMELIA GLASER: AN EARNEST PROPOSAL TO DMITRI NABOKOV

1 This review article first appeared in *Open Letters Monthly*, May 2008. Reprinted by permission.
2 Stefanie Marsh, "Vladimir Nabokov, his masterpiece and the burning question," *The Times*, 14 February 2008, http://entertainment.timesonline.co.uk/tol/arts_and_entertainment/books/article3364183.ece?token=null&offset=0.
3 Vladimir Nabokov, *Novels, 1955–1962* (New York: Library of America, 1996) 2: 655.

4 Ramona Koval, "Should Nabokov's Unpublished Manuscript be Burned?" *The Book Show*, ABC [Australian Broadcasting Company] Radio, 15 February 2008 (transcript available at www.abc.net.au/rn/bookshow/stories/2008/2157977.htm).
5 Brian Boyd, *Vladimir Nabokov: the American Years* (Princeton: Princeton University Press, 1991), 377.
6 Lila Azam Zanganeh, "Butterflies and Other Bits of Nabokov's Life, Dispersed to the Wind," *The New York Times*, 6 May 2004.
7 Walter Benjamin, *Selected Writings*, vol. 1, 1913–1926, ed. Marcus Bullock and Michael W. Jennings (Cambridge, Mass.: Harvard University Press, 2002), 254.
8 Vladimir Nabokov: *Selected Letters 1940–1977*, ed. Dmitri Nabokov and Matthew J. Bruccoli (New York: Harcourt Brace Jovanovich, 1989), 41.
9 Ibid. 371–2.
10 The following review article appeared two years after the first article, published under the title "The Creation, and Erasure, of Laura," also in Open Letters Monthly, February 2010. Reprinted by permission. All rights reserved.
11 Dmitri Nabokov, "Acknowledgments," in Vladimir Nabokov, *The Original of Laura (Dying is Fun)*, ed. Dmitri Nabokov (New York: Knopf / London: Penguin, 2009). All page references follow this edition.
12 Edgar Allan Poe, "Annabel Lee," *Complete Stories and Poems of Edgar Allan Poe* (New York: Doubleday, 1984), 738.
13 *Editor's note:* This is a reference to "referential mania," a fictional disease that Nabokov invented and described in his short story "Signs and symbols" (1948).

MICHAEL ANTMAN: GENIUS ERASED

1 This review article first appeared in *PopMatters Magazine*, 20 November 2009. Reprinted by permission. All rights reserved.
2 Dmitri Nabokov, Introduction to Vladimir Nabokov, *The Original of Laura (Dying is Fun)*, ed. Dmitri Nabokov (New York: Knopf / London: Penguin, 2009). All page references follow this edition.

JAMES MARCUS: A CURIOSITY FOR NABOKOV'S FANS

1 This review article first appeared in the *Los Angeles Times*, 15 November 2009. Reprinted by permission. All rights reserved.

2 Vladimir Nabokov, *Selected Letters 1940–1977*, ed. Dmitri Nabokov and Matthew J. Bruccoli (New York: Harcourt, Brace, Jovanovich/Bruccoli-Clark-Layman, 1989), 562.

3 Vladimir Nabokov, *The Original of Laura (Dying is Fun)*, ed. Dmitri Nabokov (New York: Knopf / London: Penguin, 2009). All page references follow this edition.

THOMAS KARSHAN: DEATHS OF THE AUTHORS

1 This review article first appeared in *Frieze Magazine,* No. 125, September 2009. Reprinted by permission. All rights reserved.

2 Roland Barthes, "The Death of the Author," trans. Geoff Bennington, in *Modern Criticism and Theory: A Reader*, ed. David Lodge (Harlow, Essex: Longman, 1988), 168.

MARIJETA BOZOVIC: THE CRITIC'S *LAURA*

1 Yuri Leving, "Interpreting Voids: Vladimir Nabokov's Last Incomplete Novel *The Original of Laura*," *The Russian Review* 70 (April 2011): 198–214.

2 Ibid., 205. See also Leving, "Nabokov's 'Swan Song'," pp. 3–14 in this volume.

3 See Ron Rosenbaum's blog entry, titled "I Helped Save Nabokov's "Laura" and Now I'm Not Sure I Should Have" (28 April 2008), http://ronrosenbaumwriter.wordpress.com/2008/04/28/i_saved_nabokovs_laura_and_now/

4 Leving, "Interpreting Voids," 202.

5 Robert Douglas-Fairhurst, "Nabokov's Final Work Still Tricks and Teases," *The Telegraph,* 21 (November 2009). See also Amelia Glaser, "An Earnest Proposal to Dmitri Nabokov," *Open Letters Monthly,* May 2008 and February 2010, and pp. 187–93 in this volume.

6 Vladimir Nabokov, *The Original of Laura (Dying is Fun)*, ed. Dmitri Nabokov (New York: Knopf / London: Penguin, 2009), xviii.

7 John Banville, "Trump Cards: Controversy Surrounds the Publication of Nabokov's Last, Unifinished Work," *Bookforum,* Devember/January 2010. See pp. 169–73 in this volume. Jonathan Bate is more sympathetic than most when he calls Dmitri Nabokov's introduction "a neat pastiche of his father's great essay on the origins of *Lolita*" in "A Money-Spinner," *The Telegraph* 21 (November 2009).

8 Leland de la Durantaye, "Last wishes." *The Boston Review* (January/February 2010). http://bostonreview.net/BR35.1/deladurantaye.php.

9 Heller McAlpin, "A Generous Gift to Readers." *Christian Science Monitor* (18 November 2009). See pp. 178–80 in this volume.

10 See Tom Adair, "Fragments of Valediction," *The Scotsman* (21 November 2009). Adair, who calls *Laura* "an old man's fumble," writes that Dmitri "decided to flout his father's wishes, and publish these fragments, which Nabokov senior, a scrupulous perfectionist, had abandoned during that final protracted illness."

11 In Durantaye's phrasing ("Last Wishes," *Boston Review,* January/February 2010).

12 Durantaye, "Last Wishes."

13 Durantaye, "Last Wishes." And yet there are odd echoes of Kafka in *Laura* itself. Kafka, too, "complained that 'my body is too long for its weakness,' and ... had sad fantasies of being whittled away like a lump of wood, or lying on a railway track to get his head and legs amputated, so that he would take up less space in the world" (Douglas-Fairhurst).

14 Nathaniel Rich, "The Nabokov Mess," *The Daily Beast* (22 November 2009). See pp. 181–3 in this volume.

15 Ibid.

16 Banville, "Trump Cards."

17 Bate, "A Money-spinner."

18 Banville, "Trump Cards."

19 McAlpin, "A Generous Gift to Readers."

20 Alexander Theroux, "In the Cards, a Last Hand." *The Wall Street Journal,* 20 November 2009: W15. See pp. 174–7 in this volume.

21 Douglas-Fairhurst, "Nabokov's Final Work."

22 Theroux, "In the Cards, a Last Hand."

23 Rich, "The Nabokov Mess."

24 Bate, "A Money-spinner."

25 Rich, "The Nabokov Mess."

26 Douglas-Fairhurst, "Nabokov's Final Work." The terror writers feel before journalists and scholars is by no means new, but has perhaps gotten worse; Steven King even picks it as the plot for a horror novel, the 2006 *Lisey's Story,* in which a crazed academic tries to *torture* a great writer's widow into handing over the archive.

27 Durantaye, "Last Wishes."

28 Ibid. Arthur Phillips explains the title of his piece with an anecdote: in 1962 Nabokov, asked by a reporter for a glimpse of a rough draft, replied: "Only ambitious non-entities and hearty mediocrities exhibit their rough drafts. It is like passing around samples of one's sputum." "The Master's Sputum: Unfinished Nabokov Novel Now Open to Examination," *Paste Magazine* (20 November 2009).

29 Banville, "Trump Cards."

30 Theroux, "In the Cards, a Last Hand."

31 Theroux continues, "his introduction is nonsensical, snobbish and cruel and reads as if it had been translated from the Albanian."

32 Martin Amis, "The Problem with Nabokov," *The Guardian,* 14 November 2009. See pages 157–68 in this volume..

33 Ibid.

34 Ibid.

35 Banville, "Trump Cards."

36 Bate, "A Money-spinner."

37 Amis, "The Problem with Nabokov."

38 Ibid.

39 Theroux, "In the Cards, a Last Hand."

40 Amis, "The Problem with Nabokov."

41 Brian Boyd, The Last Word – Or Not?: On Some Cards Named *Laura,* pp. 243–57 in this volume.

42 James Marcus, "A Curiosity for Nabokov's Fans," *The Los Angeles Times* (15 November 2009). See pp. 198–200 in this volume. Michael Dirda agrees: "Certainly all the work of a great writer like Vladimir Nabokov ought to be available to scholars and interested readers ... But that doesn't mean *The Original of Laura* actually deserves the attention of anyone but the most rabid Nabokov fanatic," "Vladimir Nabokov, Reduced to Notes," *The Washington Post* (19 November 2009). See pp. 184–6 in this volume.

43 In 1976, the year before he died, the *New York Times Book Review* asked Nabokov what he was reading. He responded with Dante's *Inferno*, William H. Howe's *Butterflies of North America*, and his own *The Original of Laura*, an unfinished manuscript that, in his delirium, he kept reading aloud to the described dream audience. As reported in David Gates, "Nabokov's Last Puzzle," *The New York Times' Sunday Book Review* 11 November 2009, www.nytimes.com/2009/11/15/books/review/Gates-t.html?pagewanted=all&_r=0.

44 Thomas Karshan, "Deaths of the Authors," *Frieze Magazine* Issue 125 (September 2009). See pp. 201–4 in this volume.

45 McAlpin, "A Generous Gift to Readers."

GENNADY BARABTARLO ET AL.: TRANSLATING *LAURA*

1 Brian Boyd, "*The Original of Laura*," *Financial Times,* 23 November 2009.

2 Monika Fludenik, *The Fictions of Language and the Language of Fiction* (London: Routledge, 1993), 102.

3 See M. Scammell, "Translation is a Bastard Form," *Nabokov Online Journal* I (2007).

4 Umberto Eco, *Mouse or Rat?: Translation as Negotiation* (London: Phoenix, 2004).

5 Nabokov's Russian translation of *Lolita* has only 5.3% fewer words than the original, whereas normally the difference is anywhere from 14 per cent to almost 20 per cent, owing to the absence of the articles and a much lower incidence of prepositions in Russian. A large part of this anomaly in *Lolita* can be ascribed to Nabokov's attempts to render certain English terms descriptively, for the sake of precision.

6 J.H. Wisdom, *The Briton in Russia: Pocket Interpreter Containing Phrases and Travel Talk Etc.* (London: Leopold B. Hill, 1918).

7 Vladimir Nabokov, *Lolita* (New York: Vintage, 1997), 299.

8 Umberto Eco, *The Role of The Reader: Explorations in the Semiotics of Texts* (Indiana: Indiana University Press, 1984), 35.

9 Umberto Eco, *The Open Work* (Cambridge: Harvard University Press, 1989), 19.

10 Michael Wood, *The Magician's Doubts* (London: Chatto & Windus, 1994), 22–7.

11 Eric Naiman, "*The Original of Laura*, by Vladimir Nabokov," *San Francisco Chronicle* 6 December 2009, see http://articles.sfgate.com/2009-12-06/books/17182936_1_vladimir-nabokov-pale-fire-nabokov-s-son

BRIAN BOYD: THE LAST WORD – OR NOT? ON SOME CARDS NAMED *LAURA*

1 The present version of this essay is adapted from "A Book Burner Recants: The Original of Laura," in Brian Boyd, *Stalking Nabokov* (New York: Columbia

University Press, 2011). ©2011 Brian Boyd. Reprinted with permission of the author and the publisher.

2 Carl Proffer's *Keys to Lolita* (Bloomington: Indiana University Press, 1968) and Alfred Appel, Jr., *The Annotated Lolita* (New York: McGraw-Hill, 1970), of which 200 pages consisted of Appel's introduction to and notes on *Lolita*.

3 The other book on *The Original of Laura* is Yannicke Chupin and René Alladaye, *Aux origines de Laura: Le dernier manuscrit de Vladimir Nabokov* (Paris: Presses Universitaires de Paris, 2011). The special issues are the Japanese *Gunzo* 11 (2009) and the French *La Revue de Deux Mondes* (July–August 2010).

4 Chupin and Alladaye, *Aux origines de Laura*, 50.

5 It incorporates elements, therefore, of my review, "Novel in Fragments is Still Nabokov," *Globe and Mail* (Toronto), 28 November 2009, and the articles "Nabokov's Literary Legacy," *Gunzo* 11 (2009): 84–101, "Nabokov Lives On," *American Scholar* 79, no. 2 (Spring 2010): 45–58, "Du doute au délice," *La Revue de Deux Mondes* (July–August 2010): 115–26, and "A Book Burner Recants: *The Original of Laura*," in *Stalking Nabokov: Selected Essays* (New York: Columbia University Press, 2011), 385–96 – a proliferation that itself attests to the media frenzy – but adds more.

6 Brian Boyd, *Vladimir Nabokov: The American Years* (Princeton: Princeton University Press, 1991) and Brian Boyd and Yuri Leving, "Chronology of the Novel in Fragments" (see pp. 15–26 in this volume).

7 Vladimir Nabokov, *The Original of Laura (Dying is Fun)*, ed. Dmitri Nabokov (New York: Knopf / London: Penguin, 2009). All page references follow this edition.

8 Véra Nabokov to Fred Hills, 20 April 1976, Vladimir Nabokov Archives (now in Henry W. and Albert A. Berg Collection, New York Public Library).

9 Martin Amis, "Out of Style," *Look at the Harlequins!*, *New Statesman,* 25 April 1975.

10 Writing only about the first five chapters, before the more emphatic slowdown into Philip Wild's life, René Alladaye remarks: "La lecture de ces 5 chapitres met donc en évidence une étonnante alternance d'accélérations et de ralentissements" ["Reading these five chapters therefore shows an astonishing alternation of accelerations and slowdowns"], Chupin and Alladaye, *Aux origines de Laura*, 154.

11 Vladimir Nabokov, *Ada or Ardor* (New York: Vintage, 1990 [1969]), 286.

12 Chupin and Alladaye, *Aux origines de Laura*, 293: "Les deux derniers mots en particulier montrent qu'on est bien loin des euphémismes poétiques dont Humbert drapait sa prose dans *Lolita* pour évoquer le sexe féminin."

13 See *Laura*, 21–2, and a fragment from the material mentioned below.
14 Vladimir Nabokov, *Lolita* (1955; New York: Vintage, 1989), 316.
15 Ibid., 213.
16 Vladimir Nabokov, *Pale Fire* (1962; New York: Vintage, 1989), 52–3.
17 Nabokov, *Ada*, 585.
18 Vladimir Nabokov, *Conclusive Evidence* (New York: Harper and Brothers, 1951), 217.
19 "The Nabokov Prose-Alike Centennial Contest," *The Nabokovian* 42 (Spring 1999): 32.
20 Brian Boyd, *On the Origin of Stories: Evolution, Cognition, and Fiction* (Cambridge, Mass.: Belknap Press of Harvard University Press, 2009).
21 Nabokov, *Lolita*, 314–15.
22 "The Circle" in Vladimir Nabokov, *The Stories of Vladimir Nabokov* (New York: Alfred A. Knopf 1995), 371.
23 Vladimir Nabokov, *Transparent Things* (New York: McGraw-Hill, 1989 [1972]), 1.
24 Tadashi Wakashima, "Watashi no Keshikata" (The effaced I), *Gunzo* 11 (2009).
25 Martin Amis, "The Problem with Nabokov," *The Guardian,* 14 November 2009; Boyd, "Novel in Fragments."
26 William Deresiewicz, "Carded," *New Republic,* 3 February 2010.

Contributors

PAUL ARDOIN is a doctoral candidate at Florida State University, working on modernism and narratology. He is co-editor of the collection *Understanding Bergson, Understanding Modernism* (Continuum, 2013) and has recent and forthcoming work in the journals *Philosophy and Literature*; *LIT: Literature, Interpretation, Theory*; and *Transnational Literature*.

GENNADY BARABTARLO, professor of Russian at the University of Missouri, has written a number of books and articles on topics ranging from Pushkin and Tiutchev to Solzhenitsyn and especially Nabokov, concentrating mostly on Nabokov's artistic means and ends. He has translated three of Nabokov's novels and all of his English short stories into Russian. He has published original poetry and prose (collected, in part, in a 1998 book *In Every Place*). His most recent book came out in 2011 (St. Petersburg: Ivan Limbakh) under the title *Sochinenie Nabokova* ("Nabokov's Composition").

BRIAN BOYD, University Distinguished Professor of English at the University of Auckland, is the author of award-winning books on Nabokov, including the biography *Vladimir Nabokov: The Russian Years* and *Vladimir Nabokov: The American Years* (Princeton, 1990, 1991), *Nabokov's* Ada*: The Place of Consciousness* (Ardis, 1985, rev. ed. Cybereditions, 2001), and *Nabokov's* Pale Fire*: The Magic of Artistic Discovery* (Princeton, 1999). Boyd's most recent books include *Stalking Nabokov* (Columbia, 2011) and *Why Lyrics Last: Evolution, Cognition, and Shakespeare's Sonnets* (Harvard,

2012). His co-edition (with Olga Voronina) of *Letters to Véra* will appear in 2014 (Knopf/Penguin).

MARIJETA BOZOVIC is assistant professor in Slavic Languages and Literatures at Yale University. Her monograph *From* Onegin *to* Ada*: Nabokov's Canon,* is forthcoming with Northwestern Univerity Press. Recent publications include articles on Nabokov, on Ivan Goncharov's *Oblomov,* and on the Balkan avant-garde journal *Zenit,* and the introduction to a new critical volume, *After Yugoslavia: The Cultural Spaces of a Vanished Land.*

MAURICE COUTURIER is professor of English and American literature (University of Nice), has published six books on Nabokov, including the first French monograph on this author, titled *Nabokov* (1979). In 1993, 1995, and 2006 he organized international Nabokov conferences in Nice and edited the papers presented at all three events. Currently he is serving as the editor-in-chief of the Pléiade edition of Nabokov's novels. In addition to many articles in French and English on Nabokov and other English and American contemporary authors, he has published on the theory of the novel in *La Figure de l'auteur* (1995) and *Roman et censure* (1996). He has translated novels by Nabokov and by David Lodge. Couturier also authored two novels and an autobiography.

LARA DELAGE-TORIEL is lecturer at Strasbourg University, France, and is the author of a PhD thesis on Nabokov's representation of women (University of Cambridge). Besides a number of articles in the field of twentieth-century American literature, she has published two book-length studies involving cross-media analysis, one on *A Streetcar Named Desire* (Bréal, 2003) and one on *Lolita* (Editions du Temps, 2009). She has co-edited *Kaleidoscopic Nabokov: Perspectives Françaises* (Houdiard, 2009) and is, since 2011, the founding president of the French Vladimir Nabokov Society, also known as *Chercheurs Enchantés: Société Française Vladimir Nabokov.*

GALYA DIMENT is professor and Thomas L. & Margo G. Wyckoff Endowed Faculty Fellow, Department of Slavic Languages and Literatures (University of Washington) and the author of *Pniniad: Vladimir*

Nabokov and Marc Szeftel (1997; 2013 paperback edition), *Approaches to Teaching* Lolita (with Zoran Kuzmanovich; MLA, 2009), *A Russian Jew of Bloomsbury: The Life and Times of Samuel Koteliansky* (2011; 2013 paperback edition), and *The Autobiographical Novel of Co-Consciousness: Goncharov, Woolf, and Joyce* (1994). Her other books include *Between Heaven and Hell: The Myth of Siberia in Russian Culture* (1993) and *Goncharov's* Oblomov: *A Critical Companion* (2006).

LELAND DE LA DURANTAYE is professor of literature (Claremont McKenna College) and the author of *Style is Matter: The Moral Art of Vladimir Nabokov* (Cornell University Press, 2007), *Giorgio Agamben: A Critical Introduction* (Stanford University Press, 2009), and numerous articles on Nabokov. His radio commentaries include (with Brian Boyd and Ron Rosenbaum) "Should Nabokov's Unpublished Manuscript Be Burned?" ("The Book Show with Romana Koval," *ABC: Australian Broadcasting Company,* 2008) and (with Brian Boyd) "Nabokov's Unfinished Work" ("On Point with Tom Ashbrook," *NPR: National Public Radio,* 2009), both one-hour-long discussions of issues relating to Nabokov's then unpublished *The Original of Laura.*

MICHAEL JULIAR is a bibliographer, blogger, and collector. He is the author of the standard bibliography on Vladimir Nabokov, *Vladimir Nabokov: A Descriptive Bibliography* (New York: Garland, 1986) along with two self-published updates issued in 1988 and 1991. Juliar is working on a new, reconceived edition, parts of which are posted to his blog weekly. The blog, "Nabokov Bibliography: All About Nabokov in Print" (www.vnbiblio.com), is described as "a crossroads where the trivia (in both its original and modern senses) of bibliography, collecting, and commerce will meet." It also includes news of translations of Nabokov, auctions of Nabokov books, as well as comments about collecting Nabokov in Russian, English, and French and the 41 other languages in which his works have appeared.

YURI LEVING is professor and chair of Dalhousie University's Department of Russian Studies. He is the author of four books – *Marketing Literature and Posthumous Legacies* (co-authored with Frederick H. White, 2013), *Keys to* The Gift*: A Guide to V. Nabokov's Novel* (2011), *Upbringing* *by Optics: Book Illustration, Animation, and Text* (2010), *Train Station – Garage – Hangar: Vladimir Nabokov and the Poetics of Russian Urbanism* (2004, short-listed for the Andrei Bely Prize) – and has also edited and co-edited five volumes of articles: *Lolita: The Story of a Cover Girl – Vladimir Nabokov's Novel in Art and Design* (2013), *Anatomy of a Short Story* (2012), *The Goalkeeper: The Nabokov Almanac* (2010), *Eglantine: A Collection of Philological Essays to Honour the Sixtieth Anniversary of Roman Timenchik* (2005), and *Empire N: Nabokov and His Heirs* (2006). Leving has published over eighty scholarly articles on various aspects of Russian and comparative literature. He served as a commentator on the first authorized Russian edition of *The Collected Works of Vladimir Nabokov* in five volumes (1999–2001), and curated the exhibition "Nabokov's *Lolita*: 1955–2005" in Washington, DC, which celebrated the 50th anniversary of the publication of *Lolita*. Leving is the founding editor of the *Nabokov Online Journal*.

ERIC NAIMAN is professor of Slavic languages and comparative literature (University of California, Berkeley), the author of *Nabokov, Perversely* (Cornell University Press, 2010) and *Sex in Public: The Incarnation of Early Soviet Ideology* (Princeton University Press, 1997), and the co-editor of *Everyday Life in Revolutionary Russia: Taking the Revolution Inside* (Indiana University Press, 2006) and *The Landscape of Stalinism: The Art and Ideology of Soviet Space* (University of Washington Press, 2003).

ELLEN PIFER is professor emerita of English and comparative literature (University of Delaware) and the author of *Nabokov and the Novel* (Harvard University Press, 1980), *Demon or Doll: Images of the Child in Contemporary Writing and Culture* (University Press of Virginia, 2000), *Saul Bellow Against the Grain* (University of Pennsylvania Press, 1990), and dozens of essays, articles, and chapters on modern and contemporary fiction. She is the editor of *Vladimir Nabokov's* Lolita: *A Casebook* (Oxford University Press, 2003) and of *Critical Essays on John Fowles* (Gale, 1983); she has served as President (1998–2000) and Vice-President (1996–1998) of the International Vladimir Nabokov Society.

ANNA RAFFETTO holds an arts degree with a specialization in Russian language and literature. After a job as a researcher in Russian literature at

Genoa University, she started working for the publishing industry. Raffetto was a literary editor for Slavic Studies at Giulio Einaudi Publishing House (Turin) until 1999, and since then has been working in the same capacity at Adelphi (Milan). She has written essays on Anton Chekhov, Izrail Metter, Alexander Chayanov, Varlam Shalamov, and Vladimir Nabokov, and has translated both literary prose and poetry from Russian and English (Antony Pogorelsky, Dmitri Likhachev, Joseph Brodsky, and Vladimir Nabokov).

MICHAEL RODGERS has recently finished his PhD – "A Nietzschean Analysis of Vladimir Nabokov's Fiction" – at the University of Strathclyde. He works as a Graduate Teaching Assistant and is currently editing a volume titled *Nabokov's Morality Play: Ethics, Aesthetics, and Metaphysics in His Fiction,* which is derived from a symposium that he organized in 2011. His published work includes '*Lolita*'s Nietzschean Morality' (*Philosophy and Literature* 35 [2011]) and 'Relationships of Ownership: Art and Theft in Bob Dylan's 1960s' Trilogy' (*Imaginations* 3 [2012]). He has given numerous talks on Nabokov, both in the United Kingdom and in Russia, and is a contributor to *The Literary Encyclopedia*, *The Slavonic and East European Review,* and the *Nabokov Online Journal.*

RIEN VERHOEF translated more than fifty novels from English into Dutch. Among these are works by Saul Bellow, William Faulkner, John Updike, Vladimir Nabokov, David Leavitt and Graham Swift. Over the last fifteen years – since *Enduring Love* – he translated all the novels by Ian McEwan, most recently *Sweet Tooth.* In 1982 Verhoef was awarded the Dutch national translation prize, and later served as a judge for this award. Most recently Verhoef was awarded an Honorary Doctorate from Leiden University. He lives in Amsterdam, The Netherlands.

OLGA VORONINA is assistant professor of Russian at Bard College. Formerly deputy director of the Nabokov Museum in St. Petersburg, she received a PhD in Slavic literature from Harvard University. Dr Voronina is currently co-editing and co-translating Vladimir Nabokov's *Letters to Véra*, previously unpublished.

TADASHI WAKASHIMA is professor of English (Kyoto University), a founding member and organizing director of the Nabokov Society of

Japan, and chair of the Kyoto Reading Circle. He is an international master in solving chess problems. He has published four books and won the Yomiuri Prize for Literature in 2004 for *An Astigmatic Reader's Lectures on British and American Short Fiction.* He has written numerous essays and articles on Joyce, Nabokov, and other modern and contemporary writers. He has translated *Lolita, The Defense,* and co-translated *The Nabokov–Wilson Letters, Transparent Things,* and *The Stories of Vladimir Nabokov* into Japanese.

MICHAEL WOOD is Charles Barnwell Straut Class of 1923 Professor and professor of comparative literature at Princeton University. He studied French and German at Cambridge University, and has taught at Columbia University and at the University of Exeter. He has written books on Vladimir Nabokov (*The Magician's Doubts: Nabokov and the Risks of Fiction,* 1994), Luis Buñuel, Franz Kafka, and Gabriel García Márquez, as well as *The Road to Delphi,* a study of the ancient and continuing allure of oracles. A member of the American Philosophical Society and of the American Academy of Arts and Sciences, he is a regular contributor to the *London Review of Books* and the *New York Review of Books.* His recent books include *Literature and the Taste of Knowledge* (2005) and *Yeats and Violence* (2010).

BARBARA WYLLIE is deputy editor of the *Slavonic and East European Review* and is based at the School of Slavonic and East European Studies, University College London. She has contributed articles on Nabokov to *The Reference Guide to Russian Literature* (Routledge, 1998), *Nabokov at the Limits: Redrawing Critical Boundaries* (Garland, 1999), *Torpid Smoke: The Stories of Vladimir Nabokov* (Rodopi, 2000), *The Cambridge Companion to Vladimir Nabokov* (Cambridge University Press, 2005), the Wiley/Blackwell *Companion to Twentieth-Century United States Fiction* (2009) and *The Literary Encyclopedia* (www.litencyc.com). Her first book, *Nabokov at the Movies: Film Perspectives in Fiction,* was published by McFarland in 2003, and her literary biography of Nabokov for Reaktion Books' Critical Lives series was published in 2010.

Index